JUST A MOMENT
— A MEMOIR —

SCHALK BURGER SNR

AS TOLD TO MICHAEL VLISMAS

Jonathan Ball Publishers
Johannesburg · Cape Town · London

All rights reserved.
No part of this publication may be reproduced or transmitted,
in any form or by any means, without prior permission
from the publisher or copyright holder.

© Text Schalk Burger Snr 2021
© Published edition Jonathan Ball Publishers 2021

First published in South Africa in 2021 by
JONATHAN BALL PUBLISHERS
A division of Media24 (Pty) Ltd
PO Box 33977
Jeppestown
2043

ISBN 978-1-77619-084-3
ebook ISBN 978-1-77619-085-0

Every effort has been made to trace the copyright holders and to obtain their permission for the use of copyright material. The publishers apologise for any errors or omissions and would be grateful to be notified of any corrections that should be incorporated in future editions of this book.

www.jonathanball.co.za
Twitter: www.twitter.com/JonathanBallPub
Facebook: www.facebook.com/JonathanBallPublishers

All photos supplied by kind permission of the author.

Cover by MR Design
Cover photograph by Dionne Jordaan
Design by Catherine Coetzer
Set in Abril Text

CONTENTS

Foreword   v
Introduction – Charting the Soils   1

PART ONE – SPRINGBOK

1   From Racing Cars to Rugby   7
2   'Skreeborsie'   13
3   The 'Professionals' of Paarl Gimnasium Primary School   19
4   A Twist of Fate on the Touwsrivier Train   22
5   The Day I Bit Jan Ellis   26
6   The Springbok Journey Begins   33
7   The Politics of Rugby   36
8   Doc Craven   41
9   My EP Rugby Family   49
10   The First White Springbok Selected from a Coloured Team   62

PART TWO – FAMILY

11   Born a Contradiction   81
12   Goodbye, Dad   91
13   'Take Care of the Family'   99

PART THREE – FATHER

14	Only Human	**109**
15	Schalk Junior	**111**
16	René	**130**
17	Tiaan	**141**
18	Our Family Holiday Before the End of the World	**150**

PART FOUR – SOUTH AFRICAN

19	The Day Cheeky Watson Asked to Wash My Feet	**157**
20	Louis Luyt and the Fight for South African Rugby's Soul	**164**
21	Fokofpolisiekar and Our 'Flower of Scotland'	**182**
22	Poetic Justice with the Breytenbachs	**187**
23	Fake News	**192**
24	Why, My Beloved Country?	**198**

PART FIVE – FARMER

25	A Farmer at Heart	**205**
26	Of Heart Transplants and Screw Caps	**217**

PART SIX – SEDIMENT

27	South African Rugby's Coaching Dilemma	**223**
28	Goodbye, Newlands	**232**
29	My Kind of People	**234**
30	Climbing Kilimanjaro	**243**
31	Operation Save Rob	**249**
32	Raising a Springbok	**256**
33	Dreams	**263**

Acknowledgements   **270**

FOREWORD

PERSONAL CIRCUMSTANCES MADE ME extremely reluctant to accept the invitation to write the foreword to this book.

More so, by choosing me for this role, it may create the entirely incorrect impression that this book is mainly about rugby. Schalk stood firm against my resistance, and the result is here I sit, three-quarters of the way through a bottle of the finest Cape Blend, searching for inspiration to appropriately introduce *Just a Moment*, or what I would describe as Schalk's terroir – his Pictures of Life.

Schalk and I have, over the past 50 years, been acquaintances, teammates, adversaries, combatants (physically and verbally) and finally, in our latter years, close family friends. So I start reading *Just a Moment* with an attitude of, 'I know this guy so well.' Very soon, the book introduces a new frame of reference for understanding the complexities that make up this versatile man.

> *A complex wine doesn't only have one flavour through it, it starts off one way, then different notes emerge mid-palate and on the finish.*
> – Margaret Rand

The notes and reflections on his early childhood, his very 'different' love for and relationship with his parents and siblings, and his final, lasting pledge to his father to 'look after the family' are significant markers in his life and an early introduction to a renewed appreciation of Schalk.

Myra, as is her way, is quietly woven throughout the fabric of their family journey as Schalk shares their joy and the near devastations of parenting their remarkable offspring, Schalk Jnr, Tiaan and René.

Schalk is a pilot, sailor, golfer, cricketer, musician, mountaineer, promoter of the arts, businessman, arbitrator, counsellor, activist and – perhaps his over-riding passion – farmer. I have travelled with Schalk to many parts of the world and have always enjoyed the surprise of new acquaintances as they encounter this giant from Africa with the biggest hands in the world, and experience his sharp intellect, humour, libertarian nature and musical talent.

And, yes, there is some rugby. It is a ringside seat to Schalk's own career – the triumph, fun and laughter of his playing days, but also the consequences and retrospective sadness of playing rugby (as we of that generation did) in a deeply troubled and divided country. There is also a close-up view of the intrigues, politics and business of rugby, in particular the emergence of professional rugby.

Schalk and I do sometimes differ on the interpretation of some of the events that shaped our rugby and also of the people in and around the game. We will vigorously debate these things, as we always do, and I will also take him on to contend that you can move forward in rugby by passing the ball.

'Who am I, and how do I live?' Schalk muses, and hopes to find the answer by writing this memoir. And so, whatever the outcome, I hope he continues to tend lovingly to the soil at Welbedacht, cherish his family, enjoy his friends, laugh and play music.

Thanks, Schalk, for sharing your personal journey and taking us below the surface of what we thought we saw.

The first step that leads to our identity in life is usually not 'I know who I am' but rather 'I know who I'm not'. – Matthew McConaughey

Morné du Plessis

INTRODUCTION

CHARTING THE SOILS

I LOVE A GOOD STORY, and I'm thinking of one now, here on my farm Welbedacht in the wine-growing region just outside the Western Cape town of Wellington.

It's the story of this piece of land. A story that began 520 million years ago.

How do you even begin to tell a story of time and moments and things unexplained that shifted and moved the earth, and opened up mystical pathways for rivers such as the beautiful Berg, which runs through Wellington?

This place where I stand is the story of Paarlberg, Paardeberg, Groenberg and Kasteelberg. And the ridge of Porseleinberg. I have always loved that name. As a wine farmer, I'll tell you the name of this story. It's called terroir. And terroir influences everything around it.

The story told by terroir creates pictures of life at various periods. These pictures drift down into the soils, washed by thousands of years of wind and heat and sun and water and the cool evening breeze that blows here. These pictures, these glimpses of moments in time, are every bit a product of their elements, and the soils are the custodians of these stories. This is why I love farming so much, because the soil tells our stories.

When I came to this farm in the Boland basin, before I could plant my new cultivars to begin making wine, I went through a process called the charting of the soils. People who know more about such things than I do will tell you that this is when the topography of the land that is to be planted (a block of land, as farmers call it) is charted to indicate its various outlines relative to north, and its elevation, and gradient or fall from the highest to the lowest point. A consultant will ask you, the farmer, to dig what are known as profile holes two metres deep. He will then climb into these holes and from there will be able to read the story of the land like a beautiful book. And the stories that lie in those soils will tell you what you can plant, and how.

I remember digging those profile holes with my trusty Massey Ferguson digger. I was told that such an unwieldy machine, with its modern hydraulics, was not suited to such a delicate task. But as a man with unusually large hands, which I have used to play rugby, guitar and even execute a certain amount of finesse on the golf course, I felt my Massey Ferguson was perfectly suited to this task.

Digging your profile hole is one thing. Reading it is, quite literally, another story. If you aren't attuned to the kind of story you are reading, you won't see a thing in those soils. And if you climb into that hole expecting to read a particular type of story, you will never see the real heart of what is before you.

And so Paul Feyt came into my life. A quiet-spoken man, he has seen most of the Swartland from below ground level, having climbed into countless profile holes and read many stories of the soil in his lifetime. Paul climbed into the profile hole on my farm, armed with an archaeologist's pick, a pocket notebook, a pen and a 30-pack of cigarettes. Once at the bottom, he hunched down and began reading the book of the land before him. Every now and then his head would pop up like a meerkat for a look around, and then he'd duck down again to make more notes.

'God made this,' he told me. 'If you don't read it carefully, as you would read the Bible, you'll never know what to do with it.'

For Paul, it was an aberration to stand on a piece of land, and simply by looking at it, decide what you will plant. How could you do that when you have no idea what lies beneath? Who could ever judge a piece of land simply by scratching at the surface? Especially when what lies beneath is a story 520 million years old and part of the collective Cape Granite Suite, which is referred to as the 'parent geology' of many of South Africa's vineyards. The arrogance of man, he reasoned, who is but a passing thought on these timeless soils.

I have never forgotten this, and I have used it as the foundation of everything we do as a wine estate at Welbedacht. I am nothing but a custodian of the land here. It's been here for 250 million years, since the Malmesbury intrusion, which shaped my beloved Groenberg, and which in turn is shaped by soils from 550 million years ago when the supercontinent of Gondwanaland split. What am I but a brief, passing phase in such a great expanse of time? And I am very much like the vine that is planted in this soil. The vine is a factor of the place where it lives and breathes. Its home. Home. Who am I, and how do I live? That is something this story will hopefully bring out of me, as well as the influence on my present-day thinking of mentors such as Dr Danie Craven, who drilled into my head at every training session that you play rugby the same way you live your life.

The French say that the dear Lord provides, and we on Earth can only care for it. On our wine farm, we can only produce this year what the Earth allows us to produce. Through fires and droughts, ours is a product of the elements, and we can only live the elements and not control them.

So how do I tell this story?

Well, maybe we need to start as Paul would tell me to start: by digging below the surface of what you think you see.

I should warn you: what you find may surprise you. Some of it may even offend you. If it does, I apologise.

We'll start with the obvious. But I guarantee you that what we uncover as we dig deeper will most likely be far from what you expected.

So let's begin.

PART ONE

SPRINGBOK

1

FROM RACING CARS TO RUGBY

IT WAS NEVER MY DREAM to become a Springbok rugby player. I wanted to become a designer of Formula 1 racing cars.

In the 1960s, when I was growing up, my childhood heroes were not rugby players. They were racing drivers like Stirling Moss, Jody Scheckter and Jackie Stewart, and motorcyclists like Giacomo Agostini and Jon Ekerold. My younger brother Johann and I would cycle 70 kilometres from our home in Paarl to the Killarney racetrack in Milnerton to see my other racing heroes, John Love and Sam Tingle, take part in single-seater races. We would climb the big bluegum tree on our favourite corner of the track, named Malmesbury, to get a better view of the racing cars.

One day we saw a blue Renault Gordini totally out of control and sliding around into this corner. It belonged to a young driver named Jody Scheckter. We immediately took a liking to him purely because of the way he drove. It always looked as if he was headed for a serious accident, and then at the last moment he'd escape disaster. And with every lap he improved his position in the race.

In our minds, a hero was born through his daring, skill and youth. We spoke endlessly about his races as we pedalled the long road home. I also loved Ekerold because he had won a World

Championship as a South African privateer riding a self-modified motorcycle, and beating big brand names such as Kawasaki in the process. That kind of pioneering spirit really resonated with me. I loved that mindset of taking on the big guys and beating them.

I spent most of my childhood years tinkering with engines and opening them up and rebuilding them. I redesigned or rebuilt everything I could get my hands on. My friends who had motorbikes benefited from my curiosity, as I was constantly looking for ways to improve their performance.

I had a really fast Ford Anglia at one stage. It had a problem stopping, though, even after I acquired disc brakes from a scrapyard and ground them into place. And it had a wicked speed wobble that developed at 50 kilometres per hour. This was because the ball joints had once expended themselves in trying to get a poor-handling car full of students to corner as quickly as possible around a roundabout, with two cars in hot pursuit. One was filled with the students we were racing against. The other was a police car chasing us. The extra-big rims and tyres on my Anglia were just too much for those ball joints to handle.

I was a keen sailor growing up, and it's something that has stayed with me my whole life. Someone who really spoke to my adventurous spirit was the South African, and international, sailing legend Bertie Reed, who caught the world's attention with his performances in the singlehanded round-the-world yacht races of the 1980s and early 1990s, then known as the 'Everest of sailing'. His exploits were filled with the kind of daring adventure I loved, such as when he rescued fellow South African sailor John Martin – funnily enough, a man with whom I would cross paths in my early rugby career – whose boat was sinking after it hit an iceberg in the Southern Ocean during the 1990–1991 BOC Challenge. Reed's exploit earned him the Woltemade Cross for Bravery – then South Africa's highest civilian award for bravery.

Flying was another great passion of mine. Here it was legendary US Air Force test pilot Chuck Yeager who captured my boyhood imagination. Years later an army friend, Graham Fig, gave me a copy of Yeager's autobiography, signed by the great man, which he'd purchased at the Oshkosh air show.

It was only much later, as I approached the end of my school career, that rugby started to feature more prominently in my mind. And then it was players such as Frik du Preez, whose autobiography my dad gave me as a birthday present, and Jan Ellis, who I had the privilege of playing against in my second senior provincial rugby match, who inspired me.

I played rugby at school, but even at school sport was not my main priority. I enjoyed the academic and cultural side of school far more, and had a particular love for subjects such as maths, chemistry and accounting.

My love for culture led me to music, and I taught myself to play the guitar. I couldn't read sheet music to save my life, and still can't, but I learnt by watching people play and then memorising the chords. Then I would number the chord sequence so I could remember it. In that way I developed my own numbering system for guitar, and it's served me very well. In fact, during my schooldays I used to make a bit of pocket money giving guitar lessons to my friends. My rudimentary numbering system proved quite lucrative for me.

But my childhood dreams and aspirations were of a largely technical nature. How does an engine work? How can I build a faster motorbike? How do you navigate a yacht around the world?

That was my world, and those were the dreams in the mind of a boy from Paarl. The ultimate dream was to finish school and then raise enough money to travel to England, study at the Birmingham School of Design (later Birmingham Polytechnic) and work for Tyrrell Racing designing racing cars. Tyrrell was the famous Formula 1 team, founded by Ken Tyrrell, that dominated motor racing in the early 1970s with Jackie Stewart as driver, as well as other greats such as Jody Scheckter and Jacky Ickx.

It's safe to say that Springbok rugby was quite far down my list of priorities when I was growing up.

My brother Johann, who at that stage was impressing as a highly talented provincial cross-country and track athlete, shared this dream with me. So when I completed school, he was adamant that I couldn't leave for England without him. I still had to complete my compulsory national service, so we agreed that I'd do my time in the army and wait for him to finish school, and then we could leave together. That would also give us enough time to save the money we needed.

And then my life changed direction completely. I was about to embark on a path with as many twists and turns as the racetracks I loved.

It was a phone call in September 1974 from Dr Danie 'Doc' Craven, during my army days, that changed my life.

Typically, I had my hands deep in the engine of an army truck that I was repairing when that phone call came through.

Our squad captain came to find me and said I needed to report to the commandant's office at 10 am. The commandant was on the phone when I arrived. He handed me the receiver and said, 'Doc Craven wants to talk to you.'

My response was, 'Who?'

Of course I knew who Doc Craven was, but only by reputation. My rugby had started to move in a direction after school, but in my mind it wasn't at the point where I should be receiving a phone call from the great Doc Craven. So I was a little confused as to whom the commandant was talking about.

'But I'm not sick,' I said. The commandant just shook his head and handed me the phone.

'Hello,' I said, and the voice on the other end announced, 'This is Dr Craven from Maties rugby. Mannetjie, what are your plans next year?'

I told him I planned to travel to England to work for Tyrrell designing racing cars.

'Resieskarretjies,' he said. 'Hoe op aarde is jy so geïnteresseerd in resieskarretjies?' (How on earth are you so interested in racing cars?)

I explained my dream to him.

'So you don't want to play rugby?' he said. 'I've been told you're Springbok material, and I know you won't become a Springbok unless you come and play rugby in Stellenbosch.'

He asked whether I would consider studying at Stellenbosch, and I told him I'd need a bursary to do that. We grew up poor, as I'll explain later, so whether it was pursuing my dream in England or going to study in Stellenbosch, money was always going to be a problem.

Doc Craven ended the conversation by saying that I should speak to the commandant about bursary options, and leave the rest to him.

When I put down the phone, the commandant said to me, 'Burger, how many young men get that kind of offer? Doc Craven wants you to come to Stellenbosch.'

I had a real problem at this stage, as I had been tested to study either engineering or medicine at university, and both these academic options were no longer open for entry. The applications had closed in June that year. Economics was another field I had considered.

But Doc's phone call made me think twice about my plans. The commandant informed me about the South African Railways Bursary, which was one of the best in those days. I decided to apply for the bursary, and to my surprise I got it. And that's how I ended up going to Stellenbosch to play rugby for Maties under Doc Craven, and studying commerce.

I have a painting in the living room of our home of Doc Craven, painted by the renowned Pierre Volschenk, who was commissioned by the University of Stellenbosch to also produce a commemorative bronze statue of the legendary man. It depicts him from behind, standing with his dog, Bliksem, at his side as they both look out onto a rugby field. I often look at the painting and wonder how different my life would have been had Doc Craven not come into it when he did – had it not been for that phone call.

It also meant that Johann's and my paths started to split as we embarked on two very different journeys. I was now off to Stellenbosch to take my rugby career to the next level under Danie

Craven. I really didn't know what to say to Johann about the change in plans. I loved my brother dearly and we had handled our difficult family issues together.

We decided that it was perhaps best that he go and study, but this was also easier said than done, because he'd barely scraped by in school. However, we managed to get him into the Wellington Teachers Training College, where he qualified as a teacher.

But then his life took a different turn as he joined the army, where he would go on to become one of South Africa's most decorated Recces (the renowned Special Forces division of the South African Defence Force). And, in our own ways, we would both be exposed to the power, influence and skulduggery of South African politics.

In my case, politics almost ended my rugby career before it even began. My senior rugby career was a tumultuous, roller-coaster journey. As Doc Craven himself once said to me, 'Burger, wherever you are, drama seems to be nearby.'

2
'SKREEBORSIE'

DOLF VISSER WAS ONE of the best coaches I ever had. He had to have been a visionary, especially when it came to me, because nothing about who I was on a rugby field during primary school at Paarl Gimnasium could ever have suggested that I would one day become a Springbok.

I was a gangly young athlete who suffered from asthma. Severe asthma. In Sub B (Grade 2) I spent nearly a year out of school because I had contracted double pneumonia as a complication of my asthma. I spent three months in the Red Cross War Memorial Children's Hospital in Cape Town. A professor at the hospital told my mother that he thought my condition might improve if I did sport at school. It then happened that my teacher, Mr Visser, intervened and said he thought rugby would be an excellent choice for me. And that's how I started playing rugby.

My mother taught Mr Visser how to prepare my old-fashioned asthma pump, and he was more than happy to carry it with him and take on this responsibility for me. And so began my rugby career.

But perhaps I should clarify that my career began more with a wheeze than a bang. My nickname on the rugby field was 'Skreeborsie' (whistling chest), because I would always play flat out, and then my chest would begin to wheeze because of the asthma. And that's when Mr Visser would run onto the field with the asthma pump, into which you poured the medication. Years later, he told me that he was surprised how he didn't do permanent damage to me, because it was always a guessing game as to how much medicine you had to put into the pump; when he was anxious or my chest was wheezing more than normal he would unintentionally put a bit more medicine into the bowl. He was a bit worried that he might have overdosed me at times. At least there was no drug testing taking place.

I started my rugby career playing at prop, believe it or not. It was later in my school career that I moved to lock, and then to eighthman.

Although sport wasn't my main priority at school, I soon grew to love expressing myself on the sports field. And there was one overriding reason for that. The sports field is the most incredible leveller. It didn't matter what neighbourhood you grew up in or what size house you lived in. And that meant a lot to a poor boy from the wrong side of Paarl.

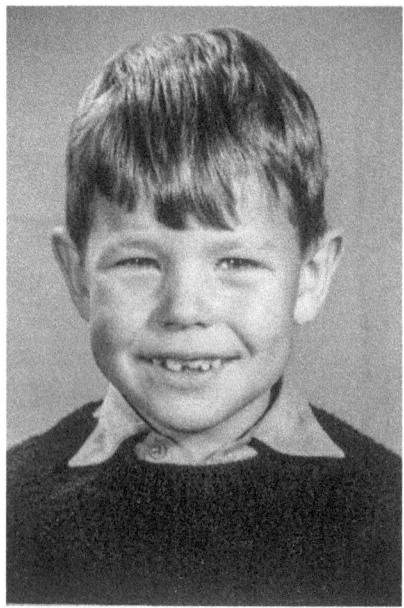

Me in Sub A (Grade 1) at Blackheath Primary, where we used to be four classes in one classroom. I sometimes went to school by donkey. The only clothing I knew was a khaki shirt and khaki pants.

'SKREEBORSIE'

I am the eldest child in our family, and my three siblings were all very good in their respective sports. Johann was a Western Province and South African champion in the 800 metres and 1 500 metres. The first cross-country race he ever ran at school was a trial for the Western Province schools team. And he won. But I remember him coming home that day and we asked him where he'd finished overall. He said, 'I don't know. We'll have to see.' In those days you had to listen to the radio to get the sports results. So we all listened carefully for the results, and there was a report about a Johann Burger who had impressed everybody by winning the Western Province cross-country trials.

My sister, Laura, was also a good runner. But my youngest brother, Paul, was probably the most talented of all of us. He was a provincial athlete and also played tennis, cricket and rugby for his province. Paul was a South African champion in discus and high jump. Paul and André Pollard, the father of Springbok flyhalf Handré, were training partners for many years. Paul beat André for the gold medal in the hammer throw at the South African Championships one year.

Many of my friends, themselves top sportsmen, tell me they think Paul was probably the most prolific school sportsman Paarl has ever produced. In his second-ever South African Under-19 pentathlon he set a South African record that stood for many years. He was also an excellent tennis player. He used to play left-handed against my children and still beat them. I think he was too talented, actually, but we'll get to that later.

As for me, as I said, sport was never my first priority. But I discovered that I was fairly good at it. Apart from rugby, I was also a provincial athlete in discus, shot put and, would you believe it, high jump. My first sporting love, though, was actually cricket. It still is. The same can be said for Schalk Jnr. I think he could've had a successful career as a professional cricketer as well. He was already playing for the first team at Paarl Gimnasium when he was only in Grade 8, and he played provincial first-class cricket while still at school.

JUST A MOMENT

I've built a cricket oval at Welbedacht, and we've hosted some incredible matches where some of the international greats of the game have played when they've come to visit. I have an extensive library of cricket books, and I even planted some of the vines on my farm according to the principle of how a cricket pitch must be laid out – from north to south, to make the most effective use of the influence of the sun.

But, unfortunately for my own cricket career, my father banned me from playing the game at school. When I questioned him about this, he simply said, 'One day I'll tell you what the English did to our forefathers.' And that was it. My mother, on the other hand, had plans of her own. It was well known that I had the biggest school bag in my grade at Paarl Gimnasium. My mother bought me a really big one so that she could pack my cricket kit and my books into the same bag without my father noticing. So I played what little cricket I could. My dad obviously found out about it later. He never took it further, but without my father's encouragement in this area, I naturally didn't pursue the game as much as I could have. I played first-team cricket as an opening bowler and number-eight batsman. I loved opening the bowling with my friend Lochie Slabber, who was originally from Rhodesia and whose father had built him his own cricket nets.

My rugby career started off at prop. My first match was in 1965 for Paarl Gimnasium Primary versus North End Primary in Paarl, and I played against a guy by the name of Hurter (no joke), who was the biggest boy I'd ever seen in my life. He was easily twice my size. He scrummed me so hard I couldn't turn my neck the following day. I remember my dad taking a mixture of salt and vinegar in a cloth and winding it around my neck to help it heal, which was a pretty good treatment in those days except that for the next three days at school, I had this salt-and-vinegar smell coming off me, as if I'd been working in a fish-and-chips shop.

However, my aunts were horrified that I was playing rugby. They came to watch a game I played against CBC (Christian Brothers' College) in Cape Town but left after only 30 minutes. My one aunt wrote me a long letter explaining how she couldn't believe her nephew was playing this barbaric and gladiatorial game. But, true to both my aunts, there was always an opportunity to pass on a lesson. So in the letter my aunt said that if I really was intent on playing rugby, she wanted to leave me with a thought: she believed that to be a good gladiator, the desire to win must always be greater than the fear of losing. I put that up on the wall of our home for my children in later years, and to this day I believe my aunt knew a heck of a lot more about rugby than she let on.

The night before that CBC game my dad had a few of his friends over to our house, and they decided that I needed something extra so I could 'bugger up those Englishmen' the next day. So I was subjected to an impromptu scrumming session in our kitchen against these men. My face was scratched red from the stubble on their chins, and I can clearly recall that distinctive smell of nicotine and brandy that was almost like a cologne for men in those days. To this day I remember that smell and am taken back to that little kitchen of ours.

I'll never forget our meeting at the church in Paarl – the Toringkerk, as we called it – at 6.45 am and then travelling by bus to the

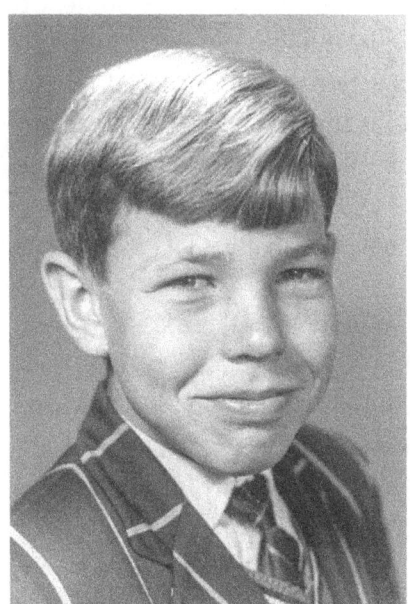

A school photo of me in 1965, proudly wearing my Paarl Gimnasium uniform.

game. My father also drove to the city to watch the match and drive me home afterwards. On the way back it was his routine to stop off at the Klapmuts Hotel bar. It was a routine that would eventually become his undoing. Any boy who grew up as the child of a hotel-bar dad kind of knows this routine. You sit in the car while Dad kuiers.

The owner of the Klapmuts Hotel was Issy Hodes, a cheerful old man who knew how to keep his customers happy when they passed through this sleepy little town. He was a great friend of all the farmers. He owned two Great Danes that were nearly as tall as I was. It was the first time I had ever seen such a massive dog, and I was astounded. Normally, on the piece of grass next to the hotel, the kids whose dads were in the bar would play a little rugby game while we waited. But there was no game on this day, so I sat in the car with my window open, waiting for something to be sent out from the bar. I was starving after my first full rugby match.

My father sent out a pie and Coke for me, and I was busy eating the pie when the one Great Dane casually put his head through my window and took a bite. I was so surprised at how big the dog was that I just froze and watched him take this enormous bite out of my pie. Eventually, my dad came out of the bar and we drove home. Up until this point my father had said nothing about my game. Finally, I plucked up the courage to ask him how he thought I'd played.

'You did okay for the first 15 minutes,' he said. 'But then you went quiet and I don't know why. You were all over your opponent in the scrum.'

'But Dad, there was a reason for that,' I told him. 'You don't know who the ref was.'

'Who was the ref and why does it matter?' he asked.

'The other prop I was scrumming against started crying, Dad. The ref asked him why he was crying, and he said, "Brother, this other guy is hurting me in the scrums." They were brothers, Dad, and I honestly thought the ref was going to moer me for hurting his brother.'

'Schalk,' my dad said. 'At CBC, all of the teachers are called brothers by the pupils.'

3

THE 'PROFESSIONALS' OF PAARL GIMNASIUM PRIMARY SCHOOL

MY RUGBY CAREER STARTED to gather a bit of momentum in 1968, during Standard Five (Grade 7), when I was made captain of the Under-12 A rugby team.

That year came a major announcement. Paarl Gimnasium Primary School would be selecting a team to travel to Pretoria to play against the mighty Afrikaanse Hoër Seunskool (Affies). I knew immediately that I wouldn't be able to go. As a family, we never had the money for extras such as this.

It was an important tour for the school. But on the day of the announcement, as we were collecting our bicycles at the bike shed, I turned to my best friend, Arrie Slabbert, and said, 'This is a stuff-up. I'm going to have to tell Mr Visser that I can't tour because my mom doesn't have the money.'

Arrie said to me, 'Listen, Schalk, I heard my dad praying for money last night because my sister is at university and he took our last savings to pay for her education. So I can't go either.' Arrie's father was a policeman, and we were both dead scared of him. Arrie said there was no way he was even going to bother asking his dad for the money. I said I was also not going to ask my mom, because it would just make her sad.

So we arranged to go and meet Mr Visser together to break the news to him. Mr Visser heard us out and then said he couldn't have his captain and star player not go on this tour. 'Leave it with me,' he said. Anyway, the next thing we know, Mr Visser tells us we're going on tour and not to worry, it's been paid for.

It was a great tour. Arrie actually has a small article from *Beeld* newspaper about it. There's a photo of our team with the headline 'Paarl Gimnasium beats Affies'. And the article mentions tries by Arrie Slabbert and Schalk Burger.

But the real highlight for me was a visit to the Impala aircraft factory in Kempton Park. It blew my mind watching these people build an aircraft, and it fuelled my fascination with engines and mechanics even more.

For years neither of us knew how Mr Visser had arranged for us to go on that tour – until we visited him shortly before he passed away.

In June 2013, I contacted Arrie, who had become very wealthy as a manufacturer of shoes and other leather products, and informed him that Mr Visser was living in Moorreesburg, but that he was very ill. I suggested we go and see him. So Arrie and I travelled out there, and I took some of my wine along. Mr Visser wasn't in a good way at all. I opened up some wine and we started to lift his spirits a bit. And that's when Arrie, in all seriousness, said, 'Sir, this is a good time to clarify something.' So now Mr Visser and I are wondering what on earth Arrie is on about.

You see, Arrie used to sit to the right and behind me in class, and he would regularly crib from me. On one occasion in Standard Four (Grade 6), Mr Visser heard me saying something to Arrie. I had disrupted his class while he was talking, so he took me outside and gave me a hiding, saying, 'You're the class captain and should know better. Why were you talking?' I didn't want to split on Arrie, so I never told Mr Visser and just left it at that, apologising for the mistake.

'Sir,' Arrie said to Mr Visser during our visit, 'you remember that day in class when you took Schalk outside and gave him a hiding for talking while you were teaching?'

'Yes, I do. Very well,' said Mr Visser.

'Well, I'd like to tell you that I was to blame.'

'How?'

'Well, it was because of me that Schalk was talking. He was actually asking me a question.'

Mr Visser was a bit puzzled by this.

'What could Schalk have been asking you, Arrie?'

'Sir, he asked me, "Arrie, have you finished copying? Can I turn my page?"'

To this day, once a year Arrie sends me a nice leather belt or a pair of shoes with a note saying, 'Thanks for getting me through primary school.'

During our visit, Arrie asked Mr Visser if he had paid for us to go on that tour. Mr Visser said he would've loved to have done so, but he also didn't have the money at the time, and it was someone else who paid. Arrie asked who, but Mr Visser said he had sworn never to tell, because that's what the donor had requested. Then he thought for a few seconds and said, 'Well, the man is dead now, so I suppose I can tell you.'

There was a man who used to sell ink to the schools, which we all used to have on our desks. His surname was De Villiers, but his nickname was 'Ink' so he was known as Ink de Villiers. He had paid for the two of us to go.

After hearing this, Arrie said to Mr Visser, 'Sir, does that make Schalk and me the first two professional rugby players in the history of Paarl Gimnasium and South Africa?'

We had such a good laugh about that, and the timing could not have been better, as our dear Mr Visser, who used to give me my asthma medicine on the side of the field, passed away two weeks after our visit.

4

A TWIST OF FATE ON THE TOUWSRIVIER TRAIN

IT TOOK 25 STITCHES to keep me out of the Western Province Craven Week team. The first time, that is. When I was 17 years old.

My rugby career was moving along steadily at school, and in 1973, when I was in matric, I made it through to the final stages of the Western Province Craven Week trials. But in my second-last trial match, I bumped heads with a player from Paul Roos Gimnasium named Harry Erasmus. It opened up a huge gash above my eye, which required 25 stitches. Dr Daantjie Greeff stitched me up and said the only way I could possibly play in the final trial would be if he bandaged my whole eye closed to keep the wound from opening again. Which he did. So I played that final trial game, in the rain at Bishops, with one eye.

Although I was in the A team, I didn't get selected. The lock who was selected in my place was a Wynberg Boys' High player by the name of John Martin, who went on to become a Springbok sailor instead. Along with Bertie Reed, he is one of South African sailing's most decorated yachtsmen.

So, having not made the Western Province Craven Week team, in June of that year I was included in a Paarl Gimnasium team that toured Pretoria for three games, with the main game once more against Affies. We were en route to Pretoria and had reached Touwsrivier when the train suddenly stopped. There was a man running down the platform shouting: 'Is there a Schalk Burger on the train?'

I was in a compartment with my friends, playing cards, when we heard him. I identified myself to the man, who said I needed to go to the stationmaster's office because there was a phone call for me. It's amazing how, throughout my rugby career, there have been some last-minute phone calls that have changed my plans. This was another of them.

When I took the call in the stationmaster's office, it was our school principal, Mr Gouws. He informed me that John Martin had suffered a bacterial infection and had been withdrawn from the Western Province team, and I had been selected to take his place. I was told to get off the train immediately and return to Paarl as quickly as possible. Mr Gouws would send a teacher to collect me.

Of course I was delighted at my inclusion. But I also felt really bad about dropping my teammates, who were waiting on the train. I don't like leaving people in the lurch, and I carried this outlook into my senior rugby days as well. As I'll point out later, it played a major part in my decision whether or not to accept my first Springbok call-up.

So, standing in the stationmaster's office, I told Mr Gouws that I couldn't drop my teammates; they were also counting on me. I decided that I would ask them to vote on whether or not I should go to Craven Week. Mr Gouws was astounded, because at that point Paarl Gimnasium had no representation in the Western Province Craven Week team, and I was now the school's only chance. But he let me go ahead with the vote. I walked back to the train and told my teammates what had transpired, and asked them to vote on the matter. Amazingly, the vote was evenly split. So I made up my mind that I would stay on the train with them. That's when one of my friends, Kippie Immelman, came out of the toilet and asked what was going on. We told him about the split vote.

'Well,' he said, 'I vote that Schalk goes to play for Western Province. I've always wanted to brag about having a mate who played Western Province Craven Week rugby.'

That Western Province Craven Week side was a really talented team, and, playing in the worst conditions, we won all of our games. I made some great friendships there. Those that stand out for me are: Skip Krige, who was our captain; Rob Louw, who I'll say more about later; Harry Erasmus; Danie van Niekerk, who a year later would make his senior provincial debut for the North Western Cape as fullback while doing his national service; and Peter Kirsten, who was sublime in the tricky conditions. I'll never forget the 45-metre drop kick he converted on a field that was little more than a mud pit. He became an outstanding cricketer, but I'm sure he would've become a Springbok rugby player had he not injured his knee, and if he had played on regular tours.

This was also the first time I was exposed to the politics of rugby. Western Province were the host union and we had made it to the Saturday unbeaten, so everybody naturally thought we would be playing the main game at a packed Coetzenburg Stadium in Stellenbosch. Our coach also used this to motivate us to play better, and we were all well aware that a good performance increased our chances of one day playing senior provincial rugby and then hopefully for the Springboks.

Then suddenly that Thursday we were told that we would not be playing in the final game. I remember Peter Kirsten had a big issue with this. I just wanted to play anyone, to be honest. But sanity prevailed and when the final draw was made, we were down to play the final game of the tournament – against Transvaal. Well, we were pumped up, and with Peter Kirsten leading the charge, we trounced them 36–7.

And that's how I ended up playing Craven Week rugby for Western Province (WP) – my first provincial-representative rugby. But if you look at the photo of that team, I'm the only one who doesn't have a WP blazer, because there was never one made for me. To this day, I don't have one. In the photo I'm actually wearing a Far North team blazer, which was light blue and the closest we could find to the WP blue. And somebody's head is in front of me, covering the emblem.

From there, my rugby career started to move quite quickly in a certain direction. I soon found myself playing in age groups above my own, and going up against the real hard men of the game, such as Hennie Coetzee and Hendrik Schräder. And the legendary Jan Ellis, who would become my first real rugby hero – and the only man I ever bit on a rugby field.

5

THE DAY I BIT JAN ELLIS

JAN ELLIS HIT ME so hard that my teammates told me I was walking around the field in a daze for a few seconds.

But let's go back a few years first.

At the end of my matric year, I was asked to play for Paarl in the Bailey Cup final against Stellenbosch's Van der Stel Rugby Club. I was only 17 years old, and here I was, playing for the Paarl first team. Both my dad and my brother Johann also played first-team rugby for Paarl. We won that final against a good Van der Stel team, and with the great WP flank Rooies van Wyk as our captain. I was now headed on a path where I was playing rugby at a much higher level than my age group.

I think it was a good experience for me. I'd always felt I was a bit of a softie at school, and being around men at such an early age helped me toughen up quite a bit. The army was also good for me in that sense; say what you like about the army, it gets you to think in a particular way and forces you to become more organised in your life.

That's not to say that there weren't challenges for a young kid playing against men. Senior rugby was hard, and they beat the living daylights out of me. You have to remember that in those days there weren't nearly as many rules around discipline and safety as there are in the game today, and the referees were also nowhere near as strict in policing incidents. Throwing a punch was actually considered a healthy part of the game.

I wasn't a fighter by nature, but in those club games I learnt very quickly that it was an eye for an eye and a tooth for a tooth on the rugby field. You had to learn to hit back harder than you got hit. To this day, people who followed my rugby career think I was this big bruiser who loved a good fight on the field. And yes, I did get into some good scraps in my time. But I always joke that I just had a really unlucky record of connecting very well with the punches I did throw. And they happened to be punches that landed on some pretty big-name players.

I actually considered giving up a sport at school because I didn't like the physicality of it. The only sport my father actively encouraged Johann and me to take was wrestling. We both hated it. When I was in Standard Three (Grade 5), I was already having to wrestle boys in Standard Five (Grade 7) because of my size.

One day, Johann complained to me that the wrestling was just hurting him too much. I was also gatvol of it. One guy in particular really hurt me every time we wrestled. I told Johann that if this guy hurt me again, I was going to bite him. Johann resolved to do the same to whoever hurt him next.

Anyway, a few days later, after Johann and I had made our decision, my dad arrived in his bakkie to pick us up from wrestling. We were waiting outside the hall on our own. We climbed in and he asked where the rest of the wrestlers were. I told him the wrestling had been cancelled, but he clearly didn't buy my story. He stopped the bakkie and went inside the wrestling hall. That's when I turned to my brother and said, 'Oh, hell, Johann. We're in big kak now.'

A few minutes later my dad came storming out, shouting, 'Julle blerrie bliksems!' (You little buggers!) He'd found out that I'd bitten the guy who was hurting me, and my brother had done the same to his opponent, and the coach had chased us out. It was one of the biggest hidings I can ever remember getting from my father. The good thing, though, was that we were both thrown out permanently,

so at least that was the end of wrestling for us. Although I must say, for any budding young rugby player, there is no better sport than wrestling for toughening up your upper body.

It was only years later, while studying at the University of Stellenbosch, that I participated in wrestling again. In fact, the first major sports event my wife Myra, then my girlfriend, came to watch me take part in was a wrestling match. I was up against a Western Province wrestler, and I somehow managed to put a great throw on him early on in the bout. It dislocated his shoulder, and I was declared the winner. When the referee held up my hand, I was, of course, extremely proud to have achieved this great victory in front of my girlfriend. But when I looked around, she was gone. It turned out that Myra was in the bathroom throwing up because she'd never seen a dislocated shoulder before.

As much as I disliked wrestling as a kid, I followed in my father's

The 8th South African Infantry Battalion receiving the freedom of Upington in 1974. I am leading the platoon as anchor marcher (far right). Next to me is my good friend the cricketer Garth le Roux, who four years later went on to become the Kerry Packer Series' player of the series.

footsteps and taught all my children to wrestle. It actually came to help Schalk Jnr in the most unlikely way.

Schalk was playing for the Springboks against the All Blacks at Kings Park in Durban during the 2007 Tri-Nations. Myra and I were watching on TV. In the 40th minute, Schalk was tackled just short of the try line and pinned on his back. I saw him put his right leg out, and he swung himself right around like you do in wrestling to create some leverage for yourself, and it allowed him to score the try.

My dad would've loved that story.

Anyway, while I was in the army I was posted to Upington, and was selected to play rugby for the North Western Cape senior team. Once again I was being pushed into teams above my age group. I was fine with this, but I told my father that I was playing Under-20 rugby. Even though my parents had separated by this time, my dad still had a limited presence in my life, and he was very much against my playing senior rugby at too young an age, because he had done the same thing and had suffered a serious back injury that basically ended his rugby career. I thought I had everything under control with the story I'd told my father.

My first match for North Western Cape was against Griquas at the Danie Kuys Stadium in Upington. They had a few big names in their team, and none more so than Piet Visagie, the Springbok flyhalf who had been the hero of the 1968 series against the British Lions. He was bidding to make a comeback so that he could be part of the 1974 Lions tour to South Africa.

I was selected as eighthman and my direct opponent was Van As Jordaan, who knocked me out twice in that game. I was so rattled that I can hardly remember anything else about this match other than tackling Piet Visagie, and that when he fell to the ground he shouted in agony that his knee was badly injured. Well, because of that injury he never did get to play against the 1974 Lions, and I felt really bad about it. I had no other intention but to stop him, although I wasn't in much of a state to think too much about anything given the working over I had received from Van As Jordaan.

A young boy who watched this match was a Sub B (Grade 2) pupil from the Kalahari who was in the hostel at a local school in Upington. His name was Tiaan Strauss, and we'd end up playing 22 seasons together at Western Province. It's funny how this game mixes time and people together.

So I was quite chuffed with myself for having stepped up a notch in the sport I was now starting to really love. Until I arrived for practice one Tuesday afternoon.

As I walked into the clubhouse, our North Western Cape coach, Chummie Jankielsohn, who later became quite a coaching legend at

Maties in Stellenbosch, said I wasn't allowed to be there and should leave immediately. My father had read in the *Paarl Post* about this 18-year-old who had been selected to play Currie Cup rugby for the North Western Cape – Schalk Burger. And that was it. He wrote a letter to the provincial union effectively banning me from playing.

In the letter he told Chummie I was under age and, in his opinion, not legally eligible to have made such a decision without his consent. He threatened to take the union to court if they allowed me to play. Part of me was angry with him, in the sense that I questioned his right to decide the future of my rugby career when he wasn't even in my life. But another part of me accepted that I had promised him I wouldn't play above my age group, and I had broken that promise. And I suppose, as my father, he was just trying to protect me.

So Chummie dropped me from the team. I phoned my dad so that we could talk it over. I apologised for lying to him, but I also told him that I'd thought it over carefully, and that I was already playing senior rugby against most of these players in the army. And yes, they were knocking me around quite a bit, but I was also getting hold of a few of them. I told my dad I could handle it, and he eventually accepted that.

So here I was, playing Currie Cup rugby at the age of 18. Unbeknown to me, it drew the kind of attention that would soon lead to that phone call from Doc Craven.

Then, in 1974, I had the opportunity to play against my rugby hero, Jan Ellis, who was playing for South West Africa (now Namibia). Jan was a veteran of 38 Tests for the Springboks and was a fearsome flank. He is easily regarded as one of the greatest Springboks of all time, and a player who was instantly recognisable not only for his physical style of play but also for his trademark red hair. For years he held the record for most tries by a Springbok forward. He was an incredible player with a supreme physical presence and an iron will. But when I first played against him, he was in my way, and something had to be done.

We played the match in Windhoek. It was a hard match, as they all were in those days. At one point I was trying to get the ball out of a loose maul. Suddenly this hand came through, trying to pull it back. I was screaming at the referee, who did nothing. I looked at this white, freckled hand and didn't immediately know who it belonged to, although I should have. But that didn't matter. This hand was stopping me from getting the ball. So I bit the hand. It was the silly reaction of a frustrated 18-year-old playing Currie Cup rugby against a bunch of tough and very experienced men.

After biting this rogue hand, the next thing was I had the daylights punched out of me. Clearly, Jan didn't take kindly to having his hand bitten by some whippersnapper. My teammates said I was walking in the wrong direction on the field for a few seconds.

I eventually became very good friends with Jan, until the day he died. He owned a sports store in Windhoek. In fact, I'd visited his shop with our coach Chummie before the game to get a new pair of boots. Mine were in tatters. When Jan saw the size of my feet, he said to Chummie, 'This kid doesn't want a big pair of boots, or even the box the boots come in. Those feet need the bloody ship that brought them here.'

6

THE SPRINGBOK JOURNEY BEGINS

I MADE THE DEFENCE FORCE Under-20 team in 1974. That same year, it was announced that the first South African Under-21 side would be selected. It was to be called the Oribis, and a tour to South America was planned for 1975. Imagine playing trials over a two-year period today.

That team was the product of Doc Craven's vision and foresight. Doc knew that the future of the Springbok team would involve the inclusion of 'non-white' players, even if the politics of the day prevented this. In his mind, the Oribis team was going to be the first South African national team to include players of colour. That was his vision, but unfortunately it never became a reality.

I desperately wanted to be part of the Oribis, because of the opportunity to visit South America, and I was grateful when I was selected. Gysie Pienaar and I were the only two players from the Defence Force to make it into the side. Nic Boje, the father of the South African cricketer Nicky Boje, was the coach, and Jannie Krige, of the Kanonkop wine estate family, was our manager. It was a fabulous team, and some of my fondest rugby memories are from that time.

Nic was very polite and well spoken. He was a real team man, and he showed me that you've also got to have a bit of fun and enjoy what you're doing. I remember countless evenings with Nic leading us in the singing of the much-loved French children's song 'Alouette': 'Alouette, gentille alouette …'

It's incredible to think that nine senior Springboks came out of that Oribis side: me, Theuns Stofberg, Rob Louw, Divan Serfontein, De Wet Ras, Dirk Froneman, Gysie Pienaar, Shaun Povey and Edrich Krantz.

When I made the team, the Paarl community did a great thing for me. They held a collection so that I would have some spending money for the trip, and handed it over to me at a ceremony held at the Paarl Rugby Club. It was a gesture that touched me deeply.

I had always felt that the Paarl community was split between those who lived above Main Road and those who lived below. I felt this even more when many of my mates from school would go on holiday to Hermanus with their families and I would stay behind to look after their farms for them. It was a way for me to earn a bit of extra money, as I grew up on the wrong side of Main Road. I won't say there was ever a feeling of injustice or bitterness or anything of that sort. I'd learnt early on to simply get on with things and not dwell too much on the unfair aspects of life. But it was nevertheless a feeling that always remained with me.

My Oribis selection also meant that my son Schalk Jnr and I would later become the first father and son to have played for the South African Under-21 team. Schalk Jnr made the South African Under-21 team in 2002. Interestingly enough, Gysie Pienaar and his son Ruan became the second such father-and-son pairing.

So the Oribis went to South America in 1975 and we had an absolute ball. It was a whirlwind trip involving everything from a shooting at a hotel (an assassination attempt on a trade union leader who was staying there) to making the most incredible friends. We also met Alfredo Stroessner, the notorious president of Paraguay who made the country a haven for exiled Nazis.

When we arrived at Montevideo, the capital of Uruguay, I received a telegram from my mother informing me that she had read the story of the Uruguayan rugby team whose chartered aircraft had crashed in the Andes in October 1972. Because of this, she urged me to please not fly over the Andes with the team but to rather take a train to Santiago in Chile. It goes to show that a mother never stops looking out for her children, no matter how old they are. I didn't take the train, purely because I didn't want to be separated from the team. But I never told my mom that.

The world of rugby is an amazing family. The lock I played against on that leg of the tour was Nando Parrado. He and Roberto Canessa were the two members of that Uruguayan team who decided to walk out from the crash site rather than wait to be rescued. We actually played against many of the survivors of that horrific tragedy, in which only 16 of the original party of 45 survived. It was still a terrible time for them. The Roman Catholic Church had not yet pardoned them for their acts of cannibalism, and they suffered great emotional turmoil as a result.

I had wanted to be a part of the Oribis team because I thought it would be fun, and I was right. It was an amazing time for all of us, and to this day we still have an annual reunion of that first South African Under-21 team.

After the tour, I returned to the University of Stellenbosch to complete my first year of studies. But the twists and turns of life still had a few surprises in store for me. It shows you that no matter what your own plans are, sometimes life takes you in another direction.

And mine was about to take a turn that nobody expected.

7

THE POLITICS OF RUGBY

THERE WAS A TIME when I felt those quaint, narrow streets in Stellenbosch were choking me.

In my days playing rugby in Stellenbosch, it became quite clear to me that there was a privileged route to success. As a student, I was quite outspoken in my political beliefs against the National Party regime, which had a stronghold in Stellenbosch. Now, I know what you're thinking. These days, everybody claims to have been an anti-apartheid activist. Nobody ever voted for the National Party, it seems, which makes you wonder how on earth they ever came to power in the first place. But let me clarify.

The Springbok Dawie de Villiers was chairman of Die Ruiterwag, which was the youth wing of the National Party. Many of the Maties rugby players of my era were members. But I didn't really hold any single political view. My close relationship with my mother meant I leaned more towards her liberal politics. My brother Johann, on the other hand, felt differently. Apart from his army duties, for a time he was also the chairman of the Junior National Party in the Western Cape. I won't say I've always agreed with his viewpoint. Maybe I felt that the tide of history always turns, and I loved him enough to want him to be on the right side when it did turn.

I had a natural inclination to rebel against the system, which got me into trouble sometimes. One such occasion was a match we played against Ikeys (the University of Cape Town). Afterwards we joined the Ikeys players for a night on the town, ending up at the Sea Point Hotel. In those days the fashion was for young people to sing songs in public. That's how we entertained ourselves – with songs. The Ikeys players were singing some highly political and liberal songs, and I suggested we all go to the police station in Sea Point and sing for the police. It seemed like a great idea at the time, but needless to say we were arrested for it.

During my time at Stellenbosch I grew to hate the political system in South Africa, which made its presence felt even in rugby in terms of Springbok selection. It irked me that your political affiliation enabled you to become a bank manager or a school principal or get a leading job somewhere. Or become a Springbok, for that matter.

At one point, I was approached to attend what I wasn't aware was a Ruiterwag meeting. On arrival in Jonkershoek, and after being asked to give a password to enter the premises, I realised I had been set up. I also realised I was definitely not correctly dressed for this meeting. All of the other attendees looked as if they were still in the army, while I was wearing my standard university gear of purple bell-bottom jeans, T-shirt and sandals. I left as soon as I could. In retrospect, I suppose if I had hung around longer it could've helped me become a Springbok a lot earlier.

I certainly wasn't the only one who was frustrated by the politics in rugby. Doc Craven once confided to me that he had left the Dutch Reformed Church in 1965, after Hendrik Verwoerd's Loskop Dam speech, which basically banned the All Blacks from touring South Africa because of the Maoris in their team. Doc Craven was a rugby man, but he was also a spiritual man. He had studied to become a minister of the church, so for him to have left the Dutch Reformed Church meant he felt very strongly about it.

During this tumultuous time, an idea of what rugby could mean for me was also crystallising in my mind. I was playing for the Maties

On my 21st birthday, in Eendrag Residence, Stellenbosch, with Francois Conradie in 1976. Francois later became one of the heroes of the Laingsburg flood, rescuing many people from the old-age home.

and WP Under-20 teams. But when we returned from the Oribis tour to South America, I arrived for practice with the Maties Under-20s and was told I should be practising with the senior team. The next Saturday I moved straight into the first team, at flank. Doc put me in at the cost of a player named Mervyn Sinclair, who later became Morné du Plessis' brother-in-law. I was still in my first year at university.

I realised that my rugby career was definitely moving in a direction. I played in the great intervarsity matches against Ikeys, and the Toyota Club Championship and Easter Weeks were phenomenal as we played to sell-out crowds and thousands of fans. I also played in two national Sevens championships. So I started to get serious about my rugby, and I set my sights on Western Province.

In 1977, the morning after an important game against Diggers in Stellenbosch, *Die Burger* announced that I was among four new players selected for the Western Province team: Wilhelm Schmidt and I were the locks, and Swys Joubert and Bob Bolus the centres. I was 21 years old. And so Western Province became the second provincial union I played rugby for, from 1977 to 1978.

But with this came the increased pressure to fit into the mould. In my mind, there was still far too much politics involved in becoming a Western Province or Springbok rugby player, and that was a game I just didn't want to play. If you toed the line, you were on the fast track to rugby royalty. But I wasn't made that way. There has always been something of the rebel in me, which at times in my rugby career cost me dearly.

The politically charged environment in Stellenbosch had reached a point where I almost felt smothered by this nationalistic fervour. At this time, the Broederbond was close to the peak of its influence in all spheres of society, including Springbok rugby. The Bond had been formed in 1918, to advance the interests of Afrikaners, and steadily extended its reach during the 1920s and 1930s. Prime Minister Jan Smuts was so opposed to the Broederbond that in 1944 he declared in Parliament that no Broeder would be allowed to work in the civil service. Richard Steyn's excellent biography, *Jan Smuts: Unafraid of Greatness*, details how Smuts saw the Broederbond and the influence it wielded in government as 'a blight that has come over South Africa', a view shared by another former prime minister, JBM Hertzog.

The problem in the Afrikaner community at the time was that if you didn't conform, then you were considered to be against them. I hated the Broederbond for one overriding reason: I didn't believe that some Afrikaners were better than others. I was already part of an economic system that made some people feel inferior to others. As a result, I had this strong belief that you had to go out there and prove yourself, and not just benefit from coming from a certain school or family. That's what I'd always loved about sport: the equality of the sports field.

So, against the increasingly political backdrop of playing rugby in Stellenbosch, I made up my mind that I wanted out. After completing my studies, the terms of the Railways Bursary dictated that I would have to go to Johannesburg to work for the railways for a period of time. But Johannesburg wasn't the out I was looking for. I saw a job advertised for an international business management graduate trainee at General Motors in Port Elizabeth (PE), and I applied. Lo and behold, I was given the job. Soon afterwards, Gideon Huisamen, an attorney and also then the coach of Eastern Province (EP), contacted me and asked if I would consider playing rugby for EP. I told him that I had just got a job at General Motors and still had to pay off the balance of my Railways Bursary, which was about R3 000.

So he agreed to pay off the balance on my behalf if I would play for EP. I think right there I became EP rugby's first professional signing. Of course, my mate Arrie Slabbert will say we'd already reached professional status at primary school, thanks to Ink de Villiers' paying for our rugby tour to Pretoria.

Eastern Province rugby would become my new home.

I arranged to meet with Doc Craven to tell him I was moving to Eastern Province. He was furious. And that's when we had our first big falling-out. Doc said that under no circumstances was I allowed to leave Stellenbosch and the Western Province fold. According to Doc, there was absolutely no way I would become a Springbok playing for Eastern Province. That incensed me. I was done with people telling me that there was a particular system I had to be part of in order to play top-level rugby in South Africa. I was just being myself, and that didn't work for either Doc or the system.

Doc had changed my life with his phone call while I was in the army, and I was grateful for everything he had done for me. But at this time in my career, I felt the move to Eastern Province was one I had to make. Doc couldn't accept that.

Although my relationship with him had its rocky moments, it remains one of my greatest privileges to have played under Danie Craven. In my opinion, he was the most holistic coach South African rugby ever had.

And I don't believe we'll ever see his like in the game again.

8

DOC CRAVEN

IT WAS WELL KNOWN that if Doc Craven called you to his office on the Saturday morning before a match, then you were going to become a Springbok.

The reasoning behind this assumption was that rugby was everything to Doc. So for him to call you to his office before an occasion as important to him as a rugby match that day meant that he liked you and wanted to share some of his rugby wisdom with you.

So one Saturday morning I received a message to say that Doc wanted to see me. I was ecstatic. But when I entered his office, his first question was where I'd been on Friday night. I told him I played in a band with a few of my koshuis (residence) friends. In Doc's world, you didn't go out on the town the night before a rugby game. So he dropped me on the morning of the match. That almost never happened. His message to me was clear: 'Schalk, you can't serve two gods. It's either rugby or music.'

I had a good relationship with Doc Craven, even though we sometimes didn't see eye to eye. I once accused him of lying, and, as I'll explain, I believe he cost me the Springbok captaincy in 1986.

But I think what Doc saw in me was not the typical rugby player, and though he couldn't always understand this about me, on an intellectual level we had a real connection. I played first team for Maties, but that was never my whole life, even though I gave it everything and played hard. I loved rugby because I liked the challenge the game presented. I enjoyed being selected ahead of other players and then being asked to prove myself. I liked the idea of a coach entrusting me with a job, in my case at flank, and then having to execute that job.

I broke the game down into a study of what skills I needed to do the job effectively, and would throw myself into that process. I knew a coach like Craven would be forthright with me and tell me if I didn't have it, so I enjoyed the opportunity of playing under him. Many players these days don't want to be told what's right or wrong with their game.

With Doc, you had a specific job as a player and you were entrusted to do it well. He never complimented a player who scored a try, because to him you were just doing your job. I tend to cringe when today's players high-five each other after a big tackle or a turnover. What's the high-five for? The man's just doing his job. A lock takes his own ball in the lineout and gets a high-five. Why? What else is he in the team for? It's his job!

I consider myself extremely privileged, as I think any player who played under Doc will say, to have played during his time in South African rugby. These were Doc's most creative years in the game. He was hurt by what had happened in 1974 with the British Lions. We all thought that South African brawn would be good enough against the Lions, and they beat us hands down. They had moved to another level in skills development. So my time at Maties from 1975 onwards overlapped with Doc's decision that South African rugby had to evolve.

He was one of the pioneers of focused training, whereby you trained within the realms of a game. He was a great strategist, and always used to say, 'The other team is only as good as you allow them to be.' He instilled in us a philosophy that the way you live is the way you play. How you conduct yourself off the field – how you live your life, in other words – is how you will be on the field.

Doc left an indelible mark on me in terms of getting my mind and body in sync. His approach resonated with me, even though I sometimes struggled a bit to achieve those lofty ideals.

But Doc ticked all the boxes in my mind, especially with his rugby strategies. He would say, 'Whatever your opponent wants you to do the most, you do the least, and whatever he wants you to do the least, you do the most.' He would plan matches like a military assault on the enemy. The backs would know what the forwards' calls were, and vice versa. Doc would make us stand up in a team meeting and recite the calls. Everybody in the team knew everybody else's job.

He had the ability to manipulate your brain so that you understood exactly what he wanted to get across to you as a player. He was phenomenal in that way. Doc was my ideal coach, and, in my opinion, he was one of the few really outstanding coaches we've had in South African rugby. And when it comes to coaches and captains, I've pretty much seen them all. In my first match for WP, Morné du Plessis was our captain and coach. At one point at Maties, we had two captains: Jan 'Boland' Coetzee captained the forwards and Dawie Snyman the backs. While I was playing for Eastern Province, my coach was Stan Terblanche, a passionate sportsman who was also a sports writer for the *Eastern Province Herald* and who had taken over the coaching reins from Gideon Huisamen. So I've played under a few interesting coaching and captaincy scenarios. And I've played under some pretty terrible coaches. You can't always go up to a coach and say, 'You're useless.' Sometimes you just have to deal with it.

But in the era that I played, I believe I was blessed to be surrounded by highly intellectual, talented people.

Danie Craven: A theology student who also went on to study social sciences and anthropology, and obtained a BA, MA and PhD in ethnology from the University of Stellenbosch. And he became a professor of physical education as well.

Springbok coach Dr Cecil Moss: A physician who was part of the team that performed the world's first heart transplant. Doc Moss was very much a people's person. In 1986, while we were negotiating a better financial deal for us as Springboks, he allowed us to have all the meetings we needed. We used to call him 'Oumatjie', because he used to fret about everything.

James Starke: Our then chairman of selections and a man famed as much for his unshakeable loyalty as for his success in business. He was also the brother-in-law of the businessman Whitey Basson.

Professor Fritz Eloff: The former president of the Blue Bulls. A man with a BSc degree from the University of Pretoria and an MSc, which he achieved cum laude; professor and head of the department of zoology at the University of Pretoria.

Buurman van Zyl: The coach of Northern Transvaal. People make the mistake of thinking he was just a policeman, but he was a deep thinker about a variety of things.

Dawie Snyman: The coach of Western Province. We were blessed to have somebody who realised he had a highly talented team of players. His biggest priority was to muster the collective skills of all the players, and his greatest strength was that he knew us all well, because he had played with us. I don't think there's ever been a coach who achieved the kind of success he did in coaching players with whom he'd also played. His style of management and understanding of particular players was critical to the team's success.

Augie Cohen: The Springbok team doctor in those days. He was a lovely guy, always ready for a laugh, and the butt of many of our practical jokes. We would put Vaseline on his glasses and he would think he was going blind.

South African rugby was blessed with these fantastic people in leading positions in every province. And Doc Craven was certainly at the head of this list. But that's not to say that Doc and I didn't have our disagreements. We had many.

I had a few serious fights on the field with Jan 'Boland' Coetzee, later the winemaker at Kanonkop. He was always late for practice and seriously unfit. He would climb in and moer everybody. One day I'd had enough and so I hit him back. The next day I was called in to Doc's office and was banned for a week. He told me I had no respect for the older players. 'No, Doc, he has no respect for us younger players,' I said. 'Rob Louw and all of them won't fight him, but I guarantee you, Doc, if it comes down to just the two of us, I'll kill him. I won't stop.' Craven looked at me and said, 'Waar kom jy vandaan?' (Where do you come from?) It was a line he often used with me. I spent a lot of time in his office, just talking, and he'd hear my views on matters and then stare out the window and say, 'Burger, waar kom jy vandaan?'

I used to also tell him, 'Doc, you need to understand me. I'm not a rugby player. I'm just a normal guy playing rugby.'

But one of the biggest ructions in our relationship also exposed one of the major controversies in world rugby at the time.

In 1985, I was voted one of the five South African Rugby Players of the Year. Then, in 1986, as part of the centenary celebrations of the International Rugby Board (IRB, now World Rugby), a World XV was selected to play the British Lions at Cardiff Arms Park in Wales. I was the only South African selected.

This was at the height of the anti-apartheid demonstrations, so the officials decided to put both teams in the same hotel – the iconic Angel Hotel on the corner right next to Cardiff Arms Park – so that if there were any protests about my inclusion, it would affect both teams.

It was a momentous occasion, because no South African team or player had played at Cardiff Arms Park since the politically charged 1969–1970 Springbok tour. The match was played on 16 April that year, and our World XV won 15–7 in horribly wet conditions. Sadly, this match would prove to be a very brief glimpse of international rugby for the Springboks of that time, and with South Africa in such turmoil and suffering, the criticism from the global community only grew.

But that World XV Test was significant for me for another reason. Andy Haden of the All Blacks was my roommate, and as a result I found myself with a front-row seat to an event that threatened the very fabric of global rugby and set the game on a completely different path.

JUST A MOMENT

One evening in the hotel, another great All Black, Andy Dalton, came into our room. I was lying on the bed with my eyes closed, resting. I heard Dalton ask Haden if I was asleep. So I pretended to be fast asleep. And they proceeded to talk about the All Blacks' tour to South Africa as a rebel Cavaliers side in 1986. Naturally, I was intrigued, as I was well aware that most countries had been banned from touring South Africa as part of the Gleneagles Agreement (1977) and the international sporting ban imposed in response to apartheid. But then I heard Dalton and Haden saying that it was confirmed that the tour would take place later that April and May, because Doc Craven had signed the agreement. Dalton said he'd just received confirmation. And they were all going to be paid NZ$100 000 each.

Dalton was ecstatic and invited Haden to join him downstairs for a beer to celebrate. Haden put the document in his suitcase and the two left. No sooner had they gone than I jumped up and grabbed the document. I locked myself in the toilet and read it through. And, sure as hell, what Dalton had said was correct. At the bottom of the contract was Doc Craven's signature. I sneaked downstairs and had the contract photocopied. I was the only South African player who knew that payments would be made to the All Blacks. It was through an intricate contract between Sporting Contacts, Haden's company, and Ellis Park (Pty) Ltd.

When I returned home from the World XV match, I went to see Doc. I told him that I knew the South African Rugby Board (SARB) were paying the All Blacks to tour as the Cavaliers. 'So what are we going to be paid, Doc?' I asked him. Remember, as players we'd had no international tours because of sanctions, and since 1981 the SARB had been dangling the carrot of international tours in front of us. Other than in 1984, when we had the Tests against England, international rugby was non-existent for us.

Doc denied that they were paying the Cavaliers. I told him I knew otherwise, and I'll never forget the look on his face. He quietly admitted, 'I made a mistake.' Doc believed deeply in the amateur code of rugby.

Anyway, before the Cavaliers played the Springboks in the first Test at Newlands in Cape Town, Burger Geldenhuys broke Andy Haden's jaw in a warm-up match against Northern Transvaal. Andy was a former All Blacks captain, and Burger was also in the Springbok team. So Doc decided he was going to make an example of Burger and he dropped him in favour of Wahl Bartmann, who made his Springbok debut in that Test. At the same time, I was still pushing Doc on the money issue and demanding answers. And that's when Doc took the captaincy away from me and handed it to Naas Botha for the Cavaliers series.

How do I know this? Well, I was captain of the final trials team, so it was natural to assume that I would be captain of the Springbok team. But, beyond this, Naas Botha also wrote in his autobiography that it was known I was going to captain the team. And my father-in-law's best friend was a man named Alex Kellerman, who was the general secretary of the SARB at the time. He'd already told my father-in-law that I had been selected as captain for the 1986 Springbok team against the New Zealand Cavaliers.

But Doc went even further, threatening to expose me as a professional and ban me from all rugby. It was ludicrous, particularly as the SARB had sold Toyota a logo sponsorship on the Springbok jersey for R50 000 for that series. I refused to play with that logo on my jersey. I actually taped it up.

A lot of the players were in my corner on the money issue. So I registered a company called Springbok Enterprises and began signing up the players in our team, with the aim of ensuring that we also received compensation for the Tests against the Cavaliers. My friend Chris Faure, who became an attorney after his rugby-playing days, wrote up the contracts for us. All but Naas Botha, who had been selected as captain of the team, signed with us. Naas had decided he was better off on his own. So now we had this subtle power that, as a united group of players, we could decide not to play.

There was a lot of turmoil in the team during the series, as we had meeting after meeting about the payment issue. With all of this going on, our coach, Doc Moss, was obviously concerned that we were losing focus. But I told him what my good friend and South African rally-driving legend Sarel van der Merwe always said: 'Coach, when the flag drops, the bullshit stops.'

I assured Doc Moss that there would be no further business talk after the Thursday before the first Test, and that when we hit that field, we would do our job as a team. And we certainly did. We won the first Test 21–15 at Newlands. Then we lost the second Test 18–19 in Durban, but beat them 33–18 at Loftus Versfeld and 24–10 at Ellis Park to win the series. The build-up to the final Test at Ellis Park was tense. We heard reports that the Cavaliers were practising the haka and would perform it before the Test. It would be the only time the All Blacks performed the haka in a Test under a different name.

The Cavaliers also took their fair share of abuse back home, as the New Zealand public felt they'd betrayed their country for personal gain. Most of those players never recovered from being targeted in this way. As rugby players, though, we were all in the same boat. They desperately wanted to play against and beat the Springboks on home soil, and we were desperate for international rugby and the chance to play against our mightiest foe.

Amid all of this was the issue of payment, as rugby was clearly moving into the professional era, but doing so in a very amateur way. I had spent the entire Test series campaigning hard for the South African players to be paid along the lines of the Cavaliers. Then, on the Thursday night before the final Test in Johannesburg, Jan Pickard, the president of the Western Province Rugby Football Union and a representative on the IRB, and Louis Luyt arrived with cheques for each player in our team. We were only paid R5 700 each, but in 1986 that was quite a lot of money. It wasn't near the amount the Cavaliers' players received, which was all paid through Ellis Park (Pty) Ltd. But it was something that represented the principle of the matter.

And the SARB still had no clue how I'd found out about the payments to the Cavaliers.

9

MY EP RUGBY FAMILY

AFTER FOUR YEARS AT MATIES, and against the wishes of Doc Craven, I made the decision to move to Port Elizabeth and start my new job at General Motors.

Little did I know that I would get mixed up with an apartheid activist who'd spent a decade on Robben Island, I'd be threatened by the National Intelligence Service (NIS) and I'd end up losing my Eastern Province captaincy because of politics. Again.

But personally the move to Port Elizabeth gave me more freedom to be myself. And I was exposed to some memorable characters.

I'll never forget the time when a few of Eastern Province rugby's most famous raconteurs were on their way back from a fishing trip to Huisklip, just past St Francis Bay. I'm told they came through Humansdorp and then into Jeffreys Bay. And that's when they spotted the circus – Brian's Circus.

In the bakkie were Pieter Malan Cilliers and a few of his mates. And, as men often do at the end of a successful fishing trip, they came up with what they thought was a splendid idea. The bakkie belonged to Pieter and was brand new. So they thought this was as good a time as any to put it to the test – by towing away the lion cage.

They stopped at the circus. One of them climbed out of the

bakkie and was doing his best to sneak past the lion cage to see how they could hook it up. Inside the main circus tent, the show was on the go. Although the lions weren't too worried about these intruders and were generally quite placid, the boys decided that perhaps their plan was a bit *too* ambitious. Then they spotted a cage containing some Toy Pom dogs, which were obviously there to do tricks. They were pretty excitable, so the boys opened the cage and released them. The dogs ran wild, barking their way into the circus tent and disrupting the whole show.

That's when the famous Tickey the Clown came around the corner and shouted that he had seen them release the dogs. So, of course, Pieter and the team all took off after Tickey, the eyewitness to their mischievous act. I'm told he sped off at a pace, ran around the tent and into a caravan where he slammed the door shut and locked it. Then he pulled back the curtain and stuck his tongue out at them. So Pieter said to his fellow troublemakers, 'Just keep him busy.' He reversed his bakkie and hooked up the caravan. They all jumped in and took off, with Tickey in the caravan screaming blue murder.

According to Pieter, the next moment there was a loud bang and a blue flame shot up behind them. They thought the caravan had exploded. What they hadn't realised was that all the performers' caravans were wired up to the electricity supply, and then to the main circus tent. So after the blue flame there was an almighty explosion and the whole place was plunged into darkness. In the meantime they were still tearing off with this caravan behind them. To make matters worse, the struts of the caravan were obviously out, so there were sparks flying on the tar behind them as they drove. But they were now committed, so they kept up the getaway. A few kilometres later one of the bakkie's occupants said, 'Boys, hier is groot kak. We better let this guy go.'

So at the turnoff to Humansdorp they found a gravel road, reversed the caravan into the veld, unhitched it and then drove the hell out of there. As they passed Jeffreys Bay, they could see that chaos was still reigning at the circus. Of course, they resolved to not breathe a word of this to anybody.

The next day, I was on the beach with a few of these boys. We bumped into George Rautenbach's dad, Rykie, and as we were chatting he said, 'Manne, you won't believe what happened last night.' Rykie proceeded to tell us that every year when Brian's Circus came to town, he would take his grandkids to see the show. 'We were having a great time watching the juggler, and the kids were loving it, when the next minute all of these bloody poodles come charging into the tent. The juggler drops everything, and then there was this massive explosion and suddenly everything went black. The lions were roaring outside and people were screaming inside. It was chaos,' he told us.

I listened intently but was also laughing because it sounded hilarious. I only later found out that my mates were involved. This story has been kept quiet for many years, but it sums up the spirit in EP rugby during the time I was there.

There are those who say I spent too long in Port Elizabeth and it hampered my Springbok career, and maybe I did stay two years too long. But I loved it there. I loved the rugby and I loved the people. And most of all, when I started coaching there a bit, I loved how we were this underdog team trying to beat the traditional giants from Western Province or Northern Transvaal, and how we often got it right.

My time in Port Elizabeth also helped to shape my political views. And it certainly shaped my absolute intolerance for political correctness and following the crowd. To this day, I struggle to put up with people who try to be something they are not. I have always felt very comfortable in my own skin, and among my EP rugby family I felt very comfortable indeed.

Myra and I were blessed to have so many good people around us there. She will tell you that some of our happiest times were in Port Elizabeth. We didn't have any children yet, so it was a carefree time in which we had a lot of fun.

Myra and I first started dating in 1977. I knew of her before then, though. Her family had moved from PE to Paarl when her father, who was a teacher, was made principal of the WA Joubert Primary School. My brother Johann later became a teacher there.

Myra had a brother by the name of Bouwer, and he and my other younger brother, Paul, became best friends. So I was more than a little aware of this beautiful Afrikaans meisie. But in 1974 I left to do my national service, and then I went to university. While at university, Paarl Gimnasium asked if I would help their Under-16 rugby team prepare for the interschools competition. So I ended up taking Paul and Bouwer to their practices, and I saw Myra again. Suffice to say she still grabbed my attention in a pretty big way. I was dating Dawie Snyman's sister, Marie Louise, at the time. I'm pretty sure Myra was also dating somebody, although she denies it to this day. So I broke up with Marie Louise and started dating Myra.

We got engaged in 1979, the same year I started playing rugby in Port Elizabeth. Myra kept asking me when we were going to get married, and I told her that I honestly didn't know. I was playing rugby every weekend and there just wasn't an open weekend for a wedding. The first Saturday after rugby season that year fell on 6 October. Myra decided on her own that it would be the date for our wedding. It was also my birthday. She didn't want it that way, but it was the only open weekend I had. And I'm forever grateful that it was, and for the great years we've shared.

After my experience with Maties and the system in Stellenbosch, playing rugby for EP really brought back my love for the game. And I suppose it also fuelled a growing desire to play for the Springboks. Doc Craven had told me that if I ever went to Eastern Province I would never become a Springbok, and I saw that as a challenge.

I now know that if I'd left Port Elizabeth a bit earlier in my career I could probably have played Springbok rugby sooner, though truth be told there wasn't much Test rugby going on anyway because of sanctions. But I stayed with EP for as long as I did because I enjoyed it.

I decided to join the University of Port Elizabeth (UPE) rugby club, and boy did we have fun there. It was a young club, with a mixture of some incredible young talent and a few older players who just wanted to play the game, score tries, score with the girls, have a beer and some wine, and have a lot of laughs. We jacked up the coaching, and pretty soon we had a team that was beating the big club sides in South Africa and having a lot of fun at the same time, with none of the politics in rugby.

We had older players such as George Rautenbach, Boeram Venter, Gavin Cowley, Fred Dreyer, Daantjie van Schalkwyk and Chris Heunis, and then probably the most talented group of youngsters I've had the opportunity to coach and play with, among them Johan Heunis, André Johnson, Jan Boelie Serfontein, Robert Blignaut, Tino Kankowski and Fats Robertson. If not for the international sports sanctions against South Africa, many of these players would have become Springboks.

I have such fond memories of training, then going to the beach for a surf and having a beer or two with the guys before going home. The beach was a real part of the training regime of George Rautenbach and me. On most mornings we'd arrive at McArthur public swimming pool at 6 am, run the whole beach to the harbour wall and back, then catch a few waves, shower and go home. I loved living in Port Elizabeth.

I was made captain of the team in my first match for Eastern Province in 1979, ironically to play one of my former teams, North Western Cape, in Upington. In the end, I played over 70 games for Eastern Province over five seasons, and coached them as well. I really threw myself into trying to make EP a great team.

With Myra in Australia in 2001. We were following our son Tiaan, who was on a school cricket tour to Australia.

We played in the semi-finals of the Currie Cup on two consecutive occasions, in 1979 and 1980. The 1980 semi-final was against our old foe, Western Province, at the Boet Erasmus Stadium in PE. We had scored two tries to WP's nil. But their flyhalf Robbie Blair was in excellent kicking form. Despite a strong wind, he'd converted all seven penalties to keep them ahead. The referee, Johan Gouws, was also blowing us to pieces, which frustrated us. Gouws's biased refereeing ultimately cost us a deserved place in the final that year.

And that's why Morné du Plessis and I eventually came to blows in this match. But before I get into the detail of what happened, let me first clarify that I have always admired and respected Morné, and today we are very good friends. Even as a young player I always looked up to him.

Morné had left the University of Stellenbosch when I arrived in 1975, but I had wanted to meet him ever since the 1973 Craven Week. The bed I was assigned at Wilgenhof residence for that tournament had his name carved into it.

I got to know him playing for the Western Province Under-20

Me and Henry Bezuidenhout, our Eastern Province tighthead prop, playing against Northern Transvaal. In the air is my great adversary Louis Moolman, with whom I also played four Tests against the Cavaliers in 1986. At right is Piet Kruger, the Northern Transvaal prop, who also played with us against the Cavaliers.

Ready for lift-off. The angle of my hips and my hand position indicate that this was going to be a flat hard ball at number four. I was the first lock in South Africa to start using this kind of throw-in. The two Eastern Province players behind me are Andrew Johnson and Pote Human, who unfortunately never represented South Africa due to the sports sanctions. In the background (from left) are Burger Geldenhuys and Jannie Breedt of Northern Transvaal.

team, as we travelled together and attended the same post-match functions. He was my first captain at Western Province when I played my first match in the beloved blue-and-white hooped jersey against Border in East London. Wilhelm Schmidt, Swys Joubert – who now owns arguably one of the best rugby museums in the world, based at Ellis Park – and Bob Bolus also made their debuts that day. The initiation before that match was a great experience for all of us, and we really felt the magic of being a senior WP player.

Morné impressed me as someone who was different and a bit quirky, but highly intelligent. I marvelled at his public-speaking skills. He would deliver incredible speeches at the post-match functions and was always so eloquent. It's quite interesting that ever since the first moment we got to know each other, we have always spoken English to each other.

But we were always competitors first, especially when Doc Craven used me as a flank forward, which put me in the direct line to come up against Morné during a game. And in that 1980 Currie Cup semi-final, we were most definitely fierce competitors.

The biased refereeing in that match was starting to grind down all of us at EP, but perhaps I was a little more frustrated than my teammates. So when I saw Morné chatting to referee Johan Gouws during the match, complaining about what he felt was our overly physical approach to the game, it was the last straw for me. I felt that Morné's constant chats with the ref were just making him more biased against us. Morné always had the ear of the referees, and this match was no exception. Every time Morné complained to the ref, he won them a penalty. So when he again complained, and was awarded yet another penalty, I saw red. As he tapped to take a quick penalty, Morné pointed at us to suggest to the referee that we were offside. So I hit him with a thunderous tackle.

It was a spear tackle. I tipped him over and he went down hard on his shoulder. (To my embarrassment, the photo of the two of us on the ground following the tackle later appeared in the Western Province rugby centenary book.) It wasn't a nice sound when Morné hit the ground shoulder first. And that was it. That tackle basically ended Morné's rugby career. To his credit, he has never held it against me and has never said anything to me about it. We're good friends today, which I think speaks volumes about Morné's character.

I don't think his mother ever forgave me for that tackle, though. A few years ago I attended a birthday party of his. He introduced me to his mom with the words, 'Mom, do you still remember Schalk?' His mom looked at me and said, 'How will I ever forget this thug of a man?'

Make no mistake, Morné could be just as much of a hothead on the field as I was in those days. He was involved in a few punch-ups, and, like me, was also something of a rebel. He too had his clashes with the rugby authorities of the day. So we were more alike than I think we even realised back then.

A perfect example of this was the first South African club rugby match to be televised live, the Grand Challenge Final between Maties and Villagers in 1977. It was played at Newlands, and it was also the first rugby match that Myra watched me play. When her father was leaving the house that morning, he mentioned that he and his friends would not be attending the match but instead watching it on TV. He implored her that I must please not be sent off or anything silly.

Early in the second half, our Maties prop Flippie van der Merwe was sent off for hitting Bobby Murtagh, the Villagers lock. About ten minutes later, following an anticipated quick throw-in by Miles O'Brien to Morné, which I intercepted, Morné and I also came to blows. Referee Mike Kessel blew his whistle and ordered Morné off, so I commented to my teammates, 'At least we are now equal on the field,' to which the referee replied, 'I think you should also walk.' I gave him a stern look and said, 'You better think very carefully about that, ref.' He did. He sent me off as well.

The final score was 14–13, which was exactly the opposite of the number of players still left on the field for both teams.

Many years later, Morné and I had just finished a game of golf at Hermanus Golf Club and were having a beer when I saw a distinctive character who looked like Mike Kessel. I had my doubts, though, as I knew he had emigrated to Australia. But Morné confirmed it was indeed Mike. We both walked over to his table and said we'd come to settle an outstanding debt and to thank him for making us famous as the first rugby players to be sent off in the first televised club rugby match in South Africa.

Morné ended up marrying Jenny, the daughter of John Newman, who was a well-known businessman in the fishing industry. One year, we had our annual WP Rugby year-end function at Bergvliet, the Newmans' magnificent old farmhouse, and our team photo for the year was taken under one of the beautiful oak trees there. We spent the day swimming, braaiing and playing tennis. Looking at that team photo tells a story of a bygone era of amateurs having fun.

Now that Jenny has passed away, I hope that Morné is blessed with all the help he will require to fill the huge gap that she has left. They were really a close-knit couple who lived for each other. I am blessed that in the last 16 years, since they purchased their little gem of a place in Riebeek Kasteel called Drie Gieters Fontein, where Morné grows magnificent Grenache Noir grapes, which he makes into a delightful rosé, we have spent many a wonderful day together.

But back to my EP teammates.

In the late 1970s and early 1980s, EP played some really good rugby and we had a tremendous team culture. We were hard guys at EP in those days, and we used to climb into our opponents. We didn't stand back if there was a fight, and as captain I encouraged our aggressive play because we frightened a lot of the bigger teams. I'd probably describe us as an angry team. We were angry because people didn't like the style of rugby we played – except the faithful Boet Erasmus crowd, of course. We were angry because we were in the B Division. We were angry because we felt not enough EP players were being considered for Springbok selection. We were angry, full stop.

But it worked for us. I knew the other teams were scared of us, so when I started coaching at EP, I kept my team angry. We used this anger to intimidate the bigger teams. I've known some incredibly talented players who when things turned angry on a rugby field couldn't deal with it and became ineffectual. In rugby, sometimes you just have to fight fire with fire; there's no way around it. That was how the game was played in those days.

But despite the rough times we may have had on the field, I've always tried my best not to hold grudges against people. I only knew one way to play rugby, and that was flat out. I had 80 minutes to express myself on the field, and I used it as best I could. But after the game, that was it. I did my best to never carry anything that happened on the field with me when I left it. And I think that's how I was able to stay good friends with many of my fiercest opponents on the rugby field.

A good example of how I approached my rugby is the Currie Cup final I played for Western Province against Natal on 6 October 1984. Natal had made it to the final from the B Division. Can you believe it? Something like that wouldn't be possible in today's game. Their captain, Chris Faure, had played with me in the Oribis team that toured South America. He was also a lock. On the Friday evening before the match, I phoned his hotel and asked to be put through to his room. When he answered, I said, 'Hello Chris. I'd like to congratulate you on your birthday and I hope you have a good match tomorrow.' And he responded with, 'And happy birthday to you too for tomorrow, Schalk. I hope you also have a good match.'

We ended up beating Natal the next day, and I was man of the match. Chris became an attorney, and we are still good friends to this day. He is also our family attorney.

But isn't that the way sport should be played? My son Schalk has inherited this quality from me. He used to pick up a bit of flak for his friendship with the late All Blacks flank Jerry Collins. Schalk and Jerry used to go out for a meal together the night before a match. There were some people at the time who criticised him for it, but that's just the way Schalk is. And I'm proud of him for it. We're human beings first, for goodness' sake, before we're rugby players.

But there were some tough times in Port Elizabeth as well, and my rugby career suffered as a result.

I started working for General Motors, but then took up a position with South African Breweries (SAB). It was while working for SAB that I employed a man by the name of Norman Ntshinga, and that appointment cost me the Eastern Province captaincy.

Norman had come to apply for a job, and I had no idea who he was. He was a flamboyant character, and when he walked into my office, he said, 'Yes, Mr Burger, when do I begin?' That was before we'd even had an interview. So I liked him immediately and ended up giving him the job, which was basically aimed at allowing us access to the black taverns that in those days were under the auspices of the Bantu Affairs Administration Boards. These bodies controlled all clear-beer sales in the black areas.

Norman had no sooner left than my secretary phoned and said a man had stormed past her and was headed up to my office. And in walked Hendrik Roodt, the chairman of the Eastern Province selection committee but also a member of the NIS. He stormed straight to my desk and, without even greeting me, immediately asked, 'What was that communist Ntshinga doing in your office?'

I had no idea what he was talking about. I calmly told him I was considering hiring Norman. A furious Roodt said that I was not allowed to employ Norman. Of course, my response was to tell him, in no uncertain terms, that he absolutely could not come into my office and start telling me who I could and could not hire. That's when Roodt threatened that I could lose the EP captaincy if I hired Norman. We both dug in our heels, and he eventually left.

I later met Norman in secret at the Swartkops Hotel and asked him what the hell he'd been involved in to warrant a visit and a threat from the NIS. He told me that he'd once been caught distributing political pamphlets and had been sent to Robben Island for it. The funny thing is, I liked him even more because of this.

A few days after my encounter with Hendrik Roodt, a report appeared in *Die Oosterlig*, a Naspers newspaper of the time, claiming that EP were going to get a new captain. So Roodt made good on his threat. I did indeed lose the captaincy for employing a black man at SAB. Stan Terblanche, our coach at the time, claimed in the media that the change to the captaincy was made in the interests of the team and was purely a tactical move. But I knew the truth, because I'd been threatened face to face.

Norman was a great character and he was very good for our business, as he helped us make inroads into the township taverns. Through Norman I met Moki Cekesane, with whom I'm still good friends. Moki was in the cells the same night Steve Biko was held there; the same night that the security police inflicted on Biko the injuries that led to his death. The police shocked Moki so badly that night that he suffered terrible damage to his hearing.

It was also through Norman that I was exposed to the township rugby of the Eastern Province. And that's how I became involved in helping with the building of the Dan Qeqe Stadium in the township outside Port Elizabeth.

In 1980, Moki and Norman told me that sports administrator Dan Qeqe needed help to build a stadium. You see, the Bantu Affairs Administration Board had refused the Kwaru Rugby Club (the club for the KwaZakhele region) the right to play rugby in the township. Dan then decided he would build his own stadium near Zwide, which would give him the right to allow Kwaru to play there.

But one of the biggest costs was the building of a Vibracrete wall around the field. I knew Gawie Carelse, the Springbok, who had a Vibracrete wall business. So we made a deal with Gawie to build the wall. The problem, however, was how to pay for it. SAB couldn't be seen to be paying for the wall, due to the pressure the NIS were applying on us.

So I devised a plan. I told Dan to go to Gawie and sign the contract with him. Dan had a Total garage in Port Elizabeth. I told Dan that I would bring our SAB trucks to his petrol station to be filled with his diesel, and then every month, by mutual arrangement, he would overcharge SAB until he recouped the money for the wall. The police would then not be able to trace the money back to us. My close friend Johann Rupert was also involved and agreed to help pay for much of the upgrade himself.

My friendship with Norman and many of the people around him only focused the NIS's spotlight on me. It was a crazy time – I was followed, and we had to have secret meetings while we tried to help develop the rugby culture in the black community. There was even talk that one of the players on the EP team was a spy for the NIS. So I was in this environment where you never knew who was listening and who you could trust.

My time at EP exposed me to a whole different side of South Africa and its rugby. People very quickly forget the role some of us played in helping the game to grow there, or the role people like Johann Rupert played in helping us to complete the Dan Qeqe Stadium. I'm not saying it makes us any better than a whole lot of people who, in their own incredible ways, helped to take South Africa forward. A lot of good people knuckled down and got their hands dirty to make a difference. Maybe we didn't shout about it enough, or put it up in headlines like some people.

As much as I did my part to help grow the game in Eastern Province, my time there helped me to grow as a player as well. And eventually I decided that maybe I was ready to return to Cape Town and the Western Province fold.

10

THE FIRST WHITE SPRINGBOK SELECTED FROM A COLOURED TEAM

IT WAS AN INCIDENT with Nick Mallett that sparked it all.

My first Western Province practice since my move to EP, on the B field at Newlands, would result in a moment that, once again, would take my rugby career in a completely different direction.

The opportunity to return to Cape Town arose when Graeme Pollock, the great South African cricketer, asked if I'd consider becoming the regional manager of the company he was a director of, the Berden Group. The timing was right for me, and so that is how I made my way back to Newlands.

The B field practices at Newlands used to be war.

When I arrived for that practice session, Western Province had won the Currie Cup two years in a row and were undoubtedly a powerhouse of South African rugby. Dawie Snyman, with whom I'd played at Maties and Western Province early on in my career, was now the Western Province coach.

The approach to rugby practice in those days was to take the A and B teams, and sometimes even the C team, and mix them up for what was called a game of koppestamp (head-knocking). Koppestamp is a really hard practice game that includes only forwards and a scrumhalf; you're expected to go flat out, as if you're playing a match. It's a good way of teaching the players rucks and mauls, but the downside is that you run the risk of injury. During one lineout, I flattened Nick Mallett with a hard tackle. Nick was always a good, hard player. A few movements later, in a loose maul, Nick came running from the wrong side and took me out. By now things had become quite heated, and Nick's tackle made me lose it. I threw the ball away and shouted, 'Okay, you want to fight? Let's fight!' The first player I hit was Hempies du Toit. The second was Nick Mallett. I remember there being a lot of blood. The next minute Dawie Snyman came running across to me, shouting, 'Burger, off my field *now*!'

I glared at him and shouted back, 'No. You don't send me off your field. I'm walking off myself. I'm done with this team.' And I left. I was furious. I was storming back to the change room when Jan Pickard, for whom I would later work at Union Wines, asked me where I was going. I told him I was fed up and was finished with WP.

He said to me, 'Schalk, you can't leave. I've just come back from an IRB meeting in England. England are going to be touring South Africa. I want you to become a Springbok. I want you to become Paarl Gimnasium's first Springbok in 19 years.' Jan was himself a Paarl Gimnasium old boy and one of their last Springboks before I was selected, so that explained why he was keen to see me pull on a Springbok jersey. Wynand Mans, in fact, had been the school's last Springbok before me, in 1965.

But I was so angry. I told Jan I was done with Western Province, that I'd made a mistake coming back to play for them, and that I would never play for them again in my life. In fact, at that moment I was ready to walk away from rugby entirely. It's quite possible that if I hadn't received a phone call from Dougie Dyers the next morning, I would've been finished with rugby.

Dougie was the coach of the Western Province League (WPL) team, which was the coloured team. That next morning, he came and had a cup of tea with me and asked if I'd consider playing for them. Now, you need to understand that although the tide was turning in South Africa politically, this was still 1984, and the country was burning. The Cape Flats, in particular, was a war zone. But I agreed to play for the WPL. A part of me wanted to make a point to Western Province that I would do whatever the hell I liked when it came to my rugby career.

So I signed up to play for the WPL team. My captain was Pompies Williams, who later worked for me at Union Wines. To get to our practices in Elsie's River, I used to climb into the boot of Pompies' car – it was a tight fit, believe me – and they would literally smuggle me in, driving through the riots and the burning tyres in the road. Me and Paul Carstens were the only white players in that team.

But even the coloured and black players in the WPL team were under pressure. They were considered sell-outs by the South African Council of Sport (SACOS). In the fight against apartheid, SACOS was at the forefront of the international boycott of South African sport. Its motto was 'No normal sport in an abnormal society'. Incidentally, I rephrased that when I delivered a speech for Danny Jordaan at the Eastern Province Sportsman of the Year banquet Port Elizabeth in 1994. The theme for my speech was 'Abnormal sport in a normal society'. I believe in using sport to help change society.

At the time, a political debate was raging as to whether sport had a role to play in the liberation struggle. Of course I believed it did, and this is where I found common ground with men such as Steve Tshwete, Ngconde Balfour, Mvuzo Mbebe and Nelson Mandela. In my heart I was convinced sport had a role to play in our divided society. But SACOS was extremely militant in its view of maintaining sporting isolation, and I think its inflexibility on a number of issues is the reason it eventually fell by the wayside. SACOS didn't even participate in the later discussions around unity in our sport.

I saw first-hand the mixed emotions of my WPL teammates. Yes, pressure needed to be exerted on the government to change its policies. But Dougie Dyers, himself an ex-SACOS member, also had a dream, which was to give one of his players the chance to become the first coloured or black Springbok. He couldn't reconcile himself to the thought of denying one of his players that opportunity.

THE FIRST WHITE SPRINGBOK SELECTED FROM A COLOURED TEAM

Western Province days. André Skinner (at left) was a very competent lock who became a good friend of mine and Myra's while I was playing rugby in Italy. We had a fabulous tour from Italy to Wales, stopping in Munich for the Oktoberfest. André was another player who could have represented South Africa with distinction.

It was Doc Craven who had asked Dougie to help form and coach the WPL so they could perhaps change perceptions of coloured and black people in rugby. This was something I also supported from the beginning because of the opportunities it would create for the players, and man did they entertain the spectators with their incredible tries and a whole fun dynamic they brought to the game. And it also brought a bunch of new names to the game that the South African rugby public would otherwise never have heard of. I liked the idea that by playing for the league, I might be helping to change people's perceptions and help them improve their skills.

The WPL produced Errol Tobias and Avril Williams, my first 'non-white' teammates in the Springbok team of 1984. Errol had first been selected for the Springbok squad for the New Zealand tour in 1981. He was a phenomenal rugby player and certainly wasn't there just because of his skin colour. He wasn't hidden on the wings, but played flyhalf and centre. Doc Craven had tremendous respect for Errol as a rugby player.

Doc was phenomenally progressive when it came to racial integration in South African rugby. When Ali Bacher, whom I always thought of as an opportunist rather than someone who was genuinely committed to the transformation of South African sport, was still organising demo tours, Doc Craven and Louis Luyt were in Zimbabwe holding negotiations with the sports council of the African National Congress (ANC) to discuss unity in rugby and how to pave the way for the first integrated team. Doc, in particular, was heavily criticised for this by right-wing conservatives and the South African government.

That was the real work being done behind the scenes to bring about unity in our sport. I used to host many such meetings in my house in Wellington when we went through similar unification issues in 1992, and which were attended by Tshwete, Mbebe and others. We trusted each other and were determined to try to find a way through all the politics. Those meetings led to the first fully unified provincial sports council in South Africa, the Boland.

But tensions ran high and emotions were still very raw when I was about to play my second game for the WPL. It was against the North Eastern Cape in Cradock. And all hell broke loose in the press.

Cradock was *the* hotspot in the country, and would become even more so in 1985 following the abduction and murder of the Cradock Four – activists Matthew Goniwe, Fort Calata, Sparrow Mkhonto and Sicelo Mhlauli – by the security police.

When we arrived for our match, the police were everywhere. Boetie Malan, the president of North Eastern Cape rugby and later the chairman of the Conservative Party in the Eastern Cape, said ahead of the game via the press that I was not welcome in Cradock. The newspapers were reporting that Malan was going to make sure that Schalk Burger did not play. That set the tone for what was a really tense match.

The match went ahead, and we were busy beating North Eastern Cape. We had a tremendous hooker named Gordon Mitchell. He was extremely talented and an expert at throwing into the lineout. During the game, Gordon retaliated for a punch thrown at him and was sent to the cooler. We were one man short, and the referee was having a full go at us as well. Eventually Gordon came back from the cooler, but just in time for another fight to break out.

By this point I'd been shouted at and called an extremely derogatory name by the other players and some of the spectators, so I was pretty fed up myself. When that next fight broke out, I jumped up and shouted to my teammates, 'Nou moer ons hierdie Boere' (Now we kill these Boers). And I started hitting whoever was in front of me. Pine Pienaar, their captain and later a good friend of mine, said to me years later that I looked like I'd gone crazy on that field. The referee broke up the fight and I was sent to the cooler, along with Pompies Williams. Not a single player from the North Eastern Cape team was sent off. Now we were two players down.

Pompies and I were standing behind our goalposts, which is where you stood in those days if you were sent to the cooler. I remember Pompies saying to me, 'Schalk, if those North Eastern Cape bastards get close to our try line, I'm telling you now, I'm going to bloody tackle them.' Fortunately it didn't get to that and we went on to win the match, thanks to a fantastic try by Wilfred Cupido.

That evening, the traditional post-match reception was cancelled because we were essentially a coloured team. On top of that, we were a coloured team that had beaten the hosts. So we took the team bus into the local township and had our own reception at a tavern there. The next minute the owner of the tavern told me to get the hell out of there, because 'They're coming to kill you.' I didn't know who 'they' were and I didn't stick around to ask. That area was a Pan Africanist Congress (PAC) stronghold, and the PAC and their military wing, Azapo, didn't like blacks, whites and coloureds playing together in the same rugby team. They felt it undermined their efforts to force political change. So I found myself running like crazy through the bushes and over a hill with some of my teammates, and back to our hotel, where I happened to bump into Koos Basson, later to become the president of Western Province Rugby, as he was struggling to finish a bottle of red wine. I duly helped him, and we ordered another. It was a bizarre experience.

It was while playing for the WPL that I was selected for the South African Federation team to play against a touring England side in 1984. The South African Rugby Football Federation (SARFF) was an association formed by the majority of coloured rugby union clubs that broke away from the South African Coloured Rugby Football Board (SACRFB) in the 1960s. Disputes between the two high-profile SACRFB leaders, Cuthbert Loriston and Abdul Abass, led to the breakaway, and the SARFF affiliated itself to the South African Rugby Board. Doc Craven was trying everything he could to get non-racial rugby to be played, but the National Party still wanted sport to be played along racial lines.

I'd played for the Federation team once before, in 1977. Northern Transvaal were opening a new stand at Loftus Versfeld, and our Federation team of that year was going to be the first multiracial team to play at the venue. I was still at university, and there I was, playing in a mixed team against the might of Northern Transvaal at Loftus Versfeld in the heart of Afrikanerdom.

I have great memories of that 1977 Federation team. Our lock,

THE FIRST WHITE SPRINGBOK SELECTED FROM A COLOURED TEAM

Piet Boonzaaier, had started out working as a truck driver for Simba chips; we knew each other from my younger days in Paarl. He'd sometimes pass me walking along the road in Paarl and give me a lift. He'd also give me a few packets of chips to take home.

We stayed in the old Union Hotel right at the foot of the Union Buildings. It was around the same time the pope was being elected. So every night on the TV news they showed images of the Vatican and the anticipation of that momentous announcement. On the day of the match we climbed onto the team bus and our hooker, Wessel Seconds, looked out the window at the Union Buildings and said to all of us, 'Jirre, mense, is dit nie die plek waar die pous op die nuus was gisteraand nie?' (Jeez, people, is that not the place where the pope was on the news last night?)

For many of these players it was the first time they'd seen the Union Buildings, and also the first time they'd ever flown in an aeroplane. Piet was one of those who'd never flown before. I'll never forget when a reporter from *The Citizen* came to interview a few of us after one of our practices at Loftus before the match. He spoke to Piet, and Piet's English wasn't that hot.

The reporter asked him, 'Are you a Federation player?'

Piet responded proudly, 'Yes. I'm a Federation player.'

Then the reporter asked him, 'Did you guys come to Loftus to train today?'

'Train,' says Piet. 'No, buddy. We came by plane this time.'

This tour exposed me to a few new experiences, not least of which was drinking glycerine. On the morning of the match, my roommate and another great character, Turkey Shields, told me we had to find a pharmacy. I went with him and he bought a bottle of glycerine, telling me we had to drink it to help with the high altitude at which we were playing. In his words: 'Schalk, daar is fokkol Afrox hierbo in die land' (Schalk, there is fuck-all Afrox here upcountry). According to Turkey, the glycerine would smooth my throat so it wouldn't feel so dry in the Highveld air. But it also made me thirstier than I think I've ever been on a rugby field.

We arrived in the change room on the day of the match and

Cuthbert Loriston, the president of the Federation and a great character, said to us, 'Boys, we're playing the mighty Northern Transvaal at Loftus. Keep the score low and the Federation name high.' Remember, we were about to make history with this multiracial rugby match. Our coach was Abe Williams, who was later active in politics. So after Cuthbert's speech, Abe stood up and proceeded to tell us that he disliked that kind of negative talk. That's when Turkey shouted out, 'But jissus Abe, we're playing Northern Transvaal, man.' Abe went on to tell us that we had one big thing in our favour, and we were not realising it.

'Turkey,' said Abe. 'Do you know a piano?'

'Ja,' said Turkey, 'my sister plays.'

'Well, the Northern Transvaal team we are going to play, they only play on the white keys of the piano. The Federation team of today, we play on both the white and black keys.'

'But what's in our favour?' asked Turkey.

'The team that can play on both the white and black keys plays a much better harmony, Turkey.'

And that was our team talk.

We led after 18 minutes, playing at a helluva pace. We ended up losing by quite a big score, though. However, I don't think Loftus has ever seen the kind of celebrations we had there that night, with all those amazing coloured songs ringing around the stadium.

Years later, I also lost my second South African Federation game when we played England and went down by a narrow 21–23 at the Danie Craven Stadium in Stellenbosch. We should've beaten them. We were a great Federation team that year, and that day we played with a lot of heart. Errol Tobias was absolutely sublime.

That England game was played on the Wednesday. On the following Saturday, I ended up playing for the WPL against South Western Districts in a curtain-raiser to a Western Province match. That evening they were going to announce the Springbok team. But after the game I went out to a steakhouse with my friends. In my mind, there was no way that I was going to make the Springbok team.

Besides, I'd already had my fair share of disappointments when it came to expectations around becoming a Springbok.

Back in 1981, we all knew that the tour to New Zealand was probably going to be the last Springbok tour before sanctions. I really wanted to be a part of that tour, which became known as the Flour Bomb Tour. The vehement anti-apartheid protests throughout the tour overshadowed the rugby, with flour bombs being dropped on the field in Auckland.

I played in the final trials and scored two tries. The Afrikaans rugby journalist Quintus van Rooyen told me that I was definitely in the team. When the team was announced at Loftus Versfeld that evening, Theuns Stofberg was in at lock. I didn't make it. The funny thing is that Theuns never even played lock on that tour. But politics had done a 180 on me. It was clear that I was seen as a divisive figure and my outspoken views had cost me a place in the Springbok team for that tour. I was the only player who played in the A team during the trials who wasn't selected.

I was bitter about that. I felt that Johan Claassen, Butch Lochner and Nelie Smith, the Springbok selectors, still held it against me that I'd been so outspoken about the Broederbond and Ruiterwag during my time at Maties.

Not making the team was very difficult for me. I've always believed that in a team environment, if you have an opinion, let's put it on the table and discuss it. And when we walk away from the table, we're all a team again. I believe that those are the kind of individuals that make for great teams. I say this because if you don't have a strong inner core and a sense of belonging, and are comfortable in your own skin, you cannot survive tragedy and the bad things that are inevitably going to happen to you. We've been through plenty of trauma in our family, and it's that blend of spirituality and belonging, and frankly just trying to be a good human being, that gets you through.

When I was overlooked for the 1981 New Zealand tour, I contemplated going to play for Wales via my mom's ancestry. Both Cardiff and Pontypridd approached me to play club rugby in Wales, but I never pursued it.

So with those 1981 memories still fresh in my mind, that evening in 1984 I wasn't holding out much hope for Springbok selection. Especially since I wasn't even playing in the mainstream league. Furthermore, the curtain-raiser at Newlands against South Western Districts was the first time I saw Frans Erasmus play. The main game was Western Province against England and all the selectors were there. They were going to announce the team later that evening from Newlands rugby ground. You must remember that, as players, we knew it was nearly impossible to become a Springbok. The imposition of sports sanctions meant that all tours were grinding to a halt. Doc Craven always said that the day we start losing, the international teams would stop coming. So the selectors were under pressure to select winning teams, and players who had not yet played for the Springboks were finding it very difficult to break into the team.

There was a photographer, Pietie Botha, who was taking photos of couples at the restaurant where we were eating. He recognised me and came over to our table. 'Schalk Burger,' he said. 'You're in the Springbok team.'

I'd been selected to play against England the next Saturday at my old stomping ground of Port Elizabeth. Errol Tobias and Avril Williams had been selected with me. In effect, I'd gone from being left out of the Springbok team in controversial fashion to being selected as a Springbok and making history: I had become the first white player from a coloured team ever to be selected as a Springbok.

So I'm actually not a Western Province Springbok. I'm a Western Province *League* Springbok. Western Province may claim me as their Springbok because the League team was one of their substructures. But at heart, I will forever be a Western Province League Springbok.

I'm immensely proud of that.

After the second Test against England – the first two Springbok Tests I played are a bit of a blur for me, they went by so quickly – we were on the plane headed back to Cape Town. The Springbok coach, Dr Cecil Moss, was also the manager of the Western Province team.

He called me to the back of the plane and asked me if I would reconsider my decision to never again play for Western Province. He told me I'd proven myself as an excellent international player, and that Western Province could really benefit from my skills.

I told Doc Moss that I'd only consider playing for Western Province if Dougie Dyers gave me the go-ahead. I felt I had made the commitment to play for Dougie and his team in the League, and it was from there that I'd reached the pinnacle of Springbok rugby. I suppose you could say I was back on that train at Touwsrivier, asking my teammates to vote on whether or not I should go and play Craven Week for Western Province.

So when I arrived back home in Cape Town, I phoned Dougie and asked him what he thought. He was very honest with me and said, 'Schalk, they learnt a lesson with you. It will be an honour that the League can deliver a Springbok and a Western Province player.' And that's how I returned to the Western Province fold in 1984, along with André Markgraaff, later to become a Springbok coach, who was selected at the same time. We won the Currie Cup that year, and in 1985 and 1986. It was a golden period for Western Province; they won what was then South African rugby's premier domestic rugby competition five years in succession from 1982.

But by 1986 every Springbok rugby player could sense it was the end of the road as far as an international career was concerned. The vehement international reaction against apartheid was making it impossible to realise our dreams of playing Test rugby against the world's best.

In 1987 we watched the first Rugby World Cup on television. And I can guarantee you that if we'd been there, we would've won it. I have no doubt in my mind. We had a better, more balanced and mentally stronger side than the All Blacks. And we'd beaten them the year before, when they controversially toured South Africa as the Cavaliers. Only two players who were in that All Blacks team that won the 1987 Rugby World Cup did not tour South Africa in 1986, David Kirk and John Kirwan. Frankly, I think we helped to prepare the All Blacks for that World Cup victory.

For all its controversy, that Cavaliers tour was a terrific series and there was some incredible rugby played. It was an important series for us to win, not only for the Springboks but, I believe, for our country as well. There was a sense that as much as we were fighting each other internally, we were also fighting the world. In my mind it was that familiar sense of being the underdog and thinking, 'How are we going to beat these guys?'

Also, bear in mind that the All Blacks only managed to beat us in a Test series in South Africa for the first time in 1996.

But unfortunately politics disrupted our futures in the game, and we had no say in the matter.

There were so many good rugby players in the 1980s and early 1990s who didn't become the Springboks they deserved to be because of politics. I feel very sorry for those guys. A storm that had been building over Springbok rugby from about the 1950s broke over our heads in 1987, and that was pretty much it for us.

I played Springbok rugby in the isolation years, and every one of us who did will wonder what could've been if we hadn't found ourselves pulling on that beloved jersey at such a difficult time in our country's history.

But I guarantee that not a single one of us would ever regret having had the opportunity, albeit fleeting, to pull on a Springbok rugby jersey and run out in the green and gold.

Perhaps this explains my deep love and reverence for Springbok rugby and what it represents. I love everything about Springbok rugby. I have the utmost respect for that jersey.

Something about the act of physically pulling on a Springbok rugby jersey changes a man. Those fibres, which constitute what is really a rugby jersey like any other, seem to become almost magical the moment you place a Springbok emblem on them. Any Springbok who truly played for that jersey, and nothing else, will tell you the same.

I know what it takes to become a Springbok – the many interwoven factors of hard work, determination, passion and a healthy dose of luck. I was fortunate enough to play six Tests for the Spring-

THE FIRST WHITE SPRINGBOK SELECTED FROM A COLOURED TEAM

boks and another six matches in a Springbok jersey on internal tours. But politics and our increasing international isolation were a constant handbrake on my Springbok ambitions, as they were for all of us in those days.

I'd venture to say that nobody other than a Springbok who had played in that time was able to appreciate seeing that Springbok jersey slip over the head of Nelson Mandela and feel the power it unleashed upon an entire nation. For us as Springboks from that era, to see Springbok rugby make its way back into international rugby was an incredibly special moment.

When I became a Springbok, I felt vindicated: I had proven that I could be myself and still become a Springbok; it wasn't just

The first Test against the Cavaliers at Newlands in 1986, following all the pre-match controversy around my captaincy. On my chest is the Toyota logo – the first time ever that a Springbok team played with a sponsor's name on the jersey. This was part of the great debate we were having around player remuneration.

about who you knew. And, I'll be honest, I felt lucky. I was grateful to Dougie Dyers, as that phone call and the opportunity he gave me to play for the WPL team had stopped me from walking away from rugby. I also realised that if I'd stayed at Western Province after I left Maties, I could possibly have become a Springbok sooner than I did.

But these are just some of the many factors that contribute to a man pulling on the Springbok jersey for his country.

It frustrates me whenever I read about the debates around transformation in South African rugby, or about the backlash Springbok captain Siya Kolisi suffered when he said early in 2019 that he was not in favour of quotas and that he believed merit should be the only criterion of Springbok talent. Over three decades ago I played two Springbok Tests with two black players – Errol Tobias and Avril Williams (the uncle of Chester Williams). They were both magnificent players fully deserving of their places in the Springbok team. Errol in particular scored a magnificent try in the second Test against England at Ellis Park in June 1984. To call Errol a quota player would be extremely degrading to the talent that he was.

Allan Boesak and I once disagreed about Errol's inclusion in the Springbok team. He said that it helped delay the end of apartheid. I said, 'Allan, don't tell me that Errol playing for South Africa and scoring that magnificent try and being called Black Gold by the British media didn't help change this country.' Errol was magnificent.

But, in the ongoing climate of transformation in South African rugby, I often think of what old Abe Williams told us in the change room at Loftus Versfeld: 'The team that can play on both the white and black keys plays a much better harmony.' That's the question, isn't it? How do you create that perfect harmony in a team? When it comes to playing a song on the piano, if you force a key in where it doesn't belong, you hit a false note. And that's why I don't agree with quotas at the highest level of South African rugby. They do a disservice to the players of colour who make it into the team on their own merit. They are then unfairly viewed as players who would not have been there were it not for the quota system.

THE FIRST WHITE SPRINGBOK SELECTED FROM A COLOURED TEAM

The 1986 Test against the Cavaliers at Newlands also featured Springbok prop Flippie van der Merwe and the late Andy Haden, the former All Blacks captain and my roommate in Cardiff.

Don't get me wrong, I'm not saying there shouldn't be development in rugby at other levels in the game. But quotas at Springbok level are a political issue, not a sports issue. Show me a coach in modern rugby who doesn't want to win, and who will actively not select players who he knows can help him win. He doesn't exist. Do you think Doc Craven would've put up with my difficult character if I hadn't been good enough to be in his team?

Similarly, I don't have a problem that there are no quotas for white players in our national football team. But I do have a problem when South Africa, a country of 59 million people, loses a football match to Cape Verde, a country of 550 000 people. So let's get real: sports quotas are a political tool. And I'd venture to say that I've seen enough 'forward passes' in our Parliament to not want to let any politician near our rugby.

No player who becomes a Springbok wants to believe he is there for any reason other than his talent. I believe the respect within our rugby for the jersey is too great.

And that should never change.

PART TWO

FAMILY

11

BORN A CONTRADICTION

SCHALK WILLEM PETRUS BURGER grew up an Englishman.

As a young boy, I couldn't speak Afrikaans. In fact, my brothers, my sister and I grew up speaking English to one another, which we still do to this day.

My mother, Laura Mavis Richards, or just Mavis as she was fondly known, was Welsh. My father, also Schalk Willem Petrus Burger, was Afrikaans and grew up on a farm in Riebeek West, 80 kilometres outside Cape Town. Our family tree goes back to Prussia. I'm told there is a castle somewhere in Europe that belonged to my Prussian ancestors, and that with me being the oldest male successor, I should inherit it, but I've never been to see it or been able to validate this.

To make things even more interesting, my mother was a liberal and a member of the Black Sash, while my father was a member of the Gryshemde (Greyshirts), a pro-Nazi movement active during the 1930s and 1940s. Although his family supported the South African Party, which was led by great thinkers such as Louis Botha and Jan Smuts (whose family, incidentally, were the neighbours to my grandfather's farm in Riebeek West), my father himself later became a supporter of the National Party. My brother Johann even became the leader of the Junior National Party in the Western Cape and at one time dated one of PW Botha's daughters. And so I grew up in this complex, dynamic mix of culture and politics. I was born a contradiction, and I suppose you could say I've been a contrarian for most of my life.

Before she met my father, my mother had been married to an Irishman, Mick Delaney, who had been badly affected by his experiences in World War II. Like so many men, he came back desperate to forget what he'd been through, and for him the way to blissful amnesia was through a pint of Guinness. Unfortunately, he grew to love his Guinness more than his wife, and they eventually divorced.

I have a half-sister from that marriage. Her name is Gaeleen, and she's eight years older than me. I had some contact with her when I was a boy because she lived with us, but then she married quite young, to the actor Dirk Kotze, and they moved from Cape Town to Durban.

My grandfather was the first stationmaster at Salt River. And then the family history takes another turn. My grandfather is

Me and Johann with my brother-in-law Dirk Kotze, who was a renowned musician, actor and radio personality, and our first niece, Juanita.

buried on the island of St Helena. He was on a ship travelling back to Wales when he passed away at sea. So they dropped off his body on this South Atlantic island and he is buried near the tomb of Napoleon Bonaparte.

But he also lies among the many graves that are a reminder of the almost 5 000 Boers who were imprisoned on the island by the British during the Anglo-Boer War (1899–1902), sometimes called the Second Boer War. The Zulu king Dinuzulu kaCetshwayo was exiled to St Helena. The Boers and the Cetshwayo clan actually shared an interesting history, as in 1884 the clan had turned to the Boers for help against their enemy and the British-appointed ruler of Zululand, Chief Zibhebhu kaMapita. The Boers helped the clan defeat Zibhebhu, but he was later reinstated by the British. When Dinuzulu returned from exile, he continued to rebel against Zibhebhu and was eventually imprisoned.

When General Louis Botha became prime minister of the Union of South Africa in 1910, he released Dinuzulu because he felt that he had not been granted a fair trial. It goes to show that the Afrikaner and the black man have a lot more in common than they think, or than our politicians will ever allow us to believe.

My grandfather's last resting place makes me feel that I am the product not only of European history but also of the New World with its strong, rebellious attitude. And I am also, proudly, a tenth-generation Burger in South Africa.

My mother and her two sisters lived in a house in Kloof Street, Cape Town, that was known as Die Driehoek. The three of them did their bit for the war effort by joining the welcoming party for returning soldiers. They helped to feed the troops and entertained them with dances and plays to help take their minds off their long journey home and as part of their reintroduction to normal society.

Mom shaped my thinking in a great many ways. She loved to climb Signal Hill and Table Mountain; I think she had a bit of a Gypsy's free spirit about her. She often told me how she loved to run down the mountain and then slide on the pine needles or the soil in her leather shoes and pretend she was skiing on snow.

My father grew up on the farm Gloria in Riebeek West. At one stage they had an opportunity to buy the neighbouring Smuts farm, but it didn't happen. I once hosted a wine tasting in Riebeek West and told the audience this story, adding that I'm very glad my grandfather never bought that farm or I might be in the cement business today – the Smuts farm is now the site of a PPC cement factory.

My parents met at a party in 1955. I was the first-born from this marriage, followed by Johann, Laura and Paul. A boy born from a liberal-minded Welsh mother and a conservative Afrikaans father who was at war with his own country. With a half-sister of Irish lineage. And a half-brother by an Italian woman. Yes, indeed. You see, after my father completed school in Malmesbury, and around the time of the Great Depression, he studied forestry at Saasveld Forestry College. He played first-team rugby there and also a few games for South Western Districts. Eventually, he qualified as a physiotherapist and he was one of the first in the country to have an ultrasound machine, which he used in his practice in Paarl, close to where the Teacher Training College was. In fact, it was this machine that landed him in trouble with the police and which took him off to war.

My father's sympathies with the Germans during World War II were common knowledge. Afrikaners were split between those who

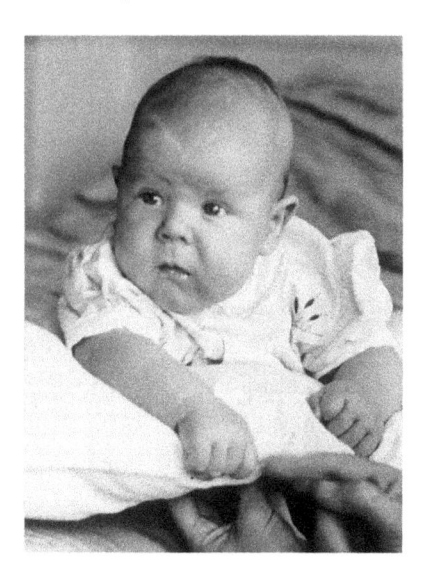

A Doc Craven lookalike? Me at four months having a good look at the world.

sympathised with Germany and those who supported Britain and the Allied cause. At that point, German U-boats were operating in the waters around Cape Town, and they often targeted Allied merchant ships carrying men and supplies to the Middle East. And, can you believe it, the police actually began suspecting my father of using his physio machine to send coded messages to the Germans, and allegedly informing them of the arrival and departure times of merchant ships. When the police started questioning him quite regularly on this, he probably decided that being thrown in prison wasn't such a romantic idea after all. So he signed up to fight in the war.

He was sent to Italy, and he played in those famous rugby games between South Africa and New Zealand near Monte Cassino. I find it quite ironic that a man who sympathised with the Germans, and then basically signed up for the war to avoid incarceration in South Africa, ended up fighting against the Germans in one of the fiercest battles of the war. Of the roughly 55 000 Allied casualties during the Battle of Monte Cassino (1944), around 800 South Africans were either killed or declared missing.

It was during his time in Italy that my father had a child with an Italian woman. So I have a half-brother. I'm told that after the war it took some time for my father to be demobilised. So I guess, as in the

Playing with cars was a favourite pastime for me and Johann. I was four years old here, behind Aunty Mayning's hotel in Sea Point.

lyrics of my favourite song, 'The Boxer', he found some comfort there. I've never met my half-brother. To be honest, I wasn't really interested in knowing more and I didn't pursue it. But my youngest brother, Paul, tracked the man down and met up with him. His name is Otello Burger. But my dad never spoke to me about that side of his life.

It was quite a complex family I was born into.

My mother's sisters were just as interesting and also had a great influence on me growing up.

The eldest, Margaret, was married to Jack Craig, a civil engineer who designed several of South Africa's harbours. Margaret wrote quite a few books. Her other sister, whom we called Aunty Mayning, didn't have any children and we would stay with her and her husband, Vivian Sampson, at their home in Sea Point whenever we visited Cape Town.

Aunty Mayning was a fascinating woman who had a phenomenal memory, and she read books that were so thick we could hardly pick them up. Like my mother, she vehemently opposed the National Party government, and constantly told us her feelings on the matter. She hated the Germans just as much because she and Uncle Vivvie (as we called her husband) had been visiting family in Prussia when war broke out in 1939. They were smuggled out through Poland, boarded a ship in the Baltic Sea and then travelled to England. From there they took a ship to Cape Town. After this arduous journey, Uncle Vivvie then promptly signed up for the war, serving as an anti-aircraft gunner with the South African forces fighting in Tobruk against General Erwin Rommel, the 'Desert Fox'. They never saw their Prussian family again, who were killed for refusing to give the Nazi salute to German officers.

Uncle Vivvie also used to tell us these fantastic stories. His father owned a share in a diamond mine in Jagersfontein in the Free State, and they were under siege by the Boers during the Second Boer War. So his parents smuggled him out of town under cover of darkness hidden in a rolled-up carpet. And during World War I, as a 16-year-old, he served on the battleship HMS *Iron Duke*, the flagship of the British fleet during the Battle of Jutland (1916), the last major naval battle fought primarily by battleships. I was captivated as he told us how they were given a few tots of rum and then locked into their gun turrets, from where they fired at the enemy for two full days. He had a tattoo on his right arm that he said was an act of remembrance undertaken by every crew member of the *Iron Duke* who survived that battle.

He told us other fabulous tales of his time in North Africa during World War II, including the Siege of Tobruk and the Battle of El Alamein. I always remember him telling us that whenever he felt a bit low he would wander over to the tents of the Afrikaner soldiers and listen to them playing their guitars and concertinas and the beautiful Boere music he so enjoyed. They would always sing 'Sarie Marais' together with the Afrikaner soldiers. And whenever he told us this story, he would immediately break into a rendition of 'Sarie Marais', and it wasn't long before Aunty Mayning joined him. That has always stayed very close to my heart.

What boy wouldn't be captivated by such tales of adventure?

Another uncle, Len Millard, was the commodore of the Royal Cape Yacht Club. He owned a yacht called *Dolphin*. It actually started out as a very big life raft, and was gradually converted into a yacht. Uncle Len had lost three fingers on his left hand in an accident when, as the commodore, he had to start a yacht race and the miniature canon they used for this had gone off prematurely while his hand was still over the barrel. In my young eyes, it gave him the look of a real seaman or pirate. We loved going out sailing with him or cleaning the yacht, and then having a sip of sherry before we went back on shore. And then Uncle Len would spend a bit more time in the local bar before taking us back to Sea Point. I got my love of sailing and navigation from him, and it has stayed with me my entire life. I also taught my children how to sail and owned two yachts of my own.

When I was 12, and Johann 10, we 'stole' my uncle's yacht and sailed around Robben Island to prove to ourselves we were man enough to handle it. Remember, we were spending most of our holidays with Uncle Vivvie and Aunty Mayning and listening to all their wonderful stories, so they really brought out the adventurous spirit in us. It was the summer of 1967, and the Six Day War in June of that year had led Egypt to close the Suez Canal. This meant that ships that normally travelled through the canal were rerouted round the Cape. So there were quite a few ships anchored in Table Bay, and the harbour security was pretty strict.

So the two of us embarked on our sailing adventure. Having just completed Standard Four (Grade 6), I put on my gruffest voice over the radio to request clearance from harbour control: 'Dolphin to harbour control, requesting permission to leave Cape Town harbour.' A few seconds later the radio crackled with the reply, 'Granted Commodore, have a safe sail,' clearly under the impression it was my Uncle Len. And we were on our way. It was all fun and games and easy sailing going out because we were downwind of a southeasterly and zigzagging between these massive ships. We took on a reach around Robben Island and were extremely proud of ourselves. We were probably carrying too much sail when we hit the waves on the northern side of the island. We saw a ferry in the distance, and the way it was ploughing into the wind and the swell should've forewarned us. We started to do a hard tack towards Blouberg Beach as we made our way back to the harbour. But coming back into this stiff wind was hard, and we were certainly not adept at sailing in those conditions. After what seemed like a lifetime, and with our last tack nearly taking us onto the beach at Paarden Island, we squeezed our way back into the harbour and were able to sail the yacht safely back to its mooring. But the tough conditions meant that we arrived back after dark.

I don't recall my mother ever being angry with me after such an incident. She seemed to take all my adventures in her stride. I believe it does wonders for children when you give them a certain amount of freedom to explore the world for themselves, although even I will admit that this particular adventure was quite a hairy one.

The stories I heard from my aunts, combined with my mother's own love for adventure, certainly shaped how I've lived my life. My

With my mother, Mavis, as she was fondly called, in front of the Welbedacht manor house, soon after the restoration of our home.

mom inspired a spirit of creativity in me; she allowed me the space to be myself and think differently about life. She also actively encouraged me to make up my own mind about things and not to be dictated to. This has served me well throughout life in my ability to connect with people of different opinions and backgrounds. It also shaped the way I raised my own children, namely, to think for themselves.

We spent some magical holidays with my aunt and uncle in Sea Point, and they introduced me to the world of books, which exposed me to a completely different side of life. I inherited my love of reading from my mother and Aunty Mayning. My mom was a very well-read woman. She would read at least two books a week. To this day I am a voracious reader. I read books that challenge my way of thinking. I search for books in second-hand shops. Friends send me books. I have a phenomenal collection of books on the Second Boer War and am a great lover of biographies and autobiographies. I'm inspired by unique individuals doing unique things. And I'm inspired by people from all walks of life. I don't read much fiction, but when I do, it is Wilbur Smith. As an African, I can relate to his books.

If there's something that intimidates me about the books I own, it's the tremendous amount of creative time the writers must have put in. People who have done extensive research about a subject and then written it down for me to read – I am honestly intimidated by that. Whenever I'm at a loss to explain something, I always turn to books and the knowledge in them. I feel very lucky to have been taught that by my mother and my aunt.

When my mother passed away, we had a small service for her on our farm. I spoke about how she never said a single negative word about me. I was never too fat or too thin, my hair never too long or too short. In her eyes, I never played a poor rugby game. To her, I could do or be anything I wanted.

And when things were really tough in our home, my mother always did her best to make sure that we children never felt second-rate or inferior to others in any way. My mom had to deal with a lot in her life. She was an extraordinary woman, given the hardship she suffered. But she guided her children wisely through a very difficult time in our family.

There is no question that she shaped the man I became.

12
GOODBYE, DAD

IT WAS 12 FEBRUARY 1987 and I had just finished a practice session with Western Province when I received a message that I needed to rush to Tygerberg Hospital, as my father was critically ill. He had been diagnosed with cancer a while back.

I'd looked after him in that time, and he'd stayed with me. He'd also spent time in Groote Schuur Hospital in Cape Town, as well as in the care of the Salvation Army. I always found that ironic: here was this staunch Afrikaner who had no time for the English, now being cared for by them.

When the cancer was at a really advanced stage, we had to admit him to Tygerberg Hospital. After receiving the news that he wasn't in a good way, I drove there as fast as I could. I ran up the stairs and through the halls, but when I reached his bedside, he had already passed away.

There he was, my dad, just lying there. My dad, with all of his faults, the mistakes he'd made, the alcoholism, the man who'd first left my life when I was only 11 years old. But still *my dad*. The man whose stubble had scratched my face while we scrummed in our kitchen. That smell of tobacco and brandy.

I kissed him on his forehead.

I was 32 years old, and it was the second time I had said a painful goodbye to my father.

The memories of World War II followed my father like smoke from a braai fire.

After the war, my father, like so many men of his time, couldn't settle down. He rented a farm called San Francisco which was located near the present Zevenwacht wine estate, and he tried everything to make a living. He sold farm equipment and fertiliser. He reared and sold turkeys. And he grew and tried to sell vegetables.

Even the snakes on the farm were considered a form of income. I remember the snake catchers coming out to the farm from Cape Town. They would dig holes about three metres by three metres and one metre deep, open all the mole runs that were there and wait for the Cape cobras to congregate in the holes. Then they would collect the cobras and pay my father before taking the snakes away to extract their poison for anti-venom.

I started catching snakes myself for the snake catchers. I also caught the moles on our farm, which used to terrorise my father by eating his vegetables. I used to go and check all my mole traps before going to school. My dad would pay me for the moles I caught, but I also used to sell them to the labourers on the farm because they viewed them as a delicacy, especially if the moles were still alive.

The small local school I went to was run by the headmaster and his wife, and they were our teachers as well. It was opposite the old Leyland car factory, in Blackheath near Kuils River, and my earliest memory of my fascination with cars was asking the teacher if I could leave the classroom to go and watch them load the cars onto trucks. I also remember being the butt of a few jokes in class because I couldn't speak Afrikaans.

Farming, though, just didn't work out for my father. Now, when I look back, I tell myself that he was just too small-scale a vegetable farmer to make a decent living from it. The farm also didn't have enough water to grow vegetables. But the reality is that my father started drinking heavily after he returned from the war, and his drinking became worse.

We moved to Paarl for what he hoped would be a fresh start. I was enrolled at Paarl Gimnasium. I loved that school, and it was very good to me. As I've said, I would definitely have labelled myself more of an academic than a sportsman. School was never difficult for me, and I loved the process of learning, especially when it involved a debate of some sort. To be honest, I think my academic strength gave me an equal footing with many of the children in my class who came from privileged areas, and who looked down on us for living in what was considered the coloured area of Paarl.

But even after moving to Paarl, my father couldn't find any peace. And that's when he went through a few bad phases in his life. I loved my dad till the day he died, but he had a drinking problem and alcohol eventually overcame him.

In Paarl, our family rented a house on the farm of Mr Costa, one of South Africa's first commercial olive farmers. It was in an area called Die Rug (The Ridge or The Back). It was in Drakenstein Road, in the so-called non-white area of town. We lived there at the height of the racial tensions in South Africa in 1966, and with many non-whites being evicted from their homes. We were slap-bang in the middle of all of this, but I never felt any animosity towards us, and the coloured people who lived close to us would even help us with food. The Moerat family, in particular, who were fruit and vegetable vendors, would always give my mom a bag of 'leftovers' to help feed our family. At night we could hear the riots and the police shooting to disperse the protestors. My mom helped a lot of the coloured parents whose children had disappeared, and I remember the confusion around whether they had been shot or taken into police custody.

I'll never forget how, years later, when Peter de Villiers was the Springbok coach, he went on about how I understood nothing of the suffering of 'non-whites' in this country, and how the coloured people especially had suffered. He told me that I'd had a privileged upbringing. That's when I told him I grew up in the coloured section of Paarl. There was nothing privileged about that. We were the stereotype of the poor white Afrikaners of the time.

Yet I felt safe in that house. It was a great environment for a boy because our back yard was basically an olive farm. But at the same time, my dad's alcoholism started to spiral out of control. I don't remember much of this. Or maybe I've buried a lot of it in my mind. I don't remember my father ever being harsh with us. My dad was a tough guy, but I was never scared of him. I never felt he was any tougher than all the other dads. You may ask what it was like growing up in a house with an alcoholic father, but, to be honest, I think I've smothered a lot of those memories. I kind of just got on with life.

My dad was a tough man. But in my eyes, that was how men were in those days. Most of my friends' dads smoked and drank. To me, that's just what a dad did. I grew up believing that the smell of alcohol and tobacco was the smell of a man.

I suppose there were those questions a boy would naturally ask as he searched for his own identity in his father's actions. Is this what a man does? Does he drink?

My dad couldn't accept that he had a problem, even when things got really bad for us as a family, as he was losing jobs because of his drinking. At one stage we had social welfare looking after us, bringing us clothing and food. Eventually, though, my dad agreed to go into rehab. By that stage we had no car, so a friend of his came to pick him up.

I remember, as I helped my father pack his suitcase to leave for Cullinan, which is where people were sent to recover from alcohol addiction in those days, that he had a particular smell about him. I thought it was the smell of a man. Little did I know that it was the smell of a broken man.

Although I knew there was something wrong, I didn't fully comprehend why he was leaving home. When he was finished packing, his friend arrived to take him to the station. I remember that it had started to rain. My mother didn't accompany my dad to the railway station. By then she'd seen two husbands suffer at the hands of alcohol. She was a soft woman, a peace-loving woman, and I think it just became too much for her. But I also believe her pure eccentricity

GOODBYE, DAD

helped her through those tough times. My mother was the kind of person who, after a day like that, would tell us to get some good rest and then try again tomorrow. She lived for the day. She gave me that, and I carried it into my sport and the way I had of playing every single rugby game flat out, and of holding nothing back.

As they were loading my father's suitcase into the car, I decided that I would ride my bicycle to the station so I could see him one last time. I wanted to say goodbye, hoping that somehow, between our house and the station, I would find the words a boy sometimes struggles to find within himself, or to even understand.

I ran to get my bicycle and cycled like mad in the rain. When I reached the station, there were quite a few of his friends on the platform saying goodbye. Many of them lived in the posh houses of Paarl. They were trying to keep things light-hearted. They were the same men who drank with my father. I remember their laughter on the platform. I'd heard that laughter before, in the bars where I'd be sent. There was only one reason why an 11-year-old boy would be sent to a bar, and that was to fetch his father and bring him home.

Eventually it was my turn to say goodbye. The rain was pelting down on the platform as I hugged my dad, and I wasn't sure any more what were tears and what were raindrops on my face.

'Schalk, you're the eldest,' he said to me. 'Take care of the family.'

The words echoed in my head as the train rolled away. I remember feeling so afraid. Many years later, I wrote a poem about it. A few of the lines I wrote explained it best:

The uptown people left softly, each in their own car,
Me alone with my thoughts, fears and the smell of a bar.

I cycled home. It was still raining hard.

As I stood out of my saddle to climb the hill to our home,
More raindrops started to appear on the handlebar chrome,
The same I thought I saw that morning on the suitcase leather,
And I realised that raindrops not only appeared because of the weather.

Those drops on the handlebars of my bicycle were more tears than rain, the same as those on my father's leather suitcase. My life changed that day. At the age of 11 you suddenly stop being a boy, and you do what your father asked you to do: 'Take care of the family.'

With the main income of the household now gone, there was no way my mother could remain in the house where we lived. So we moved into the sub-economic housing in the north of Paarl. It was in a suburb called Noorder Paarl and we rented a house from the Paarl municipality.

My mother, who had never worked in her life, got a job as a housekeeper at the local hospital. When I was 13, I started delivering newspapers to help make a bit of extra money for the family. Nicol Retief, the father of Nicol and Lambert Retief who were the later owners of the *Paarl Post* community newspaper and *Die Burger*, used to allow young scholars of all races to sell the *Paarl Post* on Friday afternoons.

On a Friday afternoon, a group of us would line up at the *Paarl Post* offices. The trick was to be in the front of the queue, because then you got your consignment of newspapers first and could head straight for the best selling points in town, especially on Main Road. I used to get my newspapers and ride at least two or three kilometres away on my bike, and start selling on the outskirts of town first.

From selling *Paarl Post* I was selected to also start delivering *Die Burger* in Paarl. The challenge was that the only route still available was the one with the steepest roads. My last delivery would be at the door of the highest house in Paarl.

And that's how I earned extra money throughout my schooldays. I'd cycle up all the steepest roads in Paarl to deliver the paper, as many of the kids didn't want to do those routes. It made me fit for school rugby, because the round trip was about 11 kilometres. On Saturdays I would have to make my deliveries very early, and also hope the newspapers wouldn't arrive late, because if we were playing a school rugby match in Cape Town, I'd have to catch the bus at 7 am. And on Sundays I did a 'double shift' of two trips delivering *Rapport*, taking over the shifts of the guys who wanted to have a lie-in. From there I'd go to church. I think all that cycling must have helped cure my asthma, as I eventually outgrew it.

There was another benefit to delivering newspapers. The Procopiou family, who were Greek, had bought Rena's café at the corner of Long Street and Main Road. They liked me because I taught them English and Afrikaans, and they let me buy from them on credit. Every morning after delivering my newspapers, I would pick up a litre of milk, a bread and, on some mornings, orange juice and take it home. On Fridays, when I was paid, I would go and settle my bill with the family. If there was a shortfall, I had to give extra Afrikaans lessons to Jannie, their youngest son.

One of the people I delivered the newspaper to was the poet MM Walters. I had to be very careful with his newspaper, especially when it rained, because if there was even a drop of water on it, he would go crazy. Then he'd contact the office and I'd be given all sorts of penalties. Normally, I would fold the paper and toss it onto the driveway or the stoep as I cycled past. But with MM Walters, I had to put it in his post box in immaculate condition.

Money was always tight in our house. Even though my aunts and uncles in Cape Town were pretty well off, I don't remember my mother ever asking for help. I'm sure they must have helped, though.

I've never thought too deeply about the effect my parents' separation had on me. They never divorced. I wrote my dad quite a few letters while he was away in rehab, which was for about nine months. In the letters, I kept saying I hoped he would come back and wouldn't be ill any more.

And he did come back, but he was never the same. He started drinking again, just as heavily. And his relationship with my mom deteriorated even further. Eventually, my dad found some work in Cape Town and moved there. Despite having a job, he never supported us with any money. I think my brothers and sister got a bit caught up in that, and later they asked him a lot of questions about that time in our lives. I went the other way. I just got on with things. I felt as if I just *had* to get on with it. In my head, I'd made a commitment to my mother to help her and my siblings.

JUST A MOMENT

Paarl Gimnasium and my education were central to my survival during that process. I could focus on other things, such as my schoolwork. That was my escape. Things were tough in our house, but my mom made do. I can't recall a single time when a friend came over to visit that, even when things were really bad, my mom didn't give him a sandwich and a cooldrink. She was great like that. And because of the way she dealt with our circumstances, I never felt embarrassed about it, or about where we lived. I know my brother Paul was embarrassed by our situation. However, it didn't bother me. You either accepted who you were or you didn't. I didn't care.

Life, though, had changed in a huge way for me back then. You come to realise that life isn't fair, that it comes with a lot of hardships. And as a boy, either you learn how to deal with it or it gets the better of you.

Of course, you don't think about it in such detail as a child. You just get on with life. You just accept that your dad isn't there, like the other dads, watching your games from the touchline. And, as much as my mom did everything for us, she was too busy surviving to attend parent-teacher meetings, and so on. You certainly think about all that when you're at your mom's memorial service, or when you take care of your father in his last few years in your own home.

Even in those quiet moments on Welbedacht, when the sun is dipping behind Groenberg, the big man that you are today remembers the day that boy rode his bicycle in the rain to the railway station.

You never forget saying a last goodbye to your father.

13

'TAKE CARE OF THE FAMILY'

MY YOUNGER BROTHER, PAUL, broke my heart.

Johann and I were always close, and he has had his share of ups and downs in life. Laura has also had her share of heartache, having been through a divorce. But Paul, who died early in 2018 from brain cancer, truly broke my heart.

Paul was supremely talented, but also a bit mixed up. When we were growing up, Johann would listen to me if I told him something. But not Paul.

I used to save some of the money from my newspaper deliveries and then buy records in Cape Town. I built my own hi-fi out of spare parts, as I loved music and had a fantastic collection of LPs. One day I came home and found that Paul had locked himself behind the glass door to the lounge, where I kept my records. He was sitting on the floor with my records. I told him not to touch them and tried to open the door. What he did next is forever etched in my memory. He took a pen and, one by one, made deep scratches on each of my records, all the time looking at me going crazy on the other side of the glass door. I threatened to kill him, but my mother had a soft spot for Paul as her youngest. He could do no wrong in her eyes. I sometimes think that because Paul was so talented and good-looking, things came too easily for him. Maybe that's why he never really found direction in life.

Years later, on the eve of Schalk Jnr's wedding, there was an incident with Paul that the media reported very poorly. The media were not aware of what our father had asked of his 11-year-old son, who had carried the words in his head all his life: 'Take care of the family.' And how, with those words, he always tried to do right by his father and his family.

According to the reports, I had assaulted Paul by throwing a table at him. Well, this is what really happened.

Paul always had a rebellious streak, and he couldn't settle down. At one stage I even employed him, and I always thought I'd been quite good to him. I tried to put him through university, but he only lasted four months.

My mother suffered from type 2 diabetes, but she was still in very good shape at the age of 88. She had a phenomenal brain and was still reading two books a week. I bought her a house in Wellington, and Paul and my sister ended up moving in with her. Laura was divorced by this time and not well off. But she and Paul didn't get along, a situation that wasn't good for my mom. I didn't like that because I wanted my mom to be happy and content.

On one occasion when I spoke to Laura, she told me that Paul had met a man in Cape Town who believed in alternative healing with crystals, and that Paul had completely bought into this. He would drive to Camps Bay supposedly to 'charge' a crystal necklace that he wore around his neck. It was crazy stuff. And he'd given my mom one of these crystals as well. But, unbeknown to me, he'd also taken my mom off her diabetic medication and was treating her with alternative medicine. Laura told me my mother also wasn't eating the right food.

I was travelling to Namibia for work, and as I landed at Hosea Kutako International Airport in Windhoek, Myra called me. She said Laura had just phoned her to say that my mom was in a bad state. She hadn't come out of her bedroom for two days. I asked Myra and my younger son, Tiaan, to go and have a look for me.

It wasn't a good situation; my mom was very ill. Myra eventually called an ambulance and got my mom admitted to Paarl Mediclinic. The resident specialist told us that she was dehydrated, which had caused her diabetes to worsen, but was being attended to by the doctor. That was just before a dinner I had to attend. After the dinner, Myra phoned to tell me that my mom had suddenly passed away.

I was broken.

Myra said that the hospital wanted to speak to me. I phoned the Mediclinic, and I'll never forget what the woman said to me: 'Wat maak ons met die lyk?' (What do we do with the body?) I asked her if it couldn't at least wait until the next day. It was almost midnight by then. She replied: 'Ons is nie 'n lykshuis nie' (We are not a mortuary). It was a brutal response to the situation.

I managed to get a flight back to Cape Town the next day. As soon as I landed, I tried to get hold of Paul, but his phone was off. Myra and I drove to the funeral parlour, where I had to take care of the arrangements. Afterwards, I asked the staff whether I could see my mother for the last time. I was shocked when they told me, 'No, you can't. There is a murder inquest around her death.' I couldn't believe what I was hearing. I was told that Paul and the police had been there before we arrived, and he had opened a murder investigation into her death.

My mind was reeling. Who on earth would want to murder my mom?

Myra and I got into the car and I again tried to get hold of Paul to find out what the hell was going on, but there was still no answer. I then phoned the specialist, whom I know, at the Mediclinic. He was in an absolute state, because Paul had stormed into his consulting rooms with the police and, in front of his patients, declared that he was a suspect in our mother's death. The general manager of the hospital then told me that Paul was demanding CCTV footage of the wards because he believed somebody had come in and murdered our mother.

It was unbelievable. The general manager also told me that Paul was making sweeping statements about me, as he believed I somehow had the power to make the CCTV footage of my mother's supposed murderers disappear. It was crazy. If my mother had indeed been murdered, I would have been the first to want to find out who did it. But of course, there was no murder. The doctors confirmed that my mother had gone into anaphylactic shock because Paul had taken her off her medication.

By that stage, I really had started to believe that my brother was mad. Bear in mind that we had no idea Paul was suffering from brain cancer. I'd suspected that something was wrong with him, but every time I asked him directly, he fobbed me off by saying he was suffering from the after-effects of a spider bite. He'd had cancer earlier in his life and had overcome it. I think he was wary of telling me the truth, because he knew I'd insist he go to hospital for treatment, which he didn't want to do. The first time Paul actually admitted to me that he had brain cancer was in January 2018. He died on 8 February 2018.

So, to be fair to him, the brain cancer was probably at an advanced stage when he was acting so crazy. For the last part of his life he refused to be called Paul Burger and went by the name of Paulo Burgaro. He believed he was Italian.

It was tragic.

Strangely enough, after my visit to the Mediclinic, it was his Italian fantasy that made me think I might find him at an Italian coffee shop he frequented in Wellington. So when I still couldn't get hold of him by phone, Myra and I drove to the coffee shop. And there was Paul, sitting on the stoep.

I sat down at his table and said to him, 'Paul, what the hell is this about mom and a murder case?' He confirmed that he had opened a case, and he vowed to send the person responsible to jail for life. Laura was also a suspect, according to him, as were Myra and Johann.

I kept trying to reason with him, begging him to let us honour our mother's memory by giving her a proper funeral without all this drama. But he was adamant. So that's when I stood up. It was a light aluminium table. I'm a big man. So, yes, I knocked that table out of the way.

Just picture this for a second. You're on a business trip in another country. Your wife phones to say that your mom is desperately ill and has been admitted to hospital. You rush back to find out that a murder case has been opened, and you're suddenly a suspect in your mother's death. By your brother's doing. Show me anybody who wouldn't be just a little frustrated with and confused by that scenario.

As I stood up, Paul picked up his phone and shouted, 'Captain, they want to kill me!' Suddenly two police officers from the nearby police station arrived to arrest me. Can you appreciate how utterly bizarre the situation was? And at a time when I was also grieving for my mother. So I left the coffee shop and went back to the farm. Schalk Jnr's bachelor party was about to take place on the farm, and he'd invited his closest friends for a cricket match on our pitch. That's when Myra phoned and said I must come to the house.

When I got there, the police had arrived and wanted to confiscate my hunting rifles. Paul had taken out a protection order against me. I wasn't allowed within two kilometres of him. It was a ridiculous situation, as Wellington is a small place. Just by going into town I was already within two kilometres of him. I was dumbfounded by what was happening.

Paul was still staying in my mother's house, claiming that she had left it to him in her will. My mother never had a will, and the house was in my name. As I've explained, I bought the house for her so that she could live in peace in her old age. But now I had to go through a lengthy court application to oppose Paul's claims and the protection order. Eventually, when the matter was heard in court, Paul didn't appear for the hearing. He'd disappeared overseas somewhere. The court order was overturned, but by then the media had reported the story, namely, that I had assaulted my brother. The day after Schalk's wedding, the front page of *Rapport* had an article about a 'broedertwis' between us.

Months later, I found out that Paul was coming back from

overseas. He had nowhere to stay, and a friend of mine said I needed to put all our issues aside and do the right thing, which was to help my brother. So I let Paul stay at my guesthouse in Wellington. He had absolutely nothing to his name.

One afternoon I went to see him there. We sat on the stoep and I showed him the ugly articles that had been written about me. He denied having said any of it. I asked him to apologise for what he'd said about me, and the lies he'd told. But he refused. I think that was the final straw for me.

'Take care of the family.' I will never forget my father's words. I believe I had tried my best to do what he'd asked. I looked after my mother in her final years. My father lived with us in his last years. I looked after Paul and Johann and Laura, and I always tried to advise them as best I could. But what Paul had done felt like a bridge too far for me. It had caused me, and my family, immense hurt.

So, on that stoep, I told Paul to leave and gave him 24 hours. Later, I was told about his cancer. He had somehow wound up in a clinic in Alexandra in Johannesburg. Laura had moved to Secunda, and she and her daughter went and fetched Paul and took him to stay with them there. And then he died. My little brother was dead.

I think Paul developed some personal issues in life because he never fulfilled his incredible potential. He was so supremely talented. It's sometimes hard for me to understand that what eventually claimed his life could occur in a brain as gifted as his.

It was just so sad. All of it.

I was reminded of what I'd written the day my father left: 'And realised that raindrops not only appeared because of the weather.'

Paul's final-year class at Paarl Gimnasium held a memorial service for him on our farm. Like most people, I hate funerals and their finality. As a Christian I hold on to the belief that the person is headed to a better place. But I cannot talk or laugh with that person again. I can't interact. I'm an emotional person, so I'm no different from anyone else when I say that funerals take a lot out of me.

Myra has helped me deal with what went unsaid between Paul and me before his death. Myra believes that the brain cancer changed Paul, and that he wasn't acting rationally in his last days.

Now, whenever I recall that day he scratched all my records, I'm not as angry as I once was. I now see only his face, not my records. And I see the smile on his face. I prefer not to think that it was the smile of a boy taking pleasure in his elder brother's heartache. It's just a smile.

But it's a smile that still makes me cry.

PART THREE

FATHER

14

ONLY HUMAN

ONE OF THE GREATEST JOYS of my life was being able to have my own children. I always wanted children.

To be able to have sons to carry on the Burger name has been a blessing, and then to add a beautiful daughter was just as much of a gift. Having the opportunity to see your kids growing up, to see how they view life, experiencing both the good and the bad that life offers – that's the greatest blessing. No material gain that you can have in life can ever match being a parent.

I always tried my utmost to keep my children out of the limelight. And, like any parent, I have done my best to shield my children from the bad things in this world. But our family is not unique in the trauma, heartache and suffering we have experienced.

There have been moments in the lives of Schalk Jnr, Tiaan and René when the bad has surpassed the good. Moments when you hear things you never expected to hear as a father, and are never prepared to hear.

The phone call you receive to tell you that your son is in hospital and has a two per cent chance of survival.

A phone call at 4 am to say that your other son has been in a horrific car accident.

Or the phone call to say that your daughter has been gang-raped.

No matter how many Springbok Tests you've played, or how many famous and influential people you call friends, or what you have achieved, life still comes at you like it does for any human being. And then you experience that moment every parent dreads, where you are helpless to do anything to protect your children. It is no longer about you and how much you can withstand on their behalf. You are forced to see what your children can withstand.

I think that's where the real success of parenting lies. It's not in the sacrifices you've made for your children, but rather in praying that everything you have instilled in them will provide that deep well from which they can draw when they need to overcome life's toughest challenges.

You are helpless, you can only watch, in anguish, and find out what your children are made of. As a father, you would give everything to take the pain away from them. But you can't. You are forced to just be there with them and watch. You watch the effects of a virus that brings your strong boy right to death's door. You are helpless to stop three angry men finding your daughter in the wrong place at the wrong time. You stare at the wreckage of a car in which your son was driving spread across a field.

And then you see the strength of your children as they fight back, pick themselves up and go forward in life again.

What my children have taught me more than anything else is that when bad things happen to them, they can make it through, and when they are restored to you, they are infinitely stronger than you ever could have been on their behalf.

15

SCHALK JUNIOR

SCHALLA, AS WE CALL HIM in our family, was born in Port Elizabeth on 13 April 1983. He was quite literally born into the game of rugby.

That evening, after rugby practice, the whole Eastern Province team and I arrived at the hospital still wearing our rugby boots. I remember Doug Jeffery leaving these big black marks on the hospital's Novilon floors. Danie Gerber was also with us. His daughter had been born in the same hospital two weeks before.

Schalk had jaundice and had been put under lights. So there we stood, all of these rugby players, looking down at my first child. Doug said later he'd never seen me prouder than I was at my first child's birth.

As a child, Schalla had us worried more than a few times. He struggled with fever fits and would regularly pass out. The doctors could never figure out what was causing it. His fever would soar to 40°C and he'd have a terrible fit. Fortunately he grew out of it, but I would describe him as a sickly child. He had encephalitis at one point and, like me, he suffered from asthma. I outgrew the asthma when I was about 14, but throughout his playing career Schalk carried an asthma pump in his tog bag and was registered with the

Schalk Jnr at eight months, and already very in love with food, music and laughter. He started walking at nine months.

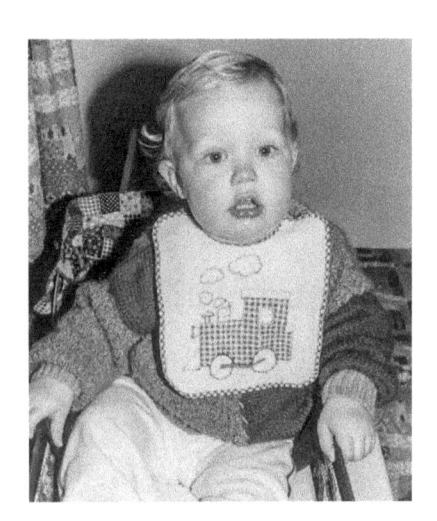

World Anti-Doping Agency for the use of asthma medication.

So from a young age Schalk kept us busy with doctors and hospitals. In fact, I don't think people realise how many operations Schalk has had on his body. In his school years he'd already had patella femoral ligament replacements in both his knees. There were subsequent knee operations, and a hand operation when he was 13 after he had severely broken four bones in his left hand and dislocated his left knee in a motorbike accident the day after he had been selected to play Under-13 cricket for Boland. I remember his teacher, Piet Krynauw, phoning to congratulate me on the selection as they were wheeling Schalkie into the operating theatre, only for me to give him the news that I didn't think Schalk would be attending what was then called the Perm Week, let alone the skiing trip I had planned for our family.

And I even had to rush him to hospital for emergency dental work when he was punched in the mouth at a high-school rugby match in his Grade 10 year in 1999. Paarl Gimnasium were playing Hoërskool Waterkloof in Paarl. After the match, Schalk was shaking hands with the players when this kid from the other team attacked him. The boy was unnaturally big and had this rage about him. He said afterwards that he was angry because Schalk had bounced him a few times during the match. He split Schalk's lip right up his face and knocked a few of his teeth out. We climbed in my car and rushed to the Mediclinic in Paarl. Schalk was holding a bloodied towel over his mouth. When the doctor had a look at him, he immediately said we would have to see a specialist, because the damage was that bad. So we rushed to Durbanville and were able to see a specialist, a university friend of mine, Dr Ottie van Zyl, who stitched him back together. So, yes, it's safe to say I've had my fair share of visits to the emergency room with Schalk.

Schalk was a tough player but always fair. He is 16 months older than Tiaan, and when Tiaan was about two, Schalk tackled him so hard he dislocated his brother's ankle.

The professional golfer Derek James can also tell you how hard Schalk tackles. A lot of professional golfers used to come and stay with us in Wellington when they were playing tournaments in the Cape. When I started working for Union Wines in 1985, we sponsored a golf tournament in Paarl. One year, Derek James and Hendrik Buhrmann were staying with us for the duration of the

A week before the announcement of the Springbok team to play the first Test against the Cavaliers, a photo in Rapport showed me, Myra, Schalk Jnr and Tiaan. The accompanying article was about my becoming the next Springbok captain, which didn't happen due to my negotiations with management about player remuneration. The photo was taken by Hoffie Hofmeister.

tournament. Derek was fond of rugby and he loved to play around with a rugby ball. So on the morning of the final round, and with Derek two shots off the lead, he was messing around on the lawn with Schalk and a rugby ball. That's when he dared Schalk to try and tackle him. Schalk must have been about 10 or 11 at the time. So Schalk tackled him. And he dislocated Derek's big toe. When I was still playing rugby, I was always the one in the team who pushed the other players' fingers back if they'd been dislocated. So I managed to get Derek's toe back in place, but of course he was in incredible pain. We sent him off to the golf course with an ice pack, his toe heavily bandaged. And, would you believe it, he went on to win the tournament – the Bastille Open –with a dislocated toe. He bogeyed the last hole but still shot a course record and won.

Golf has been another constant in Schalk's life. I'd always wanted my children to learn how to fish, hunt and play golf. I was adamant about that. The first two activities are as old as human civilisation, and the third teaches you more about yourself than any other sport I know. Schalk was only four years old when he made his first birdie at Wellington Golf Club. He hit this lovely two-iron into a par three and drained the putt.

Another time Schalk was quite badly injured was while playing for Boland Under-19 against a Wales Under-19 team in Wellington. The Welsh team had a few players who were already out of school. I saw Schalk tackle this big Welsh forward and twist his own knee in the process. He was helped off the field. I went to see him in the change room afterwards and his patella was literally sitting on the side of his knee. I phoned Spike Erasmus, who was my orthopaedic surgeon when I was still playing, and he told me to bring Schalk to his practice in Stellenbosch as quickly as possible. The operation took place the following day. I'll never forget Spike coming to see him, and Schalk telling him that he wanted to play a cricket match against Grey High School in PE in six and a half weeks' time, and would he be ready?

Spike naturally said he couldn't give any guarantees, which Schalk accepted. The following morning when we arrived at the hospital, Schalk was sitting on the side of his bed doing knee curls. He was determined to play in the opening game of the Cape Schools Cricket Week as it was going to be the first time that an Afrikaans school, Paarl Gimnasium, was going to participate.

So, six and a half weeks later, Paarl Gimnasium were chasing 220 against Grey PE, which many thought was too big a target. I was playing in the Winelands Classic golf tournament, and shortly after we'd finished our round, a friend of mine, Pietie Carstens, himself a good first-class cricketer and once president of Paarl Cricket Club, phoned me from the match. He asked where I was, and I told him I'd just finished playing golf. 'Well,' he said, 'you're going to miss a great century by your son.' I asked him what Schalk was on and he said 17. I was surprised and also concerned because I knew Schalk couldn't run properly. But something in Pietie's voice told me I needed to get to the match. I arrived at the school just in time to see Schalk hit a four that took him to 30 runs. What followed was some magnificent batting by Schalk against some great bowling, and on top of it all with a batsman who couldn't run properly but who also wanted to face all the bowling. With him on 97 runs and Paarl Gimnasium close to a momentous victory, Schalkie tried to run a ball down to the vacant third man. He touched the ball and was caught by the wicketkeeper. But he had done more than enough to show his teammates his dedication to their cause, despite his injury. It was a tired 18-year-old I saw leave the field that day.

Paarl Gimnasium made the remaining runs they needed to win. And Schalk had made yet another miraculous comeback, which would be a hallmark of his sports career.

After the match, I was having a beer with Lou Rautenbach, the well-known cricket umpire, and the Short and Wilmot families, whose children had all played for Grey PE. Lou was telling me that he had earlier watched a kid who reminded him more of Graeme Pollock than any he'd ever seen. Out of interest I asked him who this kid was, and he told me it was the opening batsman of Paarl Gimnasium. At that moment Schalk came over, kissed me on the cheek and said, 'Hello, Dad.' Lou said, 'That's your son? Man, he's going to go far.'

That was the day Schalk showed me he had everything to potentially become a great cricketer. At that stage, I would rather have had Schalk continue with a cricket than a rugby career. He was a phenomenal cricketer, as he's always had this amazing ability to concentrate for long periods of time.

Schalk was only 14 when he was playing first-division cricket in the Boland and at weekend club matches was facing bowlers such as Roger Telemachus and Henry Williams – when they weren't playing for South Africa. Throughout his high-school career, there was only one match in which he didn't play first-team cricket. When he was growing up, I always believed Schalk was more of a cricketer than a rugby player.

I remember when Ewie Cronje, Hansie's father, came to see me and said that when Schalk was finished with school, the Free State would like him for rugby and cricket, and that he'd be offered a full scholarship to study at the University of the Free State. But I didn't want that for him. I wanted him to go to university with no hang-ups and to just enjoy it. I didn't want him to feel the pressure of having to perform in any specific sport.

When you consider how Schalk ended up playing rugby instead of cricket, there are many similarities in our lives in terms of how fate intervened. In my case, it was a phone call from Doc Craven that took me on my rugby journey. In Schalk's case, it was – perhaps not so surprisingly, given his history – an injury.

Schalk had been selected as part of the final South African Under-19 training squad, but he missed out on selection to the team that went to Bangladesh for the World Under-19 Cricket Championship because he'd ruptured his bicep playing rugby the previous week. His arm had swollen to double its size. Shortly thereafter he had been selected for the South African Under-21 rugby team as a replacement, much like my own Craven Week selection. And so he joined that team after recovering from his injury. This was the same team that won the Under-21 World Championship at Ellis Park under Jake White in 2002. And, in a twist of fate, that's how Schalk became a professional rugby player instead of a cricketer.

One thing Schalk has always done very well is to grab any opportunity with both hands. In only his second year out of school he was called up to the Springbok training camp. Then, in 2003, he was in the Springbok squad for the Rugby World Cup in Australia and New Zealand. In 2004 he was voted IRB Player of the Year. It all happened very quickly. But the moment was never too big for Schalk. Whatever anyone threw at him, he would throw it back ten times harder. Excellence motivated him.

And it certainly felt as if he had this same ability with his injuries. He never moaned about any injury that befell him. He just asked what needed to be done, did it, and then got on with things. He's always had this knack for making miraculous comebacks. He's a very simple person, and he knows what works for him and what he wants.

I've always felt that he has this incredible ability to take his mind to another place when he's suffering pain, and that's how he gets through it.

Springbok coach Jake White once told me that you could put 17 stitches in Schalk's mouth and send him straight back onto the field and he'd play like there was nothing wrong, which actually happened to him in a Test match against New Zealand. He described Schalk as being like three players on the field. He is able to push through the tough times. I saw it again when he went through Kamp Staaldraad, where the Springbok team was subjected to a highly controversial, military-style training camp in preparation for the 2003 Rugby World Cup.

Consider the fact that Schalk had only been out of school for two years when he became a Springbok and was part of an experience that broke many of the (older) men around him. One of his 'tasks' during the camp was to box against his captain, Corné Krige. Schalk is not a fighter. As I've said, he's tough as nails and a hard man on the field, but he's always fair. So I know he would not have enjoyed having to box against his captain one bit. But again, he has this ability to put his head down and push through. I believe his maturity is a great factor in his rugby success.

One of his biggest injury battles occurred in June 2006. The Springboks had played Scotland in Port Elizabeth, and after the match Myra and I went out for dinner with Schalk. He told us that he had this pain in his neck. By the following Wednesday his hand had started to cramp up. That's when we discovered he was suffering from a major neck injury, which an MRI scan later confirmed. We later discovered that he had suffered the injury in the 18th minute of the Test and had played the rest of the match with a collapsed disc. Another major blow could have paralysed him. I later read how Jake White had told the media he could see that Schalk was not at his best, but that 'his work rate was still better than that of anyone else'. That's Schalk for you, I thought.

The next Saturday, he was in the operating theatre. The decision was made to fuse his sixth and seventh vertebrae. There was a chance he would never play rugby again.

While Schalk was in theatre, I couldn't just hang around the hospital. So I went for a drive. After about three hours I'd heard nothing from the hospital, and your mind starts thinking funny thoughts at that point.

Nelson Mandela phoned me and wished us luck. He was always very good to our family, and he loved Schalk dearly.

Then my friend Chris Faure phoned me. He immediately started the conversation with, 'Jeez, Schalk, it's terrible, isn't it?' I still hadn't heard anything from the hospital, and immediately thought the worst.

'What Chris? What's terrible?' I almost shouted at him. Then he told me what had happened to the flyhalf from Rawsonville Rugby Club, Riaan Loots, who had been kicked to death during a disgusting rugby match between Rawsonville and Delicious in Rawsonville.

I was shocked by what I heard, but also relieved that it wasn't anything to do with Schalk's operation. I felt that it was a premonition for me to get back to the hospital. When I returned, it had been about four and a half hours and they were wheeling Schalk out of the operating theatre.

Dr Gerhard Coetzee told us it had been a particularly difficult operation, and from what he'd seen, Schalk had injured his neck before the most recent incident, because there was about 60 per cent calcification of the discs.

While Myra and I tried to recall any previous neck injuries Schalk had suffered, it struck me that he must have injured his neck when he was in Grade 11 and rolled the bakkie on our farm. He said then that he felt some pain in his arm for some time afterwards.

Dr Coetzee told us that there had been a complication during the operation, as he had nicked a nerve. He said that Schalk would probably lose a bit of feeling in his lower left hand, but that otherwise the operation had been a success.

With Schalk back in his hospital room, Myra, Michele (Schalk's wife) and I sat by his bedside. He was still coming out of the anaesthetic. There was a TV mounted on the wall, and the Springboks were playing a one-off Test against France.

Suddenly the alarms in the room went off and the nurses rushed in with a defibrillator and other medical equipment. Then they switched off the alarm and left. We carried on watching the rugby, and again the alarm went off and the nurses rushed in. When this happened a third time, I asked them what was going on, because Schalk seemed fine while he was lying there. They said his heart rate was being monitored and it was spiking. I looked at the TV. The Springboks were on their own try line, defending for their lives against the French. Can you believe that somehow, in his subconscious, Schalk must have heard what was happening on the TV, and it was pushing up his heart rate.

Both Schalk and Tiaan loved cricket, and they were exposed to it a lot when they were growing up. We owned a box in the Newlands members' stand that we shared with some business associates and friends. Together we had underwritten the rebuilding of the stand as part of the revamping of the entire stadium. So my children were able to watch some incredible cricket, and even football matches and Aussie Rules games, while one of Myra's highlights was a Tina Turner concert that we arranged there. Schalk and Tiaan loved the cricket the most, though, because after the matches many of the players would pop in to our box and they were able to meet them.

One of Schalk's lifelong ambitions was to score a century on Newlands cricket ground, and on 21 February 2012 his dream came true in a match between the Cape Cobras cricket team and the Stormers rugby team.

Incidentally, I was part of the rebranding of the Cape Cobras. The team was playing under the name Western Province/Boland, and I thought that it needed its own identity. While I was on the board of Boland Cricket we strategised about the new name, and I asked Dawid Toua, who designed our wine labels, to come up with a new logo. We presented it to the board, and all but one member, who was afraid of snakes, loved it. Actually, the more I think about it, the Stormers rugby team should've been named the Cape Cobras. It's a great name that says a lot about the Western Cape and about our sport.

So on 21 February 2012 the Cape Cobras played the Stormers in an annual fundraiser sponsored by Pick n Pay. The Stormers needed 211 runs off 20 overs, and the rugby commentator Matthew Pearce always reminds me, whenever we meet, that Schalk scored his 100 runs that day off only 49 balls – the fastest 100-run innings ever scored at Newlands. A friend of mine recalls how afterwards Schalk, who then lived in a house exactly between the Newlands cricket and rugby grounds, walked home barefoot with his cricket gear in one hand and a beer in the other. It was mission accomplished.

Only a few days later, at Newlands rugby stadium, in a match against the Hurricanes, Schalk's dreams for the year took another turn. A double tackle left him with serious damage to nearly all the ligaments in his knee. It was back into the operating theatre and the same round of worry and rehab.

The ups and downs of life are so much harder when you watch your children suffer them than when you go through them yourself. And with Schalkie we were beginning to wonder when things would just settle down for a while.

But nothing prepared us for the time when Myra and I thought we were going to lose our son for good.

In 2013 he was busy with his pre-season training when he felt a twinge in his left calf. He went for a scan, having previously had a similar problem with his other calf that led to a ligament being removed. This time there had been some deterioration of his reflexes, and in his spinal column the doctors discovered a huge arachnoid cyst that was compressing his dura, the sheath that holds the cerebrospinal fluid (CSF) inside.

The diagnosis was that he had suffered either a severe blow or a lumbar puncture that had caused the cyst to develop. The cyst was now pushing on his spinal cord as it grew bigger. They decided to perform an operation whereby they would insert a shunt into the dura that would drain the cyst into his stomach. This would allow him to play in 14 days' time on the Australasian leg of the Stormers' Super Rugby season. The cyst was deemed too big to remove without his having to stop playing rugby completely.

And that's when the nightmare began.

It was the Friday of the Cape Epic mountain-bike race that year, and a part of the race went through our farm. I was on the farm when Michele phoned to say that Schalk was not looking well at all after the operation.

I rushed to the intensive care unit (ICU) at N1 City Hospital. Michele was there with Schalk's close friend Jean de Villiers. Gerhard Coetzee, the same neurologist who had operated on Schalk's neck, and who Schalk adored and had full faith in, arrived later. I asked him whether it wouldn't be better if Schalk remained in hospital for another night. He advised that it would be better if he went home to recover. So we loaded Schalk into the car and Michele drove him home. He was not looking good at all, and actually became ill in the car. The following day, it being a Stormers' match day, Myra and I went to Newlands and we spent the whole day at Schalk's bedside. We could hear the Newlands crowd cheering, as it was barely 300 metres from Schalk's house. But Schalk hardly reacted, and that's when I could see that my son was really not in a good way at all.

By Monday he couldn't walk and was still feeling terrible. Michele wisely had him readmitted to hospital. The only problem was that Dr Coetzee was overseas attending a conference. A Dr Wessels from the Vergelegen Mediclinic was going to take over. So Schalk was admitted to the Vergelegen Mediclinic in Somerset West.

At first, the doctors believed the increase in his bacterial count was as a result of his suffering from an external infection such as tick-bite fever or malaria. Both my sons had recently travelled with me to Botswana, so we thought it wouldn't hurt to investigate this angle.

The next day Schalk's condition deteriorated even more. The bacterial count grew and they couldn't control his temperature. I was lucky to have Dirk Hoffman, an orthopaedic surgeon in the same hospital and a dear friend of our family, come over to see how we were doing. He took a look at Schalk's scan and said he'd never seen such a large arachnoid cyst in anybody's back before. He very kindly said he would make sure the best people attended to Schalk. He brought in a physician, Dr Jan Engelbrecht, who wasted no time in trying to get to the bottom of the infection. My son was slipping in and out of consciousness at this point.

Driving home that day, I prayed that the whole episode would be sorted out and Schalk would be fine the following morning.

The following Wednesday morning I was busy chairing the Wellington Wine Route board meeting when I received an urgent call from Myra. She said Michele was beside herself and in tears, and said we'd better come soon because she thought Schalk was dying.

I'll never forget rushing away from that meeting and driving as fast as I could to Welbedacht, where Myra was already running down the gravel road to meet me. On our way to the Vergelegen Mediclinic I phoned Dr Engelbrecht and I told him that at 5 pm that day I wanted to know exactly what was wrong with Schalk and what they planned to do about it.

He said that in order to perform another lumbar puncture they would first have to remove the newly inserted shunt that was draining fluid into Schalk's stomach. Then they would have to do a barrage of tests and grow certain bacteria to try and ascertain what was killing him.

I think Dr Engelbrecht was close to telling me I was out of order, but to his credit he never did. He realised I was extremely concerned about my son's life, and he later revealed to me that he was just as concerned that Schalk wouldn't make it. Unbeknown to us, Dr Engelbrecht's wife had just undergone a mastectomy and he was working to save her life as well. His wife later confided to us in a letter that when he would disappear from her bedside, he would tell her that it was to attend to this really nice rugby player who he was desperately trying to help pull through, and he wasn't sure he would be able to do it. Life is incredibly strange like this.

When Myra and I arrived at Schalk's bedside, what met us was something you never expect to see happening to a child of yours. Michele was in tears, and Schalk was in a coma. He was making these deep groaning noises and sweating profusely. His pulse rate was over 200 and the bed was soaking wet from his sweat.

I told Michele to go to her parents' home in Stellenbosch and get some rest. I said I'd take over. As if I could do anything. But I felt I could at least help take the pressure off her and Myra.

The meeting between myself and all the doctors and specialists had been set for 5 pm. Until then, all I could do was stand at my boy's bedside and use a wet cloth to wipe the sweat off his body. A body riddled with pain and fever. I prayed that whatever was doing this to Schalk would leave his body.

In the meantime, Tiaan had driven over from the farm. He walked into the ward, saw me wiping the sweat off Schalk and was so overcome that he had to leave and go sit in the waiting room. Schalk's close friend Shaun 'Zama' Seeliger had been given the news by Michele and had immediately flown down from Johannesburg. He said that when he walked into the ward, he saw me standing there wiping Schalk, with tears streaming down my face.

At 5 pm I was standing in the foyer of the ward, ready to meet with the doctors. In the absence of Dr Coetzee, the caretaker neurologist was Dr Louis Wessels, who we found out was the son of the doctor who had operated on my brother Johann in 1 Military Hospital after he was wounded in Angola. There was also Dr Jan Engelbrecht, who was going to brief us on the way forward, Dr Dirk Hoffman, an old Oribis teammate of mine, and a colleague of his, Danie Morkel. We had to wait 15 minutes for the final result of all the tests. I felt like I was standing in the tunnel of a rugby stadium waiting for a Test match to start.

Then Dr Engelbrecht received a phone call. He seemed agitated. I remember him saying, 'Staffie. What staffie? Count? Has the pharmacy got medication?' My first thought was that a Staffie dog had perhaps bitten Schalk. The next minute Dr Engelbrecht took off at a run, and we all followed. Drips were changed and new medicine was administered. And then we were informed that Schalk had contracted staphylococcal meningitis, which accounted for his high bacterial count, and this was attacking his meninges, the protective layers around the brain and spinal cord.

In the confusion, all that the doctors could tell me was that the fact that they hadn't detected the infection earlier meant that there was a very big chance Schalk wouldn't make it, never mind ever play rugby again. His rugby career was the furthest thing from my mind. I just wanted him to live, and to see his wife and two children again.

Dr Engelbrecht took me aside and told me he would do everything he could to save Schalk. At the time I didn't know what he was going through with his own wife, and we are forever grateful for the dedication and focus he showed towards Schalk in what was an equally difficult time for him. He told me to identify everybody who had been around Schalk recently, because he wanted them to be medicated against the infection. I started making phone calls and had everybody I knew of, children included, make their way to Michele's parents' home in Stellenbosch. Dr Engelbrecht arranged for the antibiotics, and I took the medicine through to them. And then I gave them all an update on Schalk.

My son had gone into hospital as a strong 114-kilogram man. And now here he was, lying helpless and being pumped full of antibiotics and cortisone. I thought back to him as a little boy, when he used to get those fever fits. Now he was unable to move, speak or even open his eyes. It hit us all so hard.

My son. The little boy who, when I used to come home after rugby practice at nine o'clock in the evening, would wait for me in the kitchen with his little cricket bat. He would refuse to go to bed. His mom would get so angry with him, but he'd stay put until I'd spent at least 30 minutes bowling a tennis ball to him in the kitchen. My boy, whom I'd seen in hospital so many times before, who had overcome so much and had come back stronger each time.

Now he was lying in a hospital bed, in a coma and fighting for his life. And I just didn't know. I didn't know whether he would make it. I didn't know whether to pray for him to get better or to say goodbye. Poor Myra was just trying to get through each minute. We just wanted him back. Just to be healthy again.

Typical of Schalk, he made one of the most remarkable comebacks ever seen from the level of infection that he had. Within a few days he was sitting up in bed and having fun with his children and wife.

His recovery was so good that the doctors told Myra and I that we could attend the Klein Karoo Nasionale Kunstefees (KKNK), one of South Africa's biggest Afrikaans arts festivals. For years I had been a director, chairman and deputy chairman of the festival, and I really looked forward to it every year. Myra loved the KKNK and we thought that it would be the right bit of medicine for us after this period of stress with Schalk. We always rented a house in Oudtshoorn and invited friends to join us and catch up with the artists we knew. I loved sitting back and seeing so many people enjoying themselves and supporting the sometimes fragile Afrikaans entertainment industry.

While we were away, every morning at 6 am I would phone the sister on night duty and ask for an update on Schalk. Then one morning there was a shocked silence from her side. She told me that the wound in Schalk's back, where they had removed the shunt to do the lumbar puncture while trying to find the source of his infection, had broken open and his cerebrospinal fluid had literally leaked out. CSF is a clear liquid that protects the brain and spine. If the dura, which contains this fluid around the spine, develops a hole and the fluid leaks out, it affects the brain, which is surrounded by CSF. As the fluid drains out, the brain begins to sag and presses against the skull.

They would have to do an emergency operation to try and patch the leak in the dura. I woke Myra and told her we had to leave immediately. We had to get back to Schalk.

And so started Schalk's third operation. His desire to return to rugby one day ruled out the usual surgical intrusion, as it would damage too many ligaments and prevent him from ever playing again. So microsurgery was used to patch the little tear in the dura. It was a bit like putting a patch on the inner tube of a bicycle.

This procedure was done four times. Each time it was back to the hospital, an operation, recovery in ICU, moved to the normal ward, released back home, and then back in hospital again.

Poor Michele had to go through this process with the two small boys, who were by now wondering when their dad would recover. And they had bought a new house, which Michele was busy renovating.

On the fourth occasion, Schalk said: 'This is the last time. Otherwise, do a normal op and I do not have to play rugby again.'

Many medical friends were trying to help. René Truter, a radiologist friend who had attended Paarl Boys' High – the big local rival to Paarl Gimnasium – and had also matriculated in 1973, phoned me one morning and asked to see Schalkie's scans. He was attending a conference in St Petersburg, Russia, and had noticed on the programme that a specialist from San Diego was presenting a paper on dura shears in BASE (Building, Antenna, Span and Earth) jumpers – those guys who are crazy enough to jump off high places and then descend to earth using a wingsuit and parachute. René attended the presentation and afterwards spoke to the American specialist. He told her that the doctors in South Africa were battling to find the source of the leak in Schalk's back and asked if she could help.

Dr Mike Nicholas, an old friend of ours, kept a record of all

Schalk's scans and forwarded the information to René in Russia. After consulting with the specialist, he had a discussion with Schalk's medical team before the fifth and final operation. After the operation, they would keep Schalk heavily sedated for a week and keep a shunt in his dura to drain off any extra CSF pressure build-up. They believed that perhaps the reason the dura kept tearing was that Schalk's body was producing too much fluid, and the increase in pressure that resulted was too much for the newly implanted patch to hold.

By now Schalk had lost 17 kilograms. Furthermore, his resistance to secondary infections was running very low.

They did the fifth operation, and the prognosis was that it had gone well. Schalk was only conscious between 6 am and approximately 8 am. The morning after the operation, Myra and I went to visit him in the ICU. Seeing him was like something out of a movie. Schalk was awake and managed to talk to us, but he was really frail and drawn out. He was lying flat on his back, and on both his arms and legs there were big plastic bags pumped full of air that moved in a vibrating action. The whole arrangement was designed to stimulate the flow of blood so that it would not clot, as he had lost most of his body fat. Next to his head and beneath the mattress was a bag full of the fluid that was draining from his spinal column. All I could do was pray and hope that this was going to work.

And for the next few days we all prayed.

After five days they removed the drain in his back and the plastic bags, and allowed him to sit up. Our prayers were answered. Schalk went home.

He basically had to learn to walk again. But the patch has held to this day.

We celebrated Schalk's 30th birthday about three months after the actual date. He had just started going for walks, and a few runs as well. The party was a joyous affair with a lot of his rugby mates that he had been missing. We drank a good few beers and some wines, as we Burgers can do. We were all so happy that our son was slowly but surely making his comeback.

JUST A MOMENT

When everybody had left, I was saying goodbye to him and wishing him well, and saying that it was so great to see him at home with his family, when he said, 'Dad, the pain in my calf is back.' I couldn't believe it. After all he had been through. I cried all the way home to Wellington.

He went to see the doctor who had done the previous operation to remove the ligament pinching the calf muscle. Within a week Schalk had been operated on and the ligament removed. But the blessing was that if he had had this operation first, the medical team probably would never have found the arachnoid cyst that was on the point of rupturing his dura. If this had happened in a rugby match, for instance, the consequences could have been grave. So we are extremely grateful to the medical team that decided to scan his spinal column.

Sport is so competitive these days – even school sport. But I wish every parent of a talented young sportsman or sportswoman will

It was a proud moment when my friend Morné du Plessis handed over the Comeback of the Year award to Schalk Jnr at the Laureus World Sports Awards in Shanghai in 2015. At the ceremony are (from left) Schalk Jnr, his wife, Michele, me, Myra, Mika Häkkinen, Morné and his late wife, Jenny. Having wanted to design Formula 1 cars, for me, spending time with a Formula 1 hero like Mika was a treat.

believe me when I say that they should not take it too seriously. Because, believe me, nothing is as serious as seeing your child lying helpless in a hospital bed and being told that he has only a two per cent chance of survival.

Schalk made a miraculous return to rugby, and in 2015 he was honoured with the Laureus World Sports Award for Comeback of the Year. Myra and I joined him in Shanghai for the beautiful awards ceremony, and he received the award from my friend Morné du Plessis. I was in tears as Dr Mike Nicholas spoke on a video link about Schalk's condition and what our family had gone through. Mika Häkkinen, the Formula 1 driver, was sitting with us, and he said I must be very proud of my son. I replied, 'There shouldn't be an award that to win you have to put your family though a journey like this.'

I remember seeing Schalk up on stage, accepting the award, and thinking to myself, 'You came back, my boy. Not just to rugby. You came back to us all.'

16

RENÉ

A BEAUTIFUL PAINTING BY our daughter, René, hangs in our bedroom. She painted it after her brutal rape ordeal. It's a self-portrait, with her back turned to the viewer, and was the first portrait she painted after the incident. It reflected how she felt about the world, and how it had changed for her. After what she went through, there was a time when I was fearful that my brave little girl might not ever have the courage to turn around and face the world again.

I remember the day René was born like it was yesterday. Myra was booked into the Panorama Mediclinic in Cape Town to have a Caesarean the following day. That night Wellington suffered probably its worst wind storm ever. Most of the trees in our beautiful town centre were blown over. There was no electricity and it was raining cats and dogs. I thought to myself, this little girl is going to be something else if she announces her arrival in such a way.

Following the successful birth, I prepared my two sons to go and welcome their sister into the world. I took them to a clothing store and kitted them out with nice long-sleeve shirts, long trousers and docksider shoes, and bought each a tie of their choice. After washing them, we got dressed, sprayed some cologne on and went off to meet their sister. I had told them, 'When you meet a girl for the first time you have to be presentable. Make a good impression and be kind to them as they are special and will reciprocate if you do just that.'

Well, Myra was in for the surprise of her life when we opened the door of her private room, with René in the cot next to her, and the manly threesome in her life walked in, spruced up, with ties and all. We took some pictures of the boys each holding their sister, and this is how René has been in our lives ever since.

She grew up with the boys, riding a bicycle in the mountains and a scrambler motorbike at about the age of five. She loved being on our yacht and was not afraid of doing her work on the foredeck, or whatever was required of her. She shot her first buck at the age of ten. On one of our annual hunts in the Kalahari with five other families, most of whose sons were at least six years older than her, she won the prize for the best shot. And we were extremely strict about awarding the points not only for where the bullet entered the buck but also for where it exited, so as to teach the kids how important it is to preserve the meat.

After four days of hunting, all the kids would line up in the butchery and we would spend a whole day working the carcasses

My daughter René at the interschool netball match between Paarl Gimnasium and Paarl Girls' High in 2004. She was in Grade 10 and playing for the first team.

and making biltong and sausage and other cuts. I would throw all the bones in a big pot, which I could hardly stand over it was so big, and cook off all the meat for us to make venison pies and potjiekos for the ravenous children. Like the old frontier people, they learnt how to use everything from a buck, and they gained a lot of respect for the meat as they knew how difficult it was to stand for a whole day working in the butchery.

From the Kalahari we would go to Henties Bay on the Skeleton Coast of Namibia and fish off the beach. René became adept at fishing as well; when still small she would really get under Tiaan's skin by pulling out the biggest galjoen of the day. When she was battling to get the fish through the surf, she would ask me for help, so Tiaan would shout, 'Then she cannot claim the fish.' So René worked out a plan where she would walk backwards and just drag the fish out of the sea. I remember one day she caught six galjoen that each weighed over two and half kilograms. She was a very good sportsperson who played provincial tennis and netball. I'm sure her tomboy nature scared away a few potential boyfriends. But she was my ideal daughter and I loved her for it.

After school, René enrolled for a course in oral hygiene at the University of the Western Cape. Most of her classes were at the Tygerberg Hospital complex, the site where her life, and ours, changed forever.

René's ordeal was another moment that brought our family to its knees. Unfortunately, though, as is the case with so many people who experience something so horrific, many other factors around the incident were just as hurtful.

The trauma for René was extensive. There was the trauma of the rape, the anger at the mess the police made of investigating the case, the heartless intrusion of the media, and some malicious rumours questioning whether the whole incident had even taken place. It was a terrible time for all of us.

It was 5 May 2008. I was on our farm when Myra came running to me and said that René's roommate in Stellenbosch had just phoned: something bad had happened to our daughter. There were no other details. I was busy with a wine agent from the United Kingdom, and at first it didn't sound too serious. So Myra got in the car and drove to Stellenbosch. A while later she phoned me and told me that René had been raped.

There is something that happens to a father when he hears those words about his daughter. You feel as if you've been winded and you can't get any air.

I told Myra to go to the nearest police station and open a case. The tragedy is that the majority of women who have been raped don't open a case, because it's up to the victim to prove that this terrible thing has happened to her. When a woman walks in to a police station to say that she has been raped and would like to open a case, she is basically told, 'Okay. Prove it.' You only realise how broken the system is when you experience it yourself. It's shocking.

The police in Stellenbosch told my wife to go to Belhar police station because they didn't have any rape test kits left, and the incident had taken place in a different geographical area. So Myra and René had to go to Belhar police station, in one of the biggest crime hotspots in the Cape, as night was falling.

But, again, that is the reality of the situation you're dealing with as a rape victim in South Africa. You have just suffered a terrible ordeal, and then you have to suffer further indignity because of a system that doesn't support the victims.

The police took an affidavit from René, and then she and Myra drove back to our farm. René broke down. She was devastated. When I saw her, I cuddled her and said it would be all right. We spoke about a lot of things, about life in general. She went to bed early, which left Myra and I to try and process the day and how this could have happened to us, and to our only daughter.

Again, Nelson Mandela was a great support for our family. He phoned me regularly to find out how we were doing. The first phone call came a few days after the incident. In that inimitable voice, he said, 'Schalkie, Schalkie. I'm so sorry. I just want to give you a hug.' On another occasion when he phoned, I cried and he cried with me. He had great empathy for the suffering of other people. I must say, with his empathy and Zelda la Grange's incredible communication skills, they were always there to help if something went wrong or if words of encouragement were needed. I can say that in our brief conversations and over a few cups of tea, Mandela made me feel like he was the father I never had. They made a great team.

As René explained to us, she had been abducted at Tygerberg Hospital. Three men had forced her into her car and taken the N1 to an abandoned building on a farm somewhere near Klipheuwel. There they beat her, stabbed her and then gang-raped her. She escaped when her attackers heard a noise outside and went to investigate. She managed to scramble to her car and get away.

In the days that followed the incident, the media started hounding us. I will never forgive *Die Burger* and Naspers for the shocking way they conducted their reporting. They immediately reported that the sister of a well-known Western Province/Springbok flanker had been raped. Withholding her name but then making such an obvious allusion was an outrageous violation of her privacy. Who did they think they were fooling?

The well-known advocate Dup de Bruyn, a good friend of mine, very kindly offered to handle the media inquiries on our behalf after visiting our farm one day and seeing how the media were behaving.

As the days went by, the police came and took more affidavits from René, and they also took her car away for investigation. They asked me how long they could keep it, and I told them that I didn't care, as long as they made sure the forensics were done properly. I had heard so many horror stories of the poor forensics work done by the police.

During this time, René and I spoke a bit more about what had happened. The police were saying that they couldn't find the exact location where René said the attack had taken place. She was still in no state to go back to the scene herself, but she had mentioned seeing a dam where the attack occurred.

So I climbed in my car and went and looked for myself. From René's description I felt I had a pretty good idea of where the place was, because it sounded like it might be near my cricket mate Eddie Barlow's former farm. I drove to where I thought the scene might be. Before the attack, I had put new tyres on René's car, and they had a unique tread pattern. I knew this because I've always paid attention to small details. Each vehicle on our farm has a different set of tyres, each with its own unique tread pattern. The reasoning behind this is very practical. As I know which tread is on which vehicle, I can keep track of where the vehicles have been on the farm.

It didn't take me long to find the abandoned building. Next to it was a small gravel dam wall – the dam René had mentioned. And I could still see her tyre tracks on the dirt road. I put down some rocks where the tracks were and phoned the investigating officer, asking him to meet me at the site. He said he couldn't come immediately but would meet me there at 1 pm. I had some business to do in Cape Town, so I attended to that before returning to the scene at the appointed time. It was good timing because this was approximately the time the attack had taken place.

I'd expressly told the investigator that I'd found René's tyre tracks at the scene of the crime and had placed rocks to indicate where they were. As I drove back, I was shocked to see that the police vehicle had parked on the tracks. I was furious, but the police said they had found other tracks and they were busy taking photographs of these.

While we were standing there, a bakkie drove up and stopped on the dam wall. The driver climbed out and walked down the embankment towards me and the investigating officer. He recognised me and asked what had happened. And then he proceeded to tell me, in front of the police, that a few days earlier, when he was driving back to the farmhouse for lunch, he had seen a blue Citroën parked by this old house.

I said to him, 'Thank you. I think you saved my daughter's life.' His stopping and reversing to investigate confirmed what René had said about a bakkie catching the attention of her attackers. A few moments later the manager of an agricultural research centre came past. He also recognised me and, also in front of the police, asked what had happened. After telling him, I asked if he'd seen anything untoward. He told me that his workers had seen three suspicious men walking along the boundary fence that led to the Engen petrol station on the N1.

Clearly, when the bakkie stopped and reversed, her attackers went outside to look, which gave René the opportunity to make a run for her car. She told me she had been so scared that the attackers might have taken her car keys, but was relieved to find that they were still in the ignition. So she jumped in and locked the doors, and then made a quick U-turn. The tracks I'd seen backed up her version of events. I could see where they crossed, and also the skid marks that indicated a car had pulled away quickly. So I told the police to take a statement from the manager of the research centre, which they did. I was now hopeful that we would get to the bottom of the case and catch René's attackers.

In the meantime, the media were starting to make René's life hell with their phone calls. So I decided to take her to our Karoo farm, Mon Pierre. It was the right move. The farm is very remote, and it gave her the breathing space she needed to collect herself. That Saturday morning, my dear Karoo friend of many years, Jannie Olivier, came early to visit us and we went on an amazing game drive. It was as if all the antelope wanted to see René. They were out in their droves, coming very close to us in the bakkie. I could see René relaxing, and the animals she loved were having a calming influence on her.

We returned to the farmhouse, and to the most amazing Karoo hospitality. Most of the young farmers in the area had arrived and were sitting around the swimming pool. There was a big fire, fresh meat for the braai and Dominee Manus was playing a joyful song on the guitar. The first beers had already been washed down. Everyone was there to help René rebuild her life.

Then all of a sudden Henry Schoeman, who owned the local restaurant — aptly named Merino (after the sheep) – and who was managing the braai, saw a white VW driving in to the farm. I wasn't expecting anybody. As I said, Mon Pierre is very remote, and there are three gates with signage stating that it is private property, so nobody could just drive through three gates and arrive at the farmhouse by mistake.

I assumed the car belonged to the police.

The car stopped close to the farmhouse, and a man and woman got out. The man had no sooner alighted than he picked up a camera with a huge telephoto lens and started taking photos of us. Then the woman, a journalist named Marlene Malan, approached us. I rushed to the car to ask them what they were doing on my property and to tell them to leave immediately. She said they had come to speak to René to get her story of what happened. All the while the photographer was taking photographs on my property, without my permission.

René broke down and ran inside. I went after her, and Malan had the audacity to follow me – after I had told her to get back in the car – and start climbing the stairs to the house. Myra and I were astounded.

Some of my friends then grabbed the photographer's camera, removed the memory card and destroyed it.

I couldn't believe that journalists would drive about 600 kilometres from Cape Town to come and invade our privacy. It was a terrible moment for my daughter.

The following week, Dup de Bruyn phoned me and said he had bad news. The police had put Attie Trollip on René's case. In my opinion, Trollip was not a detective at all. He took over high-profile cases when the investigating officers had bungled them. Trollip had been the investigator in the Inge Lotz murder case, and it was Dup de Bruyn who had taken him apart in court and exposed the many flaws in the police's case, including the fact that the police had fabricated evidence against the accused, Fred van der Vyver.

In the book *Broken and Betrayed*, author Alan Elsdon describes Trollip as a ruthless 'fixer' willing to frame innocent people. Trollip was eventually found out. It turned out he was feeding *Rapport* newspaper with information from confidential police dockets.

So Trollip arrived on our farm to interview René. He kept

questioning her affidavit. Later, I looked at the emails that were sent by our private detective, Piet Calitz, who had offered his services free of charge, to Trollip and lead investigator Inspector Van Zyl. Trollip and Van Zyl did not investigate any of the leads that Piet dug up. A picture started to form in my mind that the police were not going to solve this.

At the same time, the Naspers journalist Tim du Plessis went on TV to claim that there was more to the whole story, and tried to suggest that I was somehow involved, and that the police were going to close the case for lack of evidence. The situation was spiralling out of control. Piet told me categorically that the police had messed up the forensics on the case. He had also tracked down René's attackers, who were living at a settlement called Bloekombos, near the scene of the attack.

That was when I demanded a meeting with Advocate Nollie Niehaus, then a senior deputy director in the Western Cape Directorate for Public Prosecutions.

The police were disputing the statement given by the farm manager, who had said that he saw the vehicle parked near the abandoned building, and had positively identified the make, colour and CN registration plates. Then Myra heard that he had been shot while transporting his workers and was in hospital. Chris Faure, our attorney, obtained another statement from him while he was in hospital, and it was identical to the one he had given to the police.

So we had all this information, only to discover that Trollip was not only disputing the facts but also had physically changed them in the police docket. This was the reason why the police wanted to close the investigation for lack of sufficient evidence. Attie Trollip, 'The Fixer', had done his job. I believe he did it in order to get back at Dup de Bruyn. The police had also refused to use any of Piet Calitz's information.

The truth is that they were saying this because they had botched the forensics, and as this was now a high-profile case, they were desperate to make it go away. During the meeting with Nollie Niehaus, and with Attie Trollip in attendance, whenever I had Attie in a corner, he would threaten to leave the meeting and would fiddle with his pens and close his files full of rubbish. I have never seen a man lie through his teeth like that, and couldn't believe that this was a senior police detective. And then we later found out the reason: Trollip had never qualified as a detective; he was simply a security policeman. In his world, the 'truth' was whatever lie suited the situation. Reading Elsdon's book reminded me that the South African system still protects these corrupt officials.

Some time after handing René's car over to the police, we inquired when we could come and collect it, only to hear that it had gone missing. The police eventually found the car, but when we went to collect it, it hadn't even been dusted for fingerprints. In all the time they had had the car, not a single fingerprint had been taken.

We collected the car, but René quite understandably said that she never wanted to drive it again. Myra noticed that the vehicle licence had lapsed while the car had been with the police. So she went to the traffic office in Wellington to renew it, only to be told that the vehicle was not on the electronic National Traffic Information System (eNaTIS). It had been deregistered. I was later informed that this is how vehicles involved in a crime are stolen. When I inquired about getting the car registered again, the local office handling such cases said we had to pay the VAT on the car and apply for registration.

I then queried the deregistration of the vehicle with the local brigadier of the South African Police Service, and told him that I was holding him responsible for the re-registration of the car. Suddenly, the vehicle was back on the eNaTIS system. Of course, this made me realise that something was seriously amiss with the whole case.

But what can you do? The police had decided to close the case, and that was that. It was incredibly frustrating, and I can't imagine how many South Africans have to go through this on a daily basis. I am not in any way taking away from the thousands of hard-working people in the police service who risk their lives to keep us safe, or the good work done by our police. But my experience also showed how the system can fail you dismally. And, unfortunately, I've had even more experience of this in my life.

It was a terrible time for us as a family, and especially so for René, who had to go on antiretroviral drugs for a period of time. I had always hoped that my daughter would become a mother one day, and one of my main concerns was how this incident would impact the rest of her life.

However, I am extremely proud of the way René has put all of this behind her. She even did a few talks about the incident, but she quickly said that she was not going to live the rest of her life defined as a victim and that she would move on, which she has done. She is happily married now to a musician, Marco Gomes, who is one of the founders of one of South Africa's best rock bands, Prime Circle. And they have given me a beautiful granddaughter, Bella.

But I still struggle to forgive those who showed such a lack of basic human empathy at a time when a young woman and her family were traumatised and hurting immensely.

17

TIAAN

MY CHILDREN ARE ALL very different. And when it comes to the boys, Tiaan and Schalk are two very different people indeed.

Early one bitterly cold September morning in 1985, Myra woke me up. I remember we had the electric blanket on. She shook me awake and said, 'My water has broken.' In my half-awake state I said, 'For goodness' sake, turn off the electric blanket. We don't want to get electrocuted.'

And so Tiaan came into our lives.

Years later, I was woken up at 4 am to be told that Tiaan had been in a car accident near our farm. He had fallen asleep at the wheel and his car had left the road and crashed, cartwheeling several times. By some miracle, he wasn't badly injured. I remember walking around the accident site, picking up pieces of the vehicle that had come loose as it had turned over and over, realising again that my children are protected by a greater hand when I am not there.

Tiaan and Schalk were close as boys and have remained so. In fact, my children are all very good friends with each other.

By the age of ten, both Tiaan and Schalk could fish and hunt well. I also took them sailing with me and hiking in the mountains. Tiaan often speaks about the wonderful memories he has of the

A boys' weekend at Kyalami. I took part in the SABC celebrity race and set a new lap record. Schalk Jnr and Tiaan were extremely proud of their old man.

Me and the boys on the exquisite Tsitsikamma coast, where I taught them to dive for alikreukel (giant periwinkle). They cut their teeth as boogie boarders and surfers at Jeffreys Bay.

three of us going to Henties Bay and fishing for 12 hours at a time. I'd use this time to talk to them about life and hear what was going on in their own lives.

I was very busy at work when they were growing up. Apart from setting up a sports marketing company, Megapro, I was doing a lot of TV work as a commentator or in-studio guest. I was spending a lot of time travelling, so I made a point of dedicating my holidays and weekends to my family. The local dominee would often mention to me that he hadn't seen us in church lately, but Sundays were an important family day for us.

We also spent some fantastic winter holidays in the Karoo or going up the Skeleton Coast to fish. Some of Tiaan's fondest memories are of the times we slept on my yacht and fished through the night, or the Sundays I'd take him and his brother to go and watch a cricket Test at Newlands.

I mentioned that Tiaan and Schalk are very different. Tiaan is unorthodox, while Schalk is more traditional. They both played cricket, but it would be Tiaan who would spray his helmet a weird metallic colour to stand out. On the sports field, Tiaan would also

Schalk Jnr's first big buck, an oryx, hunted north of Okahandja during one of our many hunting and fishing trips in Namibia. With me is my brother-in-law, Bouwer Nell, as well as Tiaan and the tracker on the farm of our friend Louis Anderson.

The one and only Otto (right), who for many years was the family's fishing guide at Henties Bay, Namibia. Here we are fishing below the dunes close to the town.

quickly react to any taunts from opponents, while Schalk was very good at ignoring them and focusing on his own game.

Both were very good sportsmen, as are all of my children, actually. René was a very good netball and tennis player. I think it helped her that she played tennis against her brothers. The rugby player Derick Hougaard spent a lot of time with us, and they would all play tennis against each other. The boys never held back when they played against René, which is why I think she surprised many of her opponents at school with how hard she could hit the ball.

Tiaan also shares my love of golf. We used to have a house at Fancourt, where he was introduced to golfers like Ernie Els and John Bland. John would give Tiaan the old Balata golf balls and tell him, 'There you go. Go and beat your old man with these balls. They spin a lot more than the modern ones.' Tiaan loved those Balata golf balls. If we came to a water hazard, he'd scratch around in his golf bag, pull out an old messed-up ball and hit that one rather than risk hitting one of his prized Balatas into the water.

Tiaan and I at the Alfred Dunhill Links Championship. He caddied for me on two occasions, and it was an incredible experience to have my son on the bag and inside the ropes in a prestigious event like this. In 2007 we came third in the pro-am, to the dismay of Myra, who was hoping to watch Schalk Jnr play against Fiji in the quarter-final of the Rugby World Cup.

One of the most special moments we shared was attending the 2007 Alfred Dunhill Links Championship tournament in St Andrews. This is undoubtedly the best place to be as an amateur golfer. During that week you play three of the best links courses in the world – the Old Course, Carnoustie and Kingsbarns – in all kinds of weather and with the nicest people you can find. For an amateur golfer it's a dream to be inside the ropes and playing alongside the professionals. Johann Rupert does not get the compliments that he should in South Africa for this tournament, and for the quality of the world leaders in sport and business who play in this event. I have only missed two of these 17 tournaments to date.

In 2007, while in France to watch Schalk play in the Rugby World Cup, I took Tiaan along as my caddie for the Alfred Dunhill tournament. After watching Schalk play against the USA in Montpellier, where he was voted man of the match, Myra joined us to fly to Scotland, and we had a great time on the golf courses there. We actually made it to the final round, and finished third overall among the amateur teams. In 2015, during the next Rugby World Cup, Tiaan was also my caddie, and these two events really stand out in my mind as great times spent with my son doing something so special.

As a rugby player, Tiaan played lock, flank and eighthman. He had great hands and was a beautiful runner with the ball. Schalk also had good hands, but he was far more physical on the field. He always played the game like a human wrecking ball. When Tiaan was in Grade 9, I picked him up from school one day and he proudly told me how he'd bounced a whole lot of players at rugby practice. I got quite agitated with him and told him not to try to play like his brother, but to play his own game, which he was very good at.

At the customary interschool derby between Paarl Gimnasium and Paarl Boys' High, Tiaan was voted man of the match. He really showed his skills under immense pressure in that game. Tiaan started in the C team when he entered high school and worked his way up to the A teams in each year. After school, he played club rugby for Wellington and they won three club championships and

Me and Tiaan at the capping ceremony of the Paarl Gimnasium first team before an interschool match against Paarl Boys' High in 2002. I'm very proud to say that he was an exceptional man of the match in a game that was won by his team with a record score of 15–0.

also played in three National Club Championships. He also played rugby for Boland Under-20.

While Schalk always made the representative teams in his age group, Tiaan would make it to the final trials but not get selected. I've always told him that there is great strength in just learning to compete.

I didn't actually want Schalk and Tiaan to attend the same school, as I didn't want them to compete with each other. They were only a little over a year apart in age, and it worried me that people would put pressure on Tiaan to be just like Schalk. I took both my sons to the school open days at Bishops, Paul Roos Gimnasium, Paarl Boys' High, Rondebosch, Boland Landbou and Paarl Gimnasium. They were never forced to go to Paarl Gimnasium because it was my alma mater. But when they both decided to attend the school, I walked a fine line trying to get Tiaan to understand that he didn't need to be like his brother, that he should just be himself. Tiaan was always very clever and did well in his studies. As far as rugby was concerned, I encouraged each one to develop their own style and play the way they felt comfortable.

Schalk was on a very different path to Tiaan. In time, both Tiaan and Schalk figured out where they wanted to be in life.

I think what ultimately convinced Tiaan that he didn't want a future in rugby was the death of Riaan Loots, who played with Tiaan at Wellington, when he was kicked to death on the rugby field in June 2006. The horrific incident happened in Rawsonville, and as Tiaan was also playing club rugby at the time, it had a profound effect on him. Tiaan had started playing club rugby after he left school, and he was coming up against the typical hard men of the club game. He'd already had his teeth knocked out. But the death of Riaan Loots was a sobering moment for him and his rugby career. As Tiaan grew older, he expressed a growing interest in our wine business, and he now runs it very successfully, having qualified in agricultural management.

Tiaan has always had a tremendous affinity for music, something he definitely shares with me. So does Schalk, who is also a very competent guitarist. I always used to tell my children that they could listen to any music they liked, as long as it was rock music. The golfer Nick Price once told me that after hearing this from me, he did the same with his son, and from that point they never had problems listening to music in the car. I travelled to London a lot when my children were growing up, and I would bring them back the latest music. I had a contact at Tower Records in Piccadilly Circus who would sell me all the latest demos and CDs of new bands trying to break through. My sons knew all the latest bands and songs years before they were released in South Africa.

I bought Tiaan his first drum kit when he was 14 years old. I never minded the noise in the house. He and a friend, Morgan O'Kennedy, formed their first band when they were still very young. They were like a young Koos Kombuis, which a lot of people liked, and they made quite a lot of pocket money. When he was in matric, Tiaan formed a band with his friend Bossie called the Flying Dakotas, and they still perform regularly together. He and his friends could play as much as they liked. I loved hearing the music.

I allowed my children a lot of freedom at a young age. Some might consider that reckless, but I think it all worked out. Sure, there were some pretty scary moments, like the incident with the jet ski on our farm dam. Schalk was driving this very powerful 130 hp jet ski with Tiaan on the back. At some point, Schalk opened the engine up full throttle, and the next minute they ramped over the dam wall and dropped almost 50 metres into the guava orchard on the other side. Tiaan was knocked unconscious, and Schalk carried him back up the dam wall. Amazingly, their injuries required nothing more than a few stiches. It happened about 200 metres from where I was standing. I remember this feeling of running faster than any man alive, and then slowing down as I neared the point of impact because I wasn't sure what was waiting for me there.

On another occasion, I'd just bought a new bakkie for the farm when Tiaan and Schalk thought it would be a great idea to teach themselves how to rally – without my knowledge. They were under age, but they decided to take the bakkie and go and visit friends on a neighbouring farm. Schalk was again the one driving. Sitting in the middle seat of the bakkie was Reghard van Dyk, a great friend of theirs who also spent a lot of holidays on the farm helping to make wine or attending to the cricket pitch. But on this occasion he was in the proverbial hot seat.

While driving, they had put the bakkie into an aggressive four-wheel-drive drift – attempting to emulate my good friend and their hero, South African rally legend Sarel van der Merwe. But they ran out of road, and the bakkie tilted onto its side, sliding further into a ditch before coming to an abrupt stop.

I had a chuckle about what must have happened next, because I had personal experience. At university, I'd also found myself sitting in a car on its side, with the driver, Francois Conradie, and Pierre Strydom. (Francois, who was from Laingsburg, became one of the heroes of the terrible flood of 1981 when he helped save people from the town's old-age home.)

The biggest problem when trying to get out of a car on its side is pushing the door open and climbing out without the door crashing down on you and possibly taking a few of your fingers with it. Schalk and the boys must have found this out for themselves.

Reghard, who was sitting in the middle, would've been the first to get out through the small window directly behind him.

We believe that it was during this incident that Schalk first injured his neck. He had Boland cricket finals that Saturday, and although he said he was feeling sore from the crash, I made him play. I told him he had a commitment to his team, and there was no way he was getting out of that commitment just because he and his brother had been stupid enough to try to slide a bakkie around a 90-degree corner. As poor Myra put it, what did I expect, with my history of racing stock cars and going on rallies with friends like Sarel van der Merwe and Nic de Waal, who would take my kids in the cars with them at breakneck speeds on gravel roads to show them what a car could really do.

At moments such as this, I would always quote my own father and tell my boys, 'Goeie idee. Kak plan' (Great idea. Shit plan).

However, I have always believed that you must give kids the space to find out who they are, and the freedom to make mistakes. If they don't push the boundaries and make mistakes, how will they ever find out what their limits are? I never raised my kids according to a manual.

18

OUR FAMILY HOLIDAY BEFORE THE END OF THE WORLD

I THINK I WAS always very good at letting my children discover their own way in life. It's so easy to say that we learn more from our mistakes than our successes. We preach this, but we are terrified of allowing our children to make mistakes.

Family holidays were the ideal occasions to let my children discover who they were, but I probably turned Myra into a nervous wreck in the process.

There was one particularly memorable holiday, which I like to call the Y2K Burger Family Holiday. It was the year of Y2K, and if you remember, the world was going to end. So I started thinking, well, what can we do as a family to really celebrate the end of the world?

I started building our own bush trailer. I named it P1, as in Prototype 1. It eventually evolved into P3, the final product. It didn't have a shower, but I managed to convince Myra to go along with my idea. And we undertook this incredible family trip to Zimbabwe, Botswana and Namibia. We covered 14 000 kilometres in five weeks in our Land Rover. In fact, we did a few incredible trips in our Land Rover.

Schalk has been a brand ambassador for Land Rover, and whenever he does a promotional talk, he says he doubts whether anybody has spent more time in the back of a Land Rover than he has on all our hunting and fishing trips together.

I tell you, if a family really wants to get to know one another, then this is the trip to do. We went everywhere. I took them to visit the ruins of Great Zimbabwe. We went up to Lake Kariba and spent time on a houseboat. Then we went to Victoria Falls. We played golf at Leopard Rock in the Zimbabwean highlands. Tiaan and Schalk rode boogie boards in the rapids of the Zambezi River.

In Botswana we camped in the Savuti, where a hyena charged us as I was taking René to bed one night. And Myra had a fit when Tiaan walked up close to an elephant in order to take a photo. We also got caught in a torrential downpour that lasted for days and turned the dirt roads to mud. I made Schalk and Tiaan wade in front of the stationary Land Rover so I could have an idea of where to drive through the deep water. I made them both carry a big stick, the rationale being that if you are surprised by a crocodile that goes for you, you give him the stick, which he then grabs thinking he's got hold of his prey.

On one occasion they were wading about 100 metres ahead of us, each with their sticks in hand, while I made mental notes of the driving line I needed to take, when they both shouted, 'Flattie!' They were referring to a flat dog, which is a slang term for a crocodile. Well, they both dropped their sticks and started to sprint back to the car. But the minute they were out of the water and on dry land running towards us, they were slipping all over the place. The slipperiest goo you will ever encounter is the wet black cotton soil of Botswana. We drove through the water, which by now was almost up to our windows, and we spotted the crocodile that had startled them. And nearby were the two sticks that were meant to save them. Schalk and Tiaan's hearts were still beating wildly as we passed that crocodile.

We also played fantastic games of car cricket. VWs were out, but a VW with a trailer was a dropped catch. I loved those car games with them. Those long road trips and the music we'd play together are some of the most special times I have spent with my children.

And I believe these things helped form my children and their views on life.

To this day, all three know exactly what they want in life. Even when I look at the relationships they've had, they have always been very serious. Both Tiaan and Schalk had one long-term girlfriend before they married them, and René married a man 11 years older than her who has three daughters, is Portuguese and a Roman Catholic, and who makes her so happy. And if they ever go boating on the dam, she is the one who reverses the boat into the water. That always makes me smile.

My children have no time for bullshit. They like having a good, solid time and spending it with good, honest people.

As a father, I didn't get everything right. I was often away from home building a business, and Myra had to handle a lot on her own. For two or three years, I spent the third week of every month in London on business. Myra did a hell of a job parenting the kids at that time. I've probably been a bit of a bad father for not spending more time at home when they were growing up. But I always

Skipper Schalk Jnr in control of our first yacht, Spindrifter, *on a broad reach on Langebaan Lagoon.*

gave them my best over the weekends and holidays.

My children also knew their father wasn't perfect. At times, we lived too much on the edge with the adventures we undertook. But if we were going to make mistakes, at least we made them together. I was with them. Many parents send their kids away on adventure camps, but I preferred to take my children on adventures with me. I taught them how dangerous a rifle is and how to shoot it properly, and how to play a big fish and read the sea.

Both Schalk and Tiaan were excellent body boarders and I remember the first time I took them each into the deep water of Supertubes at Jeffreys Bay, where we would lie in wait for the right wave to ride. They loved being in the sea, and our annual holiday to Jeffreys Bay meant they would get new kit from the Billabong surf shop, which they loved. They both developed a very good understanding of the sea, the currents and what to do if you got into trouble.

Maybe I was just being a big kid myself. But I loved my kids for giving me that opportunity. They were always up for anything. They could easily have said no, we don't want to do it. Instead, we had

Me and Schalk Jnr on the beach in front of our home in Bloubergstrand, testing the waters for some fish but mostly admiring the incredible view of Table Mountain.

some great times together. I was lucky enough to be with my kids when they shot their first buck, caught their first fish, scored a first provincial ton, played their first provincial match and, in the case of Schalk, when he played his first Springbok Test. And when he won the Laureus Comeback of the Year award.

Of course, I've doubted myself as a father many times, especially during the toughest moments in my children's lives. When things happen to my family, particularly things I don't expect or don't want to happen, it makes me doubt myself. Yes, you can try to control the environment in which your children grow up, and do your best to ensure that nothing bad happens to them. But life still comes at you.

I've also wondered about their future. If you're a first-generation creator of wealth, it's not always easy to pass this on to your children. I've perhaps created something worthwhile in my life, and hopefully my children will take it and make even more of a success of it.

However, I am forever grateful for the opportunity I was given to be a father. It was something I always wanted. And I thank my children for letting me play in their world as much as I did.

PART FOUR

SOUTH AFRICAN

19

THE DAY CHEEKY WATSON ASKED TO WASH MY FEET

MYRA AND I WERE just coming out of Makro when my phone rang. It was Graham Power of Power Construction. He was frantic. He said that he'd received a message from God and had to see me urgently. Now, I'm a Christian man, and as far as I'm concerned the Lord does not just appear with a message for me and I don't decide to hear what the message is. So I told Graham to come and see me. The message he had for me caught me completely off-guard.

The following Sunday, Graham sat down in our house and said that God had told him that his sole purpose in life was to bring the Watson and Burger families together. More specifically, Graham informed me that Daniel 'Cheeky' Watson wanted to meet with me so that he could wash my feet and begin the process of forgiveness between our two families.

All of this had its beginnings in 2007, when Cheeky went to the media calling me and Johann Rupert members of a mysterious 'third force' in South African rugby. This was at a time when Schalk Jnr and Cheeky's son Luke were vying for the same position in the Springbok team.

It was a disgusting time for all concerned. What should have been nothing more than a team selection decision became a bitter controversy. Cheeky called for the removal of the Springbok emblem, Luke said he had to stop himself from vomiting on the Springbok jersey, and the then Springbok coach, Jake White, was accused of favouring the old Afrikaners through my connections and my son's heritage. It was ridiculous.

White had already clearly stated his reasons for playing Schalk Jnr at openside flanker. 'I have five loose forwards that play consistently for South Africa,' White stated during a press conference in 2006. 'They've done consistently well. I have no say in the Stormers playing Schalk on the blindside as opposed to the openside, therefore I cannot judge Schalk Burger as a blindside flanker. He plays openside for South Africa. He was picked by the IRB as the best player in the world ... Until he loses form at openside flank for South Africa, I'm very happy that between him, Solly Tyibilika, Wikus van Heerden, Joe van Niekerk, Pedrie Wannenburg, Jacques Cronjé and AJ Venter, I've got enough cover in that position to carry forward.'

But the issue became a highly politicised melodrama. And Cheeky delighted in fanning the flames of the drama, which included making outlandish statements about a third force. If anything, the Bosasa scandal that rocked South Africa in January 2019 proved there was indeed a sinister third force at work, but it was in fact linked to the Watsons themselves rather than to me or Johann Rupert.

When it emerged that Bosasa CEO Gavin Watson, Cheeky's brother, was deeply involved in the state capture project involving former President Jacob Zuma and a host of high-ranking officials – the biggest corruption scandal in South African history – it did not surprise me one little bit. Gavin was also involved in the failed R9-billion SeaArk marine farming project in the Coega industrial development zone. The other two Watson brothers, Ronnie and Valence, were both involved in the controversial Inyanda-Roodeplaat wind farm project in the Eastern Cape, which was approved at government level despite serious concerns about its environmental impact on the bird life in the surrounding Groendal Nature Reserve. In 2019, testimony by whistleblower Angelo Agrizzi before the Zondo

Commission highlighted the conflicts of interest of various ministers with ties to Bosasa. And then you had Cheeky at the helm of Eastern Province Rugby as it descended into a pitiful state, subsequently facing charges of fraud and money laundering.

Jake White would later admit that the Watson family had approached him directly through the lawyer Brian Biebuyck (later fingered by Agrizzi as a party to the Bosasa scandal) to include Luke in the Springbok squad, even going so far as to suggest that his tenure as Springbok coach could be extended beyond the Rugby World Cup in France in 2007. White's successor, Peter de Villiers, inherited the Watson debacle. But Peter later said that Luke was not a team man, and he told how Cheeky had put immense political pressure on him to include Luke.

In his now infamous speech at a rugby festival at the University of Cape Town in 2008, Luke made the most outlandish claims. To me, it sounded like somebody desperate to create a cause for himself. He seemed to be whipping up a revolution purely to have something to define himself by. He made sweeping statements about his father and what a hero he'd been for daring to stand up against apartheid by participating in the struggle.

I can probably understand a son wanting to believe these noble things about his father. But I need to question where Cheeky's famed principles were when he played for Eastern Province against the touring All Blacks in 1976, the year of the Soweto uprising? You either stand for something or you don't – there are no half measures. Unfortunately, though, my experience of Cheeky and the rest of the Watsons, even in those days, told a radically different story.

Then Luke claimed that Doc Craven had declared that a black man would never play for the Springboks. Excuse me? I don't recall him ever saying that. Did Luke ever play under Doc? Did he spend hours having tea with Doc and talking to him? As I've already pointed out, Doc left his beloved church because of the government's stance against allowing Maori players in the All Blacks team. It was Doc who in 1975 had the vision for a South African Under-21 team which he saw as an opportunity for players of colour to eventually make their way into the Springbok team.

Luke then quoted his own father claiming that South African rugby was rotten to the core. Now, let me state this plainly: South African rugby had, and still has, plenty of issues with which to occupy itself. And yes, it always was, and still is, an arena beset with politics, backstabbing and controversy. But I found the whole 'rotten to the core' statement a bit rich coming from a family that was itself far from the perfect embodiment of the new South Africa that they purported to represent.

So, with this background, my family was now being drawn into the political cesspit that was the world of the Watsons. Schalk Jnr did his best to try to focus on what he could control, namely, his own performance in the Springbok jersey. And I am incredibly proud of the way he handled the situation and moved on in his career. I even remember the match between the Stormers and the Sharks in the Super 14 at Newlands in May 2007 when Schalk put out his hand to shake that of Luke, who was coming on as a replacement, and how Luke ignored him.

All of this was going through my mind as Graham sat before me with the request to meet with Cheeky and allow him to wash my feet.

According to Graham, our two families were from opposite poles in South Africa. The one, in his opinion, was this staunch Boere family, and the other an English family with roots in the black community.

Right there, I already knew we had a problem. I believe God knows me, my history and my family's history, including my mother's and my aunts' liberal views, and how I was raised. Graham's description was way off the mark, and because I'm not in the business of believing that God makes mistakes when He gives people messages, I knew Graham was the one who was mistaken.

So I told him, 'Jis, ou pêl, I don't think you know where I come from.'

At the end of our meeting Graham said he would like to pray for us. My poor wife was drawn into the prayer as well. Even Tiaan, who had just come from breakfast, suddenly found himself in the middle of this set-up. Graham went on and on, praying for about 20 minutes.

The next day I told Graham, 'Okay, I'll come to your house and meet with Cheeky next Sunday.' Myra said I was mad, but I decided to go. I had always admired the Watsons in a way for being open about their position on apartheid, which was not at all different from mine, and I had played against Cheeky in 1973.

Cheeky and Graham opened with prayer, focusing on the past in South Africa and that two powerful families must not be seen to be fighting, and that we should write a book together and ask for forgiveness for the sins of the past. Graham asked me if I wanted to pray, and I said, 'No, I don't understand your kind of praying with the hands in the air and occasional shout-outs. But I am here to talk, as the Lord has requested from Graham Power.'

Cheeky started by saying that we didn't know each other, and that he was glad we were having this meeting. That's when I stopped him.

'Cheeky,' I said, 'how can you say we don't know each other? At the 1973 Craven Week I stayed in the room below yours at Wilgenhof in Stellenbosch. We played the second game of the tournament against you guys. Mike Ryan, the lock, was your roommate. I was in your room on a few occasions.'

So then Cheeky rattled off this call to heaven, shouting, 'Oh, Lord, help me! I forgot, Lord! I'm a sinner!' It was crazy stuff. I further pointed out to Cheeky that I had been in their family shop several times when I played rugby in Port Elizabeth for EP. In fact, the Watsons were the biggest Crockett & Jones shoe stockist in Port Elizabeth. I'd been in there to try to find the right size shoes for myself, a problem I've had throughout my life.

'I'm a sinner, Lord!' Cheeky shouted.

Then I let him have it. 'And Cheeky, what about all the rumours surrounding the exact circumstances in which your house burnt down in Port Elizabeth, and that it was under far more questionable circumstances than your claim that it was the Broederbond's doing?'

I further asked him if he knew who was involved in the building of the wall around the Dan Qeqe Stadium and who had helped appoint Norman Ntshinga. And about my run-in with Hendrik

Roodt and the notorious security police of Port Elizabeth. 'Jeez, Cheeky, if this meeting is going to go any further, you need to be honest,' I told him.

He said, 'Schalk, all of this is all the more reason why I must wash your feet.'

I told him, 'Cheeky, I'm sorry, but you can't. I don't trust you. I think if you did that, tomorrow it will be all over the newspapers and your motives aren't right. And why on earth would you want to wash my feet? I've done nothing against you. You are the one who claimed that Johann Rupert and I were part of some ridiculous third force. But you know what, if you and your son Luke publicly apologise for the disrespect you showed the Springbok jersey, I will reconsider. So the ball is in your court.'

And that's how I left the meeting. I never heard from either Graham or Cheeky again.

I eventually figured out that Graham Power was trying to act as power broker (pardon the pun) in a deal whereby Schalk Jnr would follow his teammates and forgive Luke for the statements he had made in his speech.

I felt very strongly that the Watsons had misrepresented not only my family but also our history, and had failed to acknowledge who we actually are as a family. So that was a fundamental problem to start with.

If you take into consideration how I eventually became a Springbok, it's clear to anybody that we were far from the Afrikaans stereotype we were made out to be by Cheeky Watson and his political cohort.

In his speech at the University of Cape Town in October 2008, Luke declared that he had come from a 'disadvantaged background'. What utter nonsense. He attended Grey High School in Port Elizabeth, one of the top boys' schools in the country. For goodness' sake, it has been reported that his family's net worth was somewhere between R6 billion and R13 billion.

That's why it sickened me when they attacked the Springbok jersey the way they did, dragging my son into that mess and causing such division within our country. I know Schalk Jnr had a very hard time forgiving Luke for his comments.

Luke also said in that speech, 'I'm not going to look at what you see ... I'm not going to try and change your truth ... I will believe my truth and not the truth that you believe, so all of a sudden your reality means nothing to me ...'

Well, that may be the truest thing he's ever said, because when it comes to the Watsons, their truth, their reality, is certainly very different from mine.

The only reason I believe they could ever have come up with the idea of a third force was when Jake White was called back from the Springbok tour to the United Kingdom in 2006 to face a vote of no confidence by the SA Rugby executive, leaving then team manager Zola Yeye – a good friend and business partner of the Watsons – in charge.

Johann Rupert and I had a meeting with a few members of the SA Rugby executive, purely because there were members who, like us, were opposed to the meeting with Jake and the vote of no confidence, and who shared our view that Jake was capable of leading this team to Rugby World Cup glory the following year. But the Watsons were really going too far in trying to turn this meeting into some sinister third force in South African rugby.

I do have one very good memory of that meeting, though. Johann and I discussed a name for his first really big and prized buffalo bull. In light of all that went on at that time, it was eventually called Third Force. That name will live on, given the superb offspring it has produced for the genetic pool of South African buffaloes. The Watsons would definitely not have wanted to wash that buffalo's feet.

The reality is there really was only one third force in South African rugby at that time. And the Watsons know exactly who that was. Trying to involve me somehow was another one of those moments when my instincts and past experiences allowed me to take the only route I know – the honest one.

20

LOUIS LUYT AND THE FIGHT FOR SOUTH AFRICAN RUGBY'S SOUL

I ENJOYED LOUIS LUYT. We had some big disagreements, but I actually enjoyed his company. However, there is no doubt that he took us as close to the brink of the rugby wilderness as we've ever been in South Africa.

After the highs of the 1995 Rugby World Cup, with the game uniting the people of this country in a way never seen before, politics took us straight back to where we'd started.

On the one hand, there was the drive by the ruling ANC to transform rugby by including more black players, and on the other was the pushback by Luyt and the South African Rugby Football Union (Sarfu, formed in 1992 as the merger between the South African Rugby Board and the South African Rugby Union), who were unwilling to relinquish control of their fiefdom.

That is not to say that Louis Luyt wasn't good for South African rugby in many respects. But unfortunately he will always be remembered as the man who took Nelson Mandela to court.

The animosity had begun even before the glory of the 1995 Rugby World Cup. As Luyt increased his power, first as president of the Transvaal Rugby Union and then as president of Sarfu, those who didn't appreciate his autocratic leadership style multiplied.

Following the release of Nelson Mandela and the unbanning of liberation organisations, the negotiations between the ANC and the National Party government included South Africa's re-entry into international sport. Of course, as rugby was a major sport and also a touchstone for the Afrikaner community, heated debates raged around the future of the Springbok emblem, whether the team would still be called the Springboks and whether the national anthem and the old South African flag would be acceptable at international matches. All of these matters were under discussion. And every single one of them was like a landmine waiting to explode under the negotiation table.

I must say, I was fascinated by the events at the time, not only because I found myself at the centre of the rugby debate, but because the overall spirit of discussion in the country was something to witness. Sure, the standard of debate was sometimes poor, and it produced some incredibly heated moments. But, just think, how many countries in the world have managed to successfully sit around a table and talk their way through a major transition of power? It requires some very special people with a unique understanding of the bigger picture involved, and we were blessed to have many of those people at that massively critical time in South Africa's history.

The willingness to debate issues with people you don't necessarily agree with is something I've always admired. I've tried as much as possible to apply it in my own life.

So when it came to rugby at this explosive time, my friendship with Steve Tshwete and his allies and my cordial relationship with Luyt meant that I was in a unique position to assist in steering rugby through a very difficult transition. My involvement in the process happened via my sports marketing business, Megapro, which I'll explain more about later.

In 1992, it was announced that the All Blacks would play the Springboks at Ellis Park in the first post-isolation Test. But it was a very difficult year for South Africa. The political negotiations,

With my dear friend Steve Tshwete at a dinner. Steve should have received a lot more recognition for the role he played in creating sports unity in South Africa. A lasting impression for me was his and Nelson Mandela's incredible friendship and trust in each other's judgement.

which were being thrashed out at Codesa (the Convention for a Democratic South Africa), were on a knife-edge around several issues regarding the future of the country.

The Test against the All Blacks was set to take place in August. Then came the massacre at Boipatong on 17 June, and tensions immediately became inflamed. Mandela announced that the ANC was pulling out of negotiations with President FW de Klerk's government. Certain members of the ANC claimed that the massacre had been supported by the security forces to destabilise the negotiation process.

Then came the Test, and Luyt threw petrol on the flames by deciding to play only the Afrikaans version of the national anthem, 'Die Stem'. And some supporters flew the old South African flag. It bears noting that this was at the time still the national flag of the country, but that made it no less controversial in the eyes of the majority of the population. Of course, this incensed the ANC even further. I had pleaded with Luyt personally for him not to do that, and to wait until the country's new constitution had been drafted. I even took him a rugby jersey from newly independent Namibia, which had combined all the colours of the various federations and which they'd used during the interim phase before settling on a new jersey. I showed him this as an example of how to reach a compromise during a sensitive period.

Before the Test, Steve Tshwete, then the head of the ANC's sports committee and later to become the first minister of sport in democratic South Africa, asked me if I could try to reason with Luyt. Steve said to me that the ANC was not going to change or remove the Springbok emblem, as was feared, and that this was a decision they had taken before Mandela's release from jail. According to Steve, they had agreed that they loved what the Springbok represented as a sporting emblem. Steve wanted the Springbok to remain representative of all South African sport.

I sat down with Luyt and conveyed this to him. But the big man wasn't having any of it. I'll never forget when he said to me, 'So, Schalk, you're bringing politics into sport again.' Clearly, he still hadn't forgiven me for forcing the SARB's hand during the Cavaliers tour in 1986.

I replied, 'Doc, I trust Steve Tshwete. You even had negotiations with them about unity. If you don't trust them, why even deal with them in the way you did? But I guarantee you, Steve has told me that if you play that anthem and fly the flag, all hell will break loose.'

And Luyt said, 'Stuff it. No politician will tell me what to do.' And of course, all hell did subsequently break loose. It went on until the 1995 Rugby World Cup, during which we had a brief reprieve. It was a magical tournament for everyone in this country.

It was a very good time for me as well, because of the business I had founded: a sports marketing company. Later, this would be incorporated into Megapro, which was established with my previous lock partner and at that time family friend George Rautenbach.

When I saw that political change was coming, I believed three things were going to happen in South Africa: Nelson Mandela would be released from prison, we would have free democratic elections and we'd return to international sport. On that basis, I had decided to go into sports marketing after my rugby career ended. I knew that once we returned to international sport, there would be a market for advertising rights in stadiums.

I was right about what happened, but I had the order of events mixed up. Nelson Mandela was released a year earlier than I expected. Then came our re-entry into international sport, and only after that did we have free democratic elections.

By 1992, most of the sports federations in South Africa were busy unifying. Except for rugby. In the meantime, through Megapro and my business partner, George Rautenbach, I had been securing the advertising rights at various stadiums. We told the stadium managers, 'Give us your advertising rights, and we guarantee you that we'll triple your revenue.' Those were simple deals to make, because we could easily deliver on such a guarantee. I was also helping Boland move towards unification in sport; my house in Wellington became the meeting place for Jackie Abrams of Boland Rugby, Henry Paulse of Boland Cricket and Adam Fortuin of Boland Tennis, as well as Steve Tshwete.

Steve was greatly inspired by Nelson Mandela's belief that sport had a pivotal role to play in the liberation struggle, and we had some fascinating debates about this. I think my own experience of being denied a full Springbok rugby career because of politics somehow served as a link between me and those who were similarly denied the full reward of their sporting talents on the grounds of colour. Yes, I am white and can never claim to have suffered to the extent that my fellow black and coloured sportsmen did. But we certainly had common ground in political interference in sport, and it was politics that also meant my generation of rugby Springboks didn't play nearly as many Tests as we should have and were not able to truly fulfil our full potential.

This transitional period in our sport was a crazy time for us. Myra and I would wake up at 4 am and I'd start writing contracts, which she would type up for me. At the same time that we were drawing up business contracts for the advent of professionalism in rugby, I was also assisting lawyer Maynard Feenstra in drawing up much of the early sports marketing laws for the country.

We were literally pioneers in what today is all standard practice in the business of professional sport.

Primarily, Megapro worked at developing strategies for sports unions to become more professional, such as restructuring the ownership and funding structures for the building of stadiums, suites and electronic scoreboards. With the greater television coverage on offer, we signed up a multitude of new sponsors. With that came the creation of new brands and the drawing up of marketing plans, broadcast packages and strategic communication plans between the sponsors, broadcasters and rights holders for various sports competitions.

Merchandising was another new industry spawned by professionalism in sport, with supporters looking to buy team jerseys. Megapro invested in Signet Licensing, a specialist South African branding agency, so that we could offer sponsors and right holders control of their own merchandising. We were therefore in a position to service all the needs of sponsors and rights holders, and in the case of sponsors to ensure that the rights they had purchased would indeed be delivered on. This was new territory for everyone due to our years of sporting isolation. In quite a short space of time, Megapro obtained all the marketing rights to various rugby and cricket stadiums in South Africa. This was also the early days of M-Net SuperSport. I was their first Afrikaans rugby commentator, working with sports-broadcasting pioneers such as Russell MacMillan and Rob Orpen. I also met Hugh Bladen at this time.

We were very innovative at Megapro. We brought big screens to the stadiums, offered discounted suite leases and facilitated the first big multimillion-dollar deal in South African rugby, with tobacco brand Winfield sponsoring the South African leg of the then Super 12 competition.

Winfield – which was part of Johann Rupert's company – was previously a major sponsor of Rugby League in Australia, but that country's ban on cigarette advertising in sport had left them in a predicament. I had read about this and sensed an opportunity for South African rugby.

With Hugh Bladen, waiting for the countdown to go live in our commentary from Rotorua in 1994 during the Springbok tour of New Zealand. Moments after this photo was taken, the canvas roof caved in and doused Hugh with ice-cold rainwater.

I contacted Winfield to suggest they bring their sponsorship to South Africa, which at that stage had no laws against tobacco advertising. I had been to see Johann with Rian Oberholzer (Luyt's son-in-law and the CEO of Sarfu), and Johann had indicated to us he wanted the sponsorship in South Africa.

I was in White River, at a house I had a share in, a week after Schalk Jnr had played in the 1996 Craven Week, when I received the message that Winfield would be interested in furthering negotiations through the Rothmans Racing brand. I was accordingly invited to attend the British Grand Prix at Silverstone that Sunday. This was on Friday at 4 pm. I phoned Rian and told him to book a Saturday flight for us to Heathrow, as well as for Doc Luyt, and that I would meet them at OR Tambo International on Saturday. I drove through the night from White River back to Cape Town to pack, and then flew to Johannesburg.

Luyt quite liked the idea of going to the British Grand Prix. While we were waiting in the business class lounge to board in

Johannesburg, he told us how well he knew the legendary Formula 1 driver Jackie Stewart, and how Jackie would often stay with him when he was in Johannesburg. Luyt had been involved as a sponsor of the South African Grand Prix through his ties to *The Citizen* newspaper, which had held the naming rights from 1976 to 1978. Rian and I sort of dismissed this talk as Luyt's stretching the truth a bit. I even remember that Sol Kerzner was sitting with us, enjoying a bottle of Johnnie Walker Black Label whisky.

We arrived in London and were flown by helicopter to Silverstone, where we spent a fantastic day watching Jacques Villeneuve race to a podium finish for the Rothmans team. Johann Rupert was in the Rothmans Racing suite, as was a young South African golfer by the name of Ernie Els. After the race, we were invited to the pits to celebrate with the Rothmans crew. As we were walking over I saw Jackie Stewart, and said to Rian almost jokingly, 'There's Jackie.' That's when Luyt spotted Jackie as well. 'Hello, Jackie!' he shouted. And Jackie turned around and said, 'Hello, Dr Luyt,' and went on to ask him about his family and how they all were, and when he could come and visit again. Rian and I couldn't believe it. We had a good chuckle.

The following Monday we negotiated the Winfield rugby deal for South Africa. The next day Luyt took me for lunch at his favourite restaurant in London, the Grill Room at the Sheraton on Park Lane. He had a steak and ordered a bottle of Château Lafite Rothschild, and made me pay for it. But he was a happy man.

By bringing that sponsorship to South Africa, we not only secured a major sponsor for South African rugby, but at the same time delivered for Winfield in Australia because the Winfield on-field advertising shown during Super 12 matches in South Africa would also be broadcast in Australia.

Of course, it wasn't long before tobacco advertising was also banned in South African sport and we had to find a new sponsor. The cellular revolution had just started in South Africa and Vodacom and MTN were the main protagonists. Johann Rupert was invested in Vodacom, and with his being our previous sponsor

JUST A MOMENT

'Hello, Jackie!' The famous encounter between Jackie Stewart and Louis Luyt at Silverstone in 1996.

A day at the races: the British Grand Prix at Silverstone in 1996. From left are Rian Oberholzer, Ernie Els, Johann Rupert and myself. The race was won by the Rothmans-sponsored Williams car, driven by Jacques Villeneuve. This was the day before we concluded the Winfield deal for South African rugby.

through Winfield, it made sense for us to speak to Vodacom first.

We opened negotiations with then CEO Alan Knott-Craig and offered Vodacom the opportunity to use South Africa's rugby audience to grow its customer base. It was a natural fit, given the high LSM (Living Standards Measure) of the rugby audience, the television exposure and the opportunities professional sport now afforded sponsors to do further endorsement deals within the sport. It was a landmark deal for rugby that is still in place to this day.

Megapro was at the forefront of some other innovations as well. We miked up officials on the field and brought in the painted on-field 3-D signage. I also helped write the regulations applicable to on-field and team-jersey advertising. So we were responsible for some ground-breaking developments in South African sport and sports law. We were more than ready for international sport to resume in the country, and perfectly placed to move on it.

At the same time, the global game was now headed irrevocably into the professional era. It was a time dominated by the power play between Australian media tycoons Rupert Murdoch and Kerry Packer over who would own the biggest slice of the rugby union pie when it did indeed become a professional sport.

But no sooner was the Rugby World Cup over than we were back facing the old stumbling blocks. The national fervour had sparked a greater impetus from the ANC to transform South African rugby and allow the broader population access to the game and, most importantly, to its running. There was also the issue of player quotas and how these would be enforced in Springbok teams in the future. But Luyt clung on to the power he held in South African rugby. And he had a very significant hold on South African rugby indeed. Who will ever forget his famous fax machine? It even became a joke among rugby fans, who'd regale each other with tales of how Luyt would fire Springbok coaches via fax.

Luyt's unwillingness to budge on many of the rugby issues resulted in a stand-off between him and the National Sports Council (NSC), in particular Mthobi Tyamzashe and Mvuzo Mbebe, who were in a direct power battle with Luyt for the soul of South

African rugby. They called for his resignation, threatening that unless he stepped down, they would take rugby back into isolation and ban all incoming tours. This was easy for them to do, because they had the support of the government. So a simple letter or phone call to various embassies would've stopped those countries from playing rugby against us. The NSC's chairman, Mluleki George, tried to take over as president of Sarfu, but was heavily defeated by Luyt in an election in 1998.

The politics within rugby affected our business. Luyt didn't have much time for George Rautenbach, and he refused to work with Megapro. You see, George had earlier supported Chris van Onselen, the then deputy president of the Transvaal Rugby Union, who had stood against Luyt for the presidency of the union. Chris lost, with the result that any sports marketing rights that George had at Ellis Park were summarily cancelled by Luyt. George took Luyt to court on the matter, but lost. That's where the animosity between Luyt and George began. But Luyt still had time for me. I used to have long meetings with him. We would start at a Mozambican prawn restaurant near Ellis Park and end up at his office at Ellis Park for some brandy. We'd often talk until past midnight. He was a great raconteur and I always enjoyed listening to and debating with him. And eventually I was able to convince him to do business with us.

But the death knell for Luyt was the court case he brought against Nelson Mandela in 1998. As pressure from the NSC grew, Mandela agreed to launch a commission of inquiry into Sarfu's affairs to investigate allegations of racism and nepotism, and what was seen as the dictatorial way in which Luyt ran rugby. Luyt viewed Sarfu as a private entity and responded by taking Mandela to court over what he said was an unlawful and biased commission of inquiry.

Sarfu CEO Rian Oberholzer personally went to see Jakes Gerwel, then director-general in the Office of the President. Jakes told Rian that if he could stop Luyt's court action against Mandela, they would bestow upon Luyt the Order of the Baobab, a national award for outstanding service to the country. But Luyt dismissed the offer and went ahead with the action. It was an error on the part of judge

William de Villiers in calling Mandela to testify. The Constitutional Court later ruled that Judge De Villiers had had no right to do so.

It was a heated court case, as you would expect. At one point Mandela accused Sarfu's lawyer, Mike Maritz, of trying to portray him as a liar. This in particular incensed the NSC, and in fact turned the majority of the country and the international community against Luyt. At this point, I tell you, we were about three to five days away from being out of all international sport once again.

I decided to go and see Luyt, even though George advised me to leave it alone for the sake of our business. Of course, that thought had entered my head as well. But I felt there were bigger issues at stake here, in terms of the future of South African rugby, that transcended our business interests. So I requested a meeting with Luyt in his office at Ellis Park, reasoning that if we didn't have international sport in this country, there would be no business in any case. I also spoke with Steve Tshwete, saying, 'Steve, can you just get the NSC off Luyt's back until the vote has taken place? And long enough for me to talk to him?' (The Sarfu executive committee was due to vote on whether Luyt should step down as president of Sarfu, in light of the government's pressure and the growing intolerance of his leadership style.) I told Steve that rugby had to be given a chance to sort itself out. And if South African rugby could not get its own house in order, then the NSC could step in. But rugby had to be given a chance first.

Steve said to me, 'Schalkie, it's over to you and rugby.' And Steve, as always, was true to his word. He made the call, and the NSC was kept at bay until the vote took place.

So I went to see Luyt, and I told him in no uncertain terms that he had made a mistake. 'Please, Doc, in the interests of rugby, resign,' I said.

'You're mad, Schalk,' Luyt said. 'I have all the support in rugby.' We went back and forth on this, and he refused to back down.

I then approached Rian Oberholzer. I told him that I believed in giving somebody an honourable exit, and that he needed to work with me to give Luyt one. I still remember saying, 'You're the Moses of South African rugby now, Rian. You need to lead the sport to the Promised Land.'

Rian and I had also done our research, and we knew that Luyt did not have as much support as he claimed to keep him at the helm of South African rugby. When we confronted Luyt with this information, he disputed it, and phoned Arthrob Petersen, the Springbok team manager. Arthrob was also on the board of Boland Rugby, which at that stage was 50 per cent owned by M-Net (I had done that deal for them). While on speakerphone, Petersen said to Luyt, 'No, Doc, you've got our vote. Don't worry about a thing.' Then Luyt phoned Ronnie Masson of Western Province Rugby, who told him the same thing. Those were the two big swing votes. As Luyt ended the calls, he looked at Rian and me and said, 'And now? What do the two of you say now?' He said quite clearly that if he was voted out he would go, such was his confidence in the votes he had.

After the meeting, Russell MacMillan – then the head of SuperSport – phoned me and said we had the support of SuperSport, because they needed international rugby to grow their business. Then we sent a representative to all the rugby unions to tell them that if they didn't vote for Luyt to resign, then there would be no international rugby, and with that they'd have no income to sustain themselves. No TV rights, no advertising rights – nothing.

Russell was a tremendous ally to have as we negotiated this process. He'd been in the trenches in the Murdoch/Packer battle over the ownership of world rugby broadcasting rights, and he'd fought on our side to prevent Murdoch from taking over the South African rugby market, which was a distinct possibility at the time – especially when Luyt went behind our backs and did a deal with Murdoch. Russell made a bold move and threatened to outbid Sky, a Murdoch-owned company, for the broadcast rights to English Premier League football, which was something he could've achieved.

It was a bold time of audacious moves on everybody's part.

We also spoke to some of the 1995 World Cup-winning players and convinced them to sign contracts with us. So we had the players, who obviously were the most marketable 15 players in world rugby at the time. That kind of nerve made Murdoch and company think twice about who they were dealing with in South Africa.

A special general meeting was held at Ellis Park on 7 May 1998. It was scheduled for 10 am. At 7 that morning, we had a meeting at the M-Net offices. Representatives from Boland, Western Province and Free State also attended. Russell MacMillan told them straight that if they didn't support us, he would withdraw SuperSport's financial support for their unions. Vodacom, who were partly owned by government and a rugby sponsor, said the same.

At the time, we were busy with the deal to bring Vodacom into South African rugby as a major title sponsor. As I've explained previously, this was to replace Winfield, which was being forced out due to the new tobacco-advertising embargo. Johann Rupert advised me that Vodacom would withhold all its options to take over the sponsorship pending the outcome of the special general meeting.

As the meeting commenced, Luyt was so confident that he said, 'Why bother with a secret ballot? Let's just have a show of hands.' This was turned down. Luyt lost the vote. He was devastated. He couldn't believe it.

The first person I phoned was Steve Tshwete, and I informed him that Luyt had been ousted by vote. I said, 'Steve, now it's over to you.' And Steve made sure we were back on track with international rugby. Throughout those negotiations, whatever I asked of Steve, he did. He was a man of his word.

Then I phoned Johann Rupert, who straightaway gave me the go-ahead to do the bigger Vodacom sponsorship deal. And the third person I phoned was Russell MacMillan with the news that Vodacom was definitely in and would take over all of Winfield's rights. He was delighted.

Luyt forever after believed that Rian and I were backstabbers. But I used to go and visit him in Ballito for many years, up until his death. I'd always tell him that he could never say I wasn't honest with him. Unlike some of his so-called supporters, I didn't tell him one thing and then do another. I'd sit in his office and tell him face to face how things stood. I told him he could fight as much as he wanted, but this was a fight he was going to lose. I'd tried to make him understand that if he wasn't going to support the direction in which rugby was going, he was not going to control it.

What Luyt couldn't understand was that we weren't fighting him. We were fighting to save rugby. We were also fighting to retain control of our own game and have some say in the direction it was going to take, whether it was politically in the new democratic South Africa, or in the professional arena, especially with the threat posed by Rupert Murdoch. I find that people often confuse honesty and loyalty. People think that if you're honest with them, you're not loyal.

The Megapro years were extremely productive and exciting as we entered this new era, but also extremely taxing on me and my family. We built up a very successful company, which was eventually bought out by Primedia, but I was spending the third week of every month in London for business. Thinking back, what I should have done was to take a sabbatical.

Eventually, in 2001 I decided I'd had enough and I sold my shares. I wanted a different challenge. So I bought Welbedacht and started pursuing my passion for wine. But I also had a desire to give back through my experience in sport. I wanted to create the time to do other things with my life.

I became a director of the Western Province/Boland cricket franchise, and we set about rebranding the team as the Cape Cobras. Given my lifelong love of cricket, I take great pride in having contributed to the game in this way.

When Boland Cricket, who until then had played most of their games at the University of Stellenbosch or the Stellenbosch Farmers' Winery fields, wanted to develop their own home ground, I went to work. Hennie Liebenberg, a great rugby man, was the city clerk of the Paarl Municipality. One day he suggested that I look at what the municipality should do with the old showgrounds, as there was no agricultural show any more and vagrants were taking over. I proposed the idea of bringing Boland Cricket there. After some negotiating with regard to price and conditions, a deal was made.

Well, there were two conditions that were quite difficult. The first was that the Paarl Cricket Club, which played its matches in the Western Province league, had to join the Boland set-up. And the second was that the Stock Car Club had to end its use of the ground as an oval track.

I received the same response from both bodies when I met with them to announce the potential deal: 'How can you, who are a part of the culture of these clubs, try and tell us that this is what we should do?' I had driven stock cars at the showgrounds with the same members I was now telling to close their club; and Pietie Carstens, the president of the Paarl Cricket Club, asked how an ex-player of the club could tell them to relinquish the age-old traditions of the leagues they played in.

After many a late night, we secured the compliance of both clubs, and I told Hennie that he could go ahead with drawing up the contract. As usual, though, there were two further issues I had to sort out.

The first one was that the committee of Boland Cricket had not seen the proposed new stadium nor where their new headquarters would be. So I took them there one hot Paarl afternoon. I'll never forget when I used to compete for Boland in stock car racing on that oval track. While we were standing there, with me trying to convince the Boland officials that this was the right decision for them, I heard a car start up in the pit area. I remember Kevin Bridgens, the general manager of Boland Cricket, looking at me in shock and asking what the noise was. I told him that being the showgrounds of Paarl, there were people there who worked on cars. In the meantime, I was praying that the inevitable would not happen. Well, it did. The next minute this car came hurtling past us, throwing up a cloud of stones and dust. The cricket aficionados all turned around in disgust and exclaimed to me, 'Is this where you want us to build an international-standard cricket ground for the future?' Then another car joined the fray and these stock cars were chasing around the track. The cricket guys were aghast at what they were getting themselves into.

But, needless to say, we were eventually able to conclude the deal and make the move. And so we came to open the Boland Bank Park Cricket Ground (now known as Boland Park) with a tour match where Boland played the touring New Zealand cricket team. The three-day match had to be called off on the second day, though, when the pitch cracked in the intense December heat.

We also built the first Western Cape indoor nets there, and started the Superjuice Cricket Academy with my friend Eddie Barlow, and sponsored with Johann Rupert's kind assistance. Johann has always been incredibly willing to support a good sporting cause. The academy went on to produce several players of colour for the Proteas before the national Plascon Academy had produced one. It was a novel idea, as we joined the Western Province and Boland Cricket Associations into one body to develop talented players.

I will never forget the look on Eddie's face when he asked us as a board to come and have a look at a crazy bowler he had unearthed. There we stood as this young man ran in to bowl, and in Eddie's own words it looked as if he was stealing hubcaps off a moving car. That day we witnessed the arrival of the South African spin sensation Paul 'Gogga' Adams. I was proud of Eddie, as we had strategised together the idea of creating, in his words, cricketing excellence. Schalk Jnr was honoured to be selected by the academy.

The second issue I had to deal with was that when the time came to pay the municipality for the ground, the Boland Cricket Association had no money. Everyone involved got together to pick up the tab, to be refinanced through the development. The ground is positioned in the right place and to this day draws the most racially integrated crowd in the country.

So I experienced a very creative period in my life after Megapro. I was on the board of the Cape Cobras, Boland Rugby, Western Province Rugby, the KKNK and Rust en Vrede wine estate.

My involvement with Rust en Vrede was more an attempt to help resolve what had become a very ugly family dispute between Jannie and Jean Engelbrecht. I don't want to go into the details, because all families have their own problems and there are not many family businesses where succession takes place seamlessly. But it was a dispute that split Stellenbosch down the middle, between those who sided with Jean and those who sided with Jannie. So I became the go-between on the board and was hoping to be the catalyst that could help solve this problem. It was a difficult issue to help bridge.

But it was another element of a time in my life where I could give back in the areas I was really passionate about. The KKNK in particular was a hugely rewarding experience, as it allowed me to combine my love of music and artists with my passion to see the Afrikaans culture grow and thrive.

But, of course, it wouldn't be my story if it didn't come with its own bit of controversy.

21

FOKOFPOLISIEKAR AND OUR 'FLOWER OF SCOTLAND'

I'M A PROUD AFRIKANER. I can't be anything else.

And I consider myself extremely fortunate to have been involved with the KKNK at a time in our history when Afrikaans culture was reshaping and redefining itself.

In the roughly 11 years that I was a director of the KKNK, we experienced a period of tremendous diversity. There was a deep desire among everyone involved to take this iconic Afrikaans cultural event and broaden its participation base.

We put an incredible amount of seed money into creating new Afrikaans productions by funding contributors to produce plays. It was a time of tremendous growth in the Afrikaans arts. At one point I would guess that about 70 per cent of new Afrikaans productions were making their debut at the KKNK.

The language was evolving and finding its own place in a democratic South Africa. With the country undergoing so many dramatic changes, it was inevitable that Afrikaans would also evolve. I found it an exciting time, because Afrikaans was like this big melting pot of new ideas. I loved that. It fuelled my creative spirit and my desire to be different and challenge convention.

But, as Doc Craven always used to tell me, 'Burger, wherever you are, drama seems to follow.'

I was chairman of the KKNK when a number of religious groups informed us that a new Afrikaans rock band by the name of Fokofpolisiekar would not be allowed to take part in the 2006 KKNK. The band had always courted controversy. Their profane name alone was a step too far for some people. But when one of the band's members wrote 'fok god' on a girl's wallet when she asked for an autograph, all hell broke loose. Fokofpolisiekar were hugely popular, and the KKNK had already invited them to take part in the festival that year. But after that incident, we were under immense pressure from religious bodies to rescind our invitation. As a cultural organisation that promoted new ideas and freedom of speech in the arts, we found ourselves between a rock and a hard place.

I was invited to appear on various talk radio programmes, where I was asked to defend why we hadn't yet banned Fokofpolisiekar from taking part in our festival. I remember one particularly heated debate, on the Afrikaans talk show *Sê Wie* on RSG, hosted by Niekie van den Berg. He loved getting under people's skins. Everybody was having a go at me.

I reiterated the point that the Fokofpolisiekar incident had not taken place under the auspices of the KKNK. If it hadn't happened during our festival, how could we prevent the band from taking part? Our contract with the artists stated that they could not act contrary to the festival's rules and the Constitution of our country. But I felt strongly that we had to respect an artist's individual rights as well. Otherwise, how could we, as a cultural festival, claim to be promoting diversity in our language?

Afrikaner society was changing as fast as our country was, and with it came a flood of innovative thinking. So I wasn't defending the band's obscenity or controversial religious statements as much as I was trying to defend an idea, or the principle, that our country had made a seismic shift politically because of tolerance, and that we should have the same approach to our culture. Above all, with my diverse background, I hated the idea of censorship in any form.

But the issue didn't go away. More and more churches became involved in the debate, declaring that they would boycott the festival and ask their members to do the same. Of course, this had an impact on us, because there is a huge commercial element to the festival.

One coloured reverend in particular, Dominee Boezak, was most vocal that the band should not be allowed to take part in the KKNK. I was called to a particularly large meeting with various concerned church leaders, led by Dominee Boezak. While we were debating the issue, his cellphone rang. Would you believe that his ringtone was the New Zealand national anthem?

I was flabbergasted. I interrupted the debate right there and then and said to him, 'How can you sit here and argue with me about a South African cultural issue when you have another country's anthem on your phone?' He said that it was because of politics that he had the anthem on his phone. In the days of apartheid, many in the coloured community were great supporters of the All Blacks. To this day many still support the All Blacks rather than the Springboks, which I find ridiculous, as there is no longer any political reason for this in a democratic South Africa. The Springboks and what they represent have always been close to my heart, and I take exception to anyone who disrespects this.

On the basis of that ringtone, I stood up and told everybody at the meeting that the debate was over. I said to Dominee Boezak, 'We can talk again when you've changed that ringtone to the new South African anthem, because then we'll be speaking to each other as fellow South Africans.' And I announced to the media that Fokofpolisiekar would appear at the 2006 KKNK.

Two weeks later, I was asked to meet with Dominee Boezak again. As I walked into the meeting room, I phoned his number to check for myself if he had indeed changed his ringtone. He had.

'Right, now we can talk,' I told him.

We agreed on a compromise: the band would not use any profanity in their lyrics, and would publicly apologise for the offence they had caused, which they did. I attended their show during the festival and it was packed. They gave one of their best performances. It was the first and only time I ever attended one of their concerts.

We had a similar issue when Bok van Blerk (Louis Pepler) released his hit song 'De la Rey', which some people thought was promoting radical Afrikaner nationalism. I told the KKNK board that he had to be allowed to sing the song at the festival, notwithstanding the controversy that was raging at the time.

In defence of my decision, I cited the example of the 1991 Rugby World Cup in Britain and France. Scotland had made it to the semi-finals and were set to face England at Murrayfield. There was a big debate at the time as to whether Scotland would be allowed to play 'Flower of Scotland' as their national anthem. Bear in mind that 'Flower of Scotland' was not the official national anthem of Scotland, but it was a popular song in Scottish culture, and it had been adopted by the team. In fact, it had been sung as far back as the 1974 British Lions tour to South Africa. It's still not the official anthem of Scotland, but simply the song that represents the country at sporting events.

So there they were, about to the face their old foe, the English, at their home ground of Murrayfield, and they wanted to sing 'Flower of Scotland', a song that celebrated the Scots' defeat of the English at the Battle of Bannockburn in 1314. I had just come from a party with a bunch of New Zealand rugby players when we heard of Scotland's decision to sing 'Flower of Scotland' at the semi-final that Saturday. English politicians came out in full force, saying that it shouldn't be allowed.

I was walking down the famous Rose Street in Edinburgh before the match and people were handing out pamphlets with the lyrics of the song and encouraging all Scots to sing it. Then, on the Thursday before the match, Princess Anne announced that Scotland should be allowed to sing 'Flower of Scotland', and that she would be on the field to welcome the players and would sing it as well, as patron of Scottish Rugby. So England sang their 'God Save the Queen', and Scotland sang 'Flower of Scotland'. The former Springbok scrumhalf Garth Wright and I were in the stands, both singing 'Flower of Scotland' at the tops of our voices. England won the match 9–6 and that was that.

In 2008 I informed the KKNK board that I would accept personal responsibility for this decision and take it upon myself to make sure nothing untoward happened. And they accepted.

I arranged for extra security and even had security guards on standby. I had a conversation with Bok before his performance and told him about the 'Flower of Scotland' debate. Louis sang five or six of his best-known songs. And then he announced, 'The following song is the Afrikaans version of "Flower of Scotland",' and he delivered a beautiful rendition of 'De la Rey'. It was a tremendous success, and we had no trouble whatsoever. I think he ended up singing the song three times.

Now, you might well be wondering why I was so adamant that these songs should be sung at the festival when I'd argued so vehemently against Louis Luyt's decision to allow the old South African anthem to be sung before the 1992 Test against the All Blacks at Ellis Park. In my opinion, we weren't nearly as far advanced politically in 1992 as we were in 2008. Tensions were running high in 1992, and it was an issue of national concern, not just of cultural representation at an arts festival.

I was privileged to have spent that time with the KKNK. Seeing such a variety of artists, some of them turning up in buggered-up old cars just to live their passion for performing, really inspired me. I met supremely talented people, such as Lochner de Kock and Anton Goosen. My children grew up knowing people like Dozi and Ghapi, and many, many other great musicians, whom we entertained at our house. I often think South Africans don't always appreciate how much our musicians and artists have done to take our people and our language forward in the new South Africa.

I'm proud of the Afrikaans language and the part it plays in my own history. And I have no doubt the language will survive and continue to thrive.

22

POETIC JUSTICE WITH THE BREYTENBACHS

IF EVER THERE WAS a family that personified the diversity of South Africa, I believe it is the Breytenbach family.

Jan, the eldest of four brothers, was a military man and helped found the Recces and 32 Battalion. He was one of the most feared soldiers in South Africa's Special Forces. Cloete Breytenbach was a war correspondent and a fantastic photographer who was once named South Africa's Photographer of the Year. And then you have Breyten Breytenbach, one of our country's most renowned poets and writers, who was imprisoned for his anti-apartheid beliefs. Can you imagine a more politically diverse family?

As Cloete himself once said, one brother supported the terrorists, one brother killed the terrorists, and he took the pictures of the terrorists.

When I was young, Breyten's writing was very close to my heart. And, to be honest, I never thought I'd ever get to know him as well as I eventually did.

In the 1950s the Breytenbach family owned a house called Greyvilleas in Wellington, which they ran as a boarding house. The house was sold in 1974, and subsequently fell into disrepair. The local municipality wanted to demolish it. But a plan was developed, with the support of the Breytenbach family, to renovate the building and turn it into a museum. Several years ago, Cloete came to see me and said that the municipality was considering helping with the renovations, and would I help to set up the museum. However, word of the project had reached the media, and an article in the *Sunday Times* questioned how the Drakenstein Municipality could allocate resources to the renovation of a building that had once been the home of Jan Breytenbach, a man the article described as 'having killed so many of our people in the struggle against apartheid'.

So I got together with Professor Ampie Coetzee, another great South African (who, sadly, passed away in October 2020), and Dr Manie Rust. We looked deep into a bottle of Chenin Blanc and came up with a plan of our own. We decided that the house should be renovated and turned into a cultural centre for the Wellington community. To shift the focus from the rumour that it was being turned into a museum, we decided that it would be known as the Breytenbach Sentrum, and it would be a hub for artists, writers, musicians and other creatives to develop their talents and share ideas. We wanted to create not just a museum but a place that reflected a language that was alive and growing and in touch with its community. And every year Breyten Breytenbach would hold a writing school there.

We put the proposal to Herman Bailey, the Drakenstein mayor, and he agreed to support the idea if we could find a way to fund both the centre and the writing school, the latter of which was key for him.

The first task was to get the building done, and here Cloete played a key role. Eventually, he became the project manager and relayed all his problems to me, which were generally of a financial nature. The architect for the job, who had also helped me with my cellar, had put in quite a substantial invoice, which the project could not afford. I ended up having a meeting with the architect, and my brief to him was, 'You need to do something important for

Afrikaans, so I'm halving your quote for this project.' But we still needed substantial funding for the rest of the project, as well as for the writing school, or the municipality would go ahead and demolish the house.

And so it came about that Johann Rupert, Chris Faure (my friend the attorney), Ampie, Cloete, Breyten and I had lunch together. Early on in the lunch, Johann told Breyten how much his mother loved his work and that he would gladly fund the Breytenbach Sentrum. That evening, Schalk Jnr was playing for the Stormers at Newlands. We had had such a delightful lunch that Johann invited all of us to his suite to watch the match. The only issue was that when we left the steakhouse, we hit incredible traffic and ended up arriving at the suite with five minutes left to play in the first half. It was a special moment for Breyten, because it had been 47 years since he'd last been to Newlands. Needless to say, it was a most festive outing. After the match I had to get Ampie, Breyten and Cloete back to the steakhouse in Durbanville where they had left their vehicles. Thankfully, Myra was our designated driver, and from the back seat Breyten poured out expressions of gratitude and respect for Myra's driving, given the circumstances and our 'festive' condition.

I had the privilege of informing Cloete and Ampie that Johann had decided to also fund the writing school, and with that the Breytenbach Sentrum's future was assured. It was a successful day for all of us as part of furthering the cause of Afrikaans.

After months of hard work, we finally arrived at the grand opening of the centre. I was to be the master of ceremonies, and Frederik van Zyl Slabbert, the well-known academic and political figure, and a dear friend of Breyten's, was appointed as the patron. And that's when Cloete Breytenbach informed me of our next hurdle.

Being such a diverse family has its challenges, not least of which is trying to get all the siblings to agree on the same thing. Cloete told me that he was having a tough time ensuring that Breyten, Jan, their younger brother, Sebastiaan, and their sister, Rachel, would all be at the opening, and that each had very different views on how the proceedings should unfold. I must admit that by this point I was beginning to wonder why on earth I'd ever become involved in all this.

Jan was refusing to be present at the opening, and Breyten was starting to get cold feet himself. At a hastily arranged coffee at 11 that morning, Cloete informed me that there was no way we could have all five of them on a stage together, because, in his words, 'Hier kom groot kak.'

But we had invested so much and come so far that we couldn't stop the project at that point. So we went ahead with the opening, not knowing whether any of the Breytenbach siblings would attend. But, lo and behold, with about five minutes to go before the proceedings began, all five of them arrived.

Van Zyl Slabbert opened the proceedings and spoke from the heart, talking about how crazy this country's history is. He expressed regret at how Breyten, his friend, had been sent to prison (in 1975 he was charged with treason and sentenced to nine years under the Terrorism Act), and recalled how he had pleaded with then prime minister PW Botha to be allowed to visit Breyten in jail. On his release Breyten had gone into exile, and was not allowed to return to South Africa to even visit his sick father, all for marrying Yolande, who was of Vietnamese ancestry and as such was regarded as 'non-white' by the South African government.

Jan then spoke about his experiences, followed by Cloete. Then it was Breyten's turn. He read some beautiful poetry especially selected for the occasion. While Jan and Breyten were speaking, Cloete – who was sitting behind me on the stage – kept kicking my chair and whispering to me that Rachel mustn't be allowed to speak under any circumstances, because they had no idea what she might say.

So I introduced Rachel.

The rest of the Breytenbach family held their breath. I think even Jan, a man used to bullets flying over his head, was never as tense as he was at that moment. Rachel didn't say a single word, but instead beckoned her daughter to the podium to stand beside her and read a piece of poetry.

Then Sebastiaan stood up to talk. He said that although his brother Breyten had written several books, he too was an aspiring author, and wanted to use this occasion to announce his debut as a writer, as two of his books had just been published. It was a fantastic moment. The entire event went off incredibly well.

After the function, Cloete called over his eldest brother. 'Boet Jan,' he said. 'When the South African Army was called in to help suppress an attempted coup in the Ciskei, they gave all of the soldiers a balkie (badge). But they were never officially handed to us as part of a military ceremony.' Cloete then took a badge out of his pocket. He ordered Jan to march towards him, called him to attention and pinned this badge on his jacket. It was a surreal moment, and done quite comically. Jan then saluted Cloete, asked his brother to stand to attention, ordered him to march a few steps, removed the badge and then pinned it on Cloete's chest. And they were both laughing. Yolande and Breyten were also watching this and laughing. I found a strange irony in the situation, considering that Breyten's two brothers had once represented a system that didn't recognise their marriage.

I remember looking at Breyten and marvelling at how he could laugh at this now – at his two brothers. Jan, a career soldier and one of the most feared men in South African military history. A man who had fought for everything Breyten had fought against. A brother who believed in a system that had cost him much of his life when he was imprisoned and then exiled. And here these three brothers were, all so different from one another, laughing together.

I thought to myself, 'This country is crazy. Absolutely crazy. I'll never understand South Africa.'

It's exactly why I love South Africa so much.

But I'll never understand it.

23

FAKE NEWS

BEING WELL KNOWN, I have always tried to keep my children away from the prying eyes of the media. This comes at a price, especially in this age of fake news, and the way journalists and media institutions are manipulated by individuals.

When one member of a family is implicated in a wrongful and damaging story, the whole family suffers. It amazes me that the media has such freedom to write damaging and untruthful articles, and that it takes so much for the person who has been offended to set the record straight. Johann Rupert uses a very good saying: 'Never get into a fight with somebody who buys ink by the barrel.'

I have great respect for the media – having myself been a part of it in my days with M-Net and commentating – and the very fine journalists of the world who do their jobs properly and report facts. But my family has been the victim of some scandalously poor reporting, from the so-called falling-out I had with my brother Paul to how I allegedly tried to murder a person living illegally on my farm. René had to deal with some very hurtful reporting during her ordeal. And Schalk has also suffered at the hands of the media. I believe there should be a media tribunal in South Africa that exposes some of the horribly inaccurate reporting we've witnessed.

In 2004, Schalk had just been named the IRB Player of the Year. He was sponsored by BMW at the time, and his name appeared on the side of his car. At the beginning of 2005, he and Michele and a friend of theirs were on their way to a pub in Stellenbosch. Schalk was reversing into a parking space when a man drove into the passenger door of his car, on Michele's side. Schalk hooted, and the man reversed. And then he drove forward into the door a second time. By now Michele was screaming. Schalk jumped out, ran to the other car and shouted at the driver, whose window was open, 'Are you bloody crazy?'

While he was standing there, the man drove into his car door a third time. Schalk put his hand through the window of the man's car and pulled the keys out of the ignition. The car lurched forward and hit the door a fourth time. So Schalk, desperate to stop this from happening again, pulled the man out of his seat and through the car window. He pinned him down on the sidewalk, only to discover that the man was blind drunk.

So he had a few words with him, but left it at that and they drove home, shaken by the incident. The next morning Schalk phoned me and told me what had happened. I told him that as the car he was driving was not his, but belonged to BMW, he needed to report the incident to the police. He had the ID number and car registration of the other driver. He went to the police station to make his statement.

Two days later, *Die Son* newspaper published an article under the headline, 'IRB Player of the Year in Road Rage Incident'. In their version of events, Schalk had attacked the other driver for no apparent reason, and the man was now laying a charge of assault against Schalk.

We proceeded via the correct channels, hiring an attorney and collecting ten affidavits from people who had been at the pub and witnessed the incident. I was absolutely certain that my son was telling the truth, based on all the affidavits, which clearly stated that the other man was in the wrong and had been drunk. However, because of this incident, Schalk's passport was confiscated and there was a possibility that if the problem was not sorted out, he would not be able to travel for Super Rugby. And the article in *Die Son* turned it into a political issue as well, as the 'victim' was coloured.

As the case dragged on, I received a phone call from my friend the Italian restaurateur Emiliano Sandri. He suspected there was something fishy about the case against Schalk. He had known Schalk for years, because his own son had played provincial cricket with Schalk. And he had also overheard something worrying in one of his restaurants. A woman called Fran du Plessis, who was a director of SA Rugby and South African Airways, had told her dinner companions that the man accusing Schalk of road rage was one of her employees.

Emiliano suggested that he set up a breakfast with Fran du Plessis and myself, which I agreed to. And so I met with her at Die Wijnhuis in Stellenbosch. She proceeded to tell me the following gob-smacking story.

The man who had driven into Schalk's car, whom she was mentoring to become an accountant like herself, was in the process of converting to Islam so that he could marry a Muslim woman. On the day of the incident, he had got drunk at an office party. This was when he repeatedly drove into Schalk's car, having also parked on the wrong side of the road. But if it emerged that he had been drunk during the incident, his future wife's family would not allow the couple to marry, as consuming alcohol went against their religious principles. So the man decided to press charges against Schalk for having instigated the attack. It was a classic case of my son being framed for something he didn't do.

I asked her straight out: how could she stand by when my son is cast as the villain by her own employee? I told her we had several affidavits that proved her employee had been in the wrong, and that we were happy to go to court on the matter. Following a visit to the state prosecutor and the Stellenbosch station commander, stating our case with all the affidavits, they had to drop the trumped-up charges against Schalk. It was also the last time Schalk allowed his name to appear on a sponsored car. I now tell young players never to let their names appear on their cars; it just makes them a target.

But the damage was done. It had cost us time and money, and the accusation, albeit false, had impacted on Schalk's public image internationally. And the newspaper simply moved on, facing no consequences whatsoever.

When I wanted to evict a woman, Anneline Arendse, who is living on my farm illegally – she is actually squatting with her husband in our workers' crèche and community centre – she teamed up with a political party, the Independent Civic Organisation of South Africa, and their representative, Alvina Abrahams, just before the local government elections in 2016. She went to the media with every potential lie available, and they were willing to publish her story. I was labelled a racist. It was said that I did not pay my workers correctly and that I turned off their water for five days. And then, the most ludicrous of all, it was claimed that I had twice driven over a worker with my quad bike and assaulted him, and that he was critically injured and in the hospital.

I opened a case of crimen injuria against the media group that had run the story. I remember the Sunday morning when a Detective Sergeant De Villiers arrived at my farm and said that a case of attempted murder had been opened against me. At first I laughed, and he agreed it was laughable. But he still had to take a statement. A little later, Myra and I had to leave for a lunch date in Riebeek Kasteel. Driving out of my front gate, I saw the man whom I was alleged to have driven over, and who was purported to be in intensive care. He admitted that he had been so drunk on the Saturday of the alleged incident that he fell in front of his home, in an area unreachable by quad bike. He mentioned that Anneline Arendse and Alvina Abrahams had been with him, and they had both said that they would have this Boer locked up, they would win the election and then she would hand the farm over to the workers.

Furthermore, on the following Monday, without the so-called victim even having given a statement to the police due to his being still so intoxicated, *Die Son* ran a front-page article to the effect that Schalk Burger was being had up for attempted murder. Just think what my poor family had to go through.

And if that wasn't bad enough, every subsequent article included a comment about the Springbok rugby player's father being a racist. It is illegal to make such a statement until the person concerned has been charged and appeared in court, which obviously had not yet happened.

Well, I approached the public prosecutor's office to intervene, and after a thorough investigation of what had happened on my farm, they were not willing to go further with the trumped-up charges of Arendse and Abrahams.

But the two refused to be deterred. An NGO, Women on Farms, became involved and tried to get a protection order against me for Arendse, which I vehemently fought in court and won. But Arendse and Abrahams, claiming poverty, said they could not pay costs. Not one of these appearances was reported by the newspapers as they already knew they had made a big mistake.

And so I am busy with a case against Naspers.

The political parties involved believed that I was another one of those Afrikaner Boere, as they call us, who had baggage, and they could use this fact to score easy political points. But they forgot that I had grown up on Die Rug in Drakenstein Road, and they could not scare me politically.

What was astounding about this affair was that on three occasions statements made by workers who have been with me for over 21 years disappeared out of the police docket. Piet Calitz, my dear friend who had helped us so much with René's case, again came to my rescue. He appealed to the police's Major General Jeremy Vearey, formerly one of Nelson Mandela's bodyguards and by then deputy provincial commissioner (and the author of the delightful autobiography *Jeremy vannie Elsies*). Jeremy had also had a problem with documents of his going astray. We knew there was something going on. He put us in touch with the police anti-corruption unit, and ever since then no documents have gone missing and our dealings with the police have improved. This makes you wonder what is really going on behind the scenes in our country and how many cover-ups there are.

The evening of the launch of Jacques Pauw's book *The President's Keepers*, at his excellent guesthouse and restaurant, the Red Tin Roof, I sat and listened as he and Max du Preez, who was interviewing him, recounted some of the stories in the book as well as the threats aimed at Jacques. I looked to my left at this large mural of Mao Zedong on the wall, and thought back to friends of mine who had questioned how I could read the 'Communist literature' published by Max in *Vrye Weekblad*, and it also took me back to my own experiences.

In South Africa, the truth has become a commodity that is sometimes very well hidden, protected most of the time by the wrong people, and the media somehow wilfully overlook it. Just recall how the now-defunct public relations firm Bell Pottinger deployed the notorious 'white monopoly capital' slogan to deflect the public's focus away from the well-strategised theft campaign of the state capture brigade, and how much media exposure and traction this received, until the truth came out, though not before good citizens like Johann Rupert and his family had been demonised. I did not come through my walk of life to see such things taking place without getting involved to let the truth be told. Unfortunately, most South Africans do not know what is really going on, just like in the days of apartheid. And with social media and political correctness being the order of the day, the average person is going to know even less.

Our children will have to have strong moral compasses to weather the storms that lie ahead.

24

WHY, MY BELOVED COUNTRY?

I SPEND A LOT of time thinking about the future of my country. Like most South Africans, I am hopeful and concerned at the same time.

It seems to me that we are increasingly becoming a society where there is so much intolerance for different ways of thought. As a result, I fear that we are lacking in truly constructive thought leaders. There seems to be a lot of shouting going on, especially on social media, and very little thinking. And I find it strange that we have such a problem dealing with diversity at this time in our history. After all, diversity is nothing new to South Africa.

We have a rich history of diversity in this country. Diversity is part and parcel of who we are. But now, if I say I am a proud Afrikaner, then I am typecast. Surely there must be some recognition of the fact that not all Afrikaners are bad? Is there no place in our history to recognise that Afrikaners were among the first freedom fighters in South Africa? They died in concentration camps at the hands of an English oppressor. Afrikaners have a history in South Africa, and it doesn't help to try and write it out of the history books.

Similarly, I have a lot of respect for the African peoples of this country and their long-standing traditions, such as the Xhosa initiation ceremony. I respect this and agree that it has a place in their culture.

Perhaps it's to be expected that after such a long period of aggressive dominance by white people over all other cultures, we should still be struggling to come to terms with how we view each other. But I do believe that our success in this regard lies in a spirit of like-mindedness. That's where we need to find common ground. Like-mindedness surpasses differences in religion, politics or race. If we are like-minded, we will all work together for the same goal, regardless of our differences.

Unfortunately, the pressure of a declining ruling party has produced gross misuses of power. Rather than celebrating our differences, this is amplifying them for short-term political gain.

And this kind of thinking is exactly the trap the Broederbonders fell into. That was a period in our history where, as a South African, you were either black or white. And if you were white, you were classified even further as either Afrikaans or English. And if you were Afrikaans, you were classified even further as either driving a Ford or a Chevrolet, or drinking Castle beer or Lion beer. If you could vote, you voted either for the South African Party or the National Party.

And now we seem to be right back in that style of thinking.

A key moment in my life occurred during the Voëlvry movement of the late 1980s. This was the time when Afrikaans musicians such as Johannes Kerkorrel, Koos Kombuis and many others sang anti-apartheid songs in Afrikaans. I loved going to their shows. I was awestruck by their ability to convey through music what they were feeling inside. They helped me realise that I am an Afrikaner, and that I identified with the Afrikaner and the Afrikaner struggle of forging a new identity in a changing South Africa.

One of my favourite records of the time was David Kramer's album *Bakgat!* I loved it, and then the Afrikaans radio broadcaster and sports commentator Edwill van Aarde banned it from his radio show. I remember writing a letter to the SABC in protest. In my world, Kramer was a brilliant wordsmith who told the story of the Boland and its people so beautifully.

Then, in 1988, *Vrye Weekblad* was launched as a progressive anti-apartheid newspaper in Afrikaans. I felt it spoke to my own views about life, and I became one of the first subscribers. It meant a lot to read about stories that we knew something about and that were ignored by the major newspapers, but which eventually were proven true through the work of the Truth and Reconciliation Commission. I really have enormous respect for Max du Preez and Jacques Pauw, the Afrikaans-speaking journalists who went to such lengths to get the truth into the public domain.

The future of South Africa depends on movements and individuals like these, who honestly express who we are in the national debate. We can't just listen to one side. The disastrous Zuma presidency engendered exactly the same kind of fear of honest and open debate as we experienced under PW Botha.

I have a great deal of respect for those of our leaders who were incarcerated on Robben Island, as they had a very clear idea of the path they felt South Africa should follow. But when I listen to what many of our current politicians have to say, I'm not so sure that they have the same clear and, most importantly, unified focus.

And if I should disagree with them, I am typecast as a racist Afrikaner.

Even in my own family, my mother had very liberal views and my father was far more conservative. But a particular memory from childhood is always my own example of how there surely can still be mutual respect between such radically different viewpoints.

My aunt owned a hotel in Cape Town, and one year they put on a Christmas play. One of the waiters who was acting in the play was gay. His name was Percy. It was the first time I had ever been exposed to somebody who was gay. He was dressed in a pink tutu, and at one point he ran onto the stage and did the splits. The next minute, he was in agony. He'd dislocated his hip and was locked in this split position. The curtain was drawn so that poor Percy could be evacuated.

My dad had a Chevy Biscayne station wagon, which was a big car. So he loaded Percy into it and rushed him off to hospital. When he came back later, he said in all seriousness to my mother and aunts, 'How could you do that to me? I had to walk into a non-white hospital pushing a man in a pink tutu on a trolley.' He was so embarrassed. My mom and her sisters were crying with laughter.

I might be naive, but I sometimes wish everyone's attitude could be as simple as that. My dad's embarrassment and his inability to understand Percy's sexuality didn't stop him from taking him to hospital. It seems such a simple concept.

Maybe the best solutions always are.

PART FIVE

FARMER

25

A FARMER AT HEART

IF YOU WANT TO COUNT the number of headaches you'll have as a farmer, my experience is that you just need to count the number of pistons you have on your farm. These are the parts of machinery that really give you trouble.

But I still love being a wine farmer. I love the late afternoons, when I climb on my lawnmower and mow the lawn. The whole process triggers different sensory thoughts in me. It seems to confirm what I'd thought as a child, that somehow I would end up farming one day, and that I would love it.

I can probably thank Dawie Botha for that.

Dawie was a dear friend of mine in high school. In my eyes, his family was rich because his dad drove a Jaguar and we didn't even have a car. The Bothas owned a big farm and employed a lot of people. Dawie had to spend two hours every afternoon in his room doing homework, which I would help him with. By helping Dawie in this way, my own schoolwork improved as well.

During the school holidays I'd work on their farm and earn some much-needed pocket money. It was a table-grape farm, so in winter I'd help prune the vines. I think it was on the Bothas' farm that my interest in and love for wine farming and vines began to develop.

When the Bothas went on holiday, I'd look after their water pumps and a few other things on the farm. In that way, I began to learn quite a bit about farming. And I enjoyed it. I also learnt a lot from the Bothas' approach to farming. They were very good farmers: very particular and precise, and never afraid of doing things themselves. They weren't what we call 'bakkie-boere' – those guys who just sit in their bakkies shouting orders at their labourers. The Bothas got their hands dirty, an approach I've emulated throughout my farming career.

In later years, I bought my first motorbike from one of the Botha brothers thanks to my first-ever loan, from Dawie's father, which I paid off by working on the farm. When I was 15, Dawie and I rode our 50 cc motorbikes all the way from Paarl to Hartswater in two days, roughly a 2 000-kilometre round trip. We rode through the night. It was a great adventure.

I've always had a great desire to have my own farm.

In 1995 I bought my first farm through Wimpie Basson, an estate agent. I had been ill and had just recovered, and was about to fly overseas for work. But I had this strong urge to buy a farm that day. So I phoned Wimpie in Hermanus, and he drove over to meet me. We went to look at a few farms, and that evening I put in an offer on our farm. It was love at first sight. I'd done some research and discovered that Wellington was a good area for wine. During my time at Union Wines, I'd realised that the decomposed granite soils here were magnificent for making wine.

I'd always wanted to make my own wine, and to have a farm where my kids could grow up. It's ironic, really, because when I was growing up, I was very anti-alcohol because of my father's drinking problem. But having worked with the vines on Dawie Botha's family farm, I developed a desire to produce my own wine one day.

When I was a youngster in Paarl and delivering newspapers in the mornings, I'd cycle past the wine farms and the wine manufacturers, and I would inhale these heady aromas of brandy and budding fruit trees. I think this in its own way also sparked in me a passion to be a farmer one day.

In my vineyards with Hugo Porta, the great Argentine flyhalf who in 1982, as captain of the Jaguars, beat our Springbok team virtually single-handed. He scored all the points in their 21–12 victory over us in the second Test in Bloemfontein, and was named man of the match. He became ambassador to South Africa in 1991 and later served as his country's minister of sport.

Breaking ground at Welbedacht. I was one of the first farmers to plant my vineyards in a north–south direction, as per Dr Richard Smart's seminal book Sunlight into Wine.

I later purchased the farm Mon Pierre in the Karoo near Victoria West. It was named after a Frenchwoman's son who had died during a fire on the farm. His mother had mourned him, crying out, 'Mon Pierre! Mon Pierre!' This beautiful farm exposed me to the peculiarities of farming in South Africa. One year we had a terrible drought and I struggled to find decent land for our cattle to graze. My farm manager, Job Steenkamp, told me that he belonged to a consortium that rented municipal land near the airstrip outside Victoria West, and that I could rent the land from the municipality and let my cattle graze there.

I applied to the municipality to rent the land. Their response was that they only rented the land to 'new farmers'. I informed them that I was indeed a new farmer in the area. I even sweetened the deal by offering to fix two boreholes on the land, which they could keep at no cost to them when I no longer required the grazing for my 200 cattle. With that, I was notified that I had to appear before the municipal council.

I left Cape Town at 3 one morning and did the six-hour drive to Victoria West. I met with a man who told me that the council wanted me to better my offer. I upped the amount I was offering by 30 per cent. The man left to consult with the rest of the council. After a while, he came back and handed me a contract stipulating that I could use the land for the next three years. I went into the council chamber to sign the contract, and encountered a sea of faces shocked at the sight of me. That's when the council members informed me that 'new farmers' actually referred to 'non-white' farmers. They had a good laugh about the fact that I'd simply assumed it meant 'new in the area'.

The principles of farming, of doing things with my hands, have always appealed to me. I love working things out. I've always loved solving puzzles, and so many elements of farming are like a puzzle you have to solve. Recently, my wife bought me an old marble solitaire board game and I spent hours trying to solve it. My brain is wired to figure out any formula. I believe, whether it's in sport or business, that there is a certain formula to solving any problem, and you just need to figure it out. It relates to my love of design, which inspired me to design my own wine cellar – to the great consternation of many 'experts' in the industry.

When I announced that I would be building my own cellar, I was widely mocked by the experts. What does a lock forward know about building his own wine cellar? But I'd been in so many cellars over the years that I knew exactly what I wanted. Just as nobody could tell me not to plant my vines in the same way a cricket pitch is laid out, namely, from north to south, to make full and effective use of the sun.

Throughout my life, I've always looked towards the next horizon, always tinkering with new ideas. And now I was going to build my own cellar.

People laughed at me. My architect even brought along five engineers to say that what I wanted to build wasn't possible. But I kept insisting that I wanted to build my cellar to complement my fruit. Whenever I take people on a cellar tour, I always tell them that I built it to suit my fruit. And you know what? When it was finished, it was groundbreaking, and my critics admitted as much. I built a cellar with lifted fermenters that dramatically affect both the way the grapes are received and the whole fermentation process. It takes full advantage of the unique conditions in Wellington and the way the cool evening wind blows through, wafting off the ferment.

A big inspiration for my cellar came when I visited Charles Back's Spice Route cellar outside Malmesbury. Charles, my dear schoolfriend from the age of seven, is a great farmer, winemaker and entrepreneur, and was named the 2017 South African National Farmer of the Year.

I believed in cement fermenters coupled to a wooden basket press. The big difference in the design was that I wanted the cement fermenters to be higher than the rim of the basket press. This was so that, after the fermentation period, I could easily remove the husks in the fermenter and get them into the basket without damaging them through pumping. The idea was to be able to softly shovel them out and then press them in the basket press, which works like a coffee percolator and is very soft on the husks and pips, so you get these wonderful extractions of flavour.

The problem, though, was where to find a company to build cement fermenters, which in my design also had to be open underneath to provide storage space for bottles of wine, and sufficiently strong not to crack or break, given the stresses and strains exerted by seven tons of grapes per ferment. The design had to allow for four square metres of surface area for one metre of depth. Furthermore, I needed windows above the fermenters to allow the evening breeze to waft over the fermenting grapes and take away excessive alcohol residing there, and to allow fresh air to help cool down the top layers of the ferment for the early-morning hand punch-downs that we do.

Well, as you know by now, most of my unique plans have at least two initial problems that need solving.

The first problem was that the fermenters I wanted had never before been made in the way that I wanted them. I was given a myriad reasons why I was wrong, why the design would not work and why it was a waste of space. Even though I pointed out that I could store whatever I wanted underneath them, the engineers would still answer that it wasn't possible to build fermenters in this way.

The solution came to me one day when I drove past a big water tower. I wondered how on earth those towers were designed. At the time, Willie Enright was the director-general of water affairs in the Western Cape. I phoned him and asked him who the designer was. He told me it was a chap by the name of Peter Lister.

By way of background, by September 2004 we had got the farm rezoned, a prerequisite for building a cellar, after a four-year struggle with neighbours who opposed every possible thing. They were cooperative farmers who did not believe that Wellington was an area for making fine wines. A few years down the road, Marc Kent would be named Diners' Club Winemaker of the Year for his 2007 Boekenhoutskloof Syrah, but part of the contract I had with him was that I could not divulge to whom I was selling my grapes. Well, in winning this magnificent accolade, which was well deserved, he returned the favour by announcing that the grapes came from our farm, and more importantly from the Wellington region, which was still a ward of Paarl.

More pressing was that I was running out of time, as I wanted to start harvesting in January 2005 in my own cellar and I could not get my grand idea sorted out, albeit that I was already – along with Charles Back – importing a Marzola basket press from Spain. Those in the know told me I was mad to do that too. Anyway, I contacted Peter Lister and asked him to come and see me.

A few days later, one of my workers came to me and said he suspected there was a dead man on the farm. He took me to where the man was lying, on the grass, flat on his back, with a glass of wine held to his chest. From inside his Isuzu bakkie, playing at full blast, was one helluva piece of classical music. I woke him up, and he said, 'Hello. Peter Lister. Pleased to meet you.'

He'd arrived early for our meeting, taken out his normal lunch pack, put on some music and started to enjoy the music, the wine and the cheese. He loved the tranquillity surrounding him so much that he decided to lie down and listen to his favourite piece of classical music, during which he fell asleep. That's when I found him. From that day on, I called him Mister Lister. From his experience designing water towers for the Department of Water Affairs, he not only designed my fermenters but also built them between Christmas and New Year. And to this day they haven't had as much as a single crack.

So I've never been afraid to venture outside traditional parameters to try something new. That's what I love about good design. To me, design is the most fulfilling experience you can have. When I build something on the farm, I draw up the plans myself. But what is good design? I believe it's when practicality, aesthetics and economics are in balance for the job to be done.

My love for design extends even to my wine labels, which I write and design myself. I love using the right word at the right time, and one word I love is 'gregarious'. So when I desperately wanted to use the word on a wine label, that's how we created our Meerkat range, calling it 'South Africa's most gregarious wine'.

People don't expect a big man like me to be creatively inclined, but I like to challenge myself with design. In sport, I wanted to design my opponent's downfall. It's what excited me about sport.

I sincerely hope that I've added some value to the wine of the Wellington region and helped boost its status as a top wine region in South Africa, having been involved in the process to have Wellington officially recognised as a wine district.

In 2008 I was in the process of having my farm registered as a wine estate, which means that your final product in the bottle must be grown, made and bottled on the estate. South Africa has a very good system controlling this, all managed by the South African Wine Industry Information and Systems, a not-for-profit company. When I was applying for this classification, I became aware that there was another area that was applying to use the name Groenberg, my beloved mountain, which has granted us these unique soils, for a ward. Because Wellington was still a ward of Paarl, we could not use the name Groenberg for a ward because the demarcation rules stipulate that you cannot be a ward of a ward. So, once again, my two-pronged approach was used.

I got together the five farmers of Groenberg, with five days to go before this other application was to be decided on. We put in a bona fide application for the use of Groenberg as a ward. The letter we got back stated that we could not use it, but if Wellington became a ward, then the demarcation board would reserve the use of the name for us. This started a nine-year battle, first to get Wellington demarcated as a district, where we had to prove every title that fell within the district and the farmers had to agree with it. You can imagine the problems that we had in getting that through. Then we created five wards in Wellington, namely, Groenberg, Bovlei, Limietberg, Blouvlei and Mid-Bergrivier.

It was a joyous day when finally the new demarcation was approved, following all the statutory processes, and it was advertised in the *Government Gazette*. I would like to thank all those who helped me in the process, and especially Herman le Roux and Jannie Bosman, who stood by me through the whole difficult period. Better news was to come when Wellington twice won the prestigious Novare South African Terroir Awards' wine area of the year, in 2010 and 2016. The awards recognise wines of origin from a single vineyard, estate, ward or district. If we had not been granted the new demarcation, we could not have won.

I've read widely about wine over the years, and most of what I know about wine I taught myself or picked up when I worked in the wine industry. When I was younger, in my late twenties, I actually came very close to owning a big stake in the industry.

I was working for Jan Pickard at Union Wines when I had the opportunity to buy the company. I'd helped build the business to become a leading listed company. At the age of 29, I was on the board of a listed company and the alternate director of Picbel, the holding company. I was the youngest member of the Cape Wine and Spirit Institute and the Brandy Foundation of South Africa. I'd

With fellow Paarl Gimnasium old boy Jan Pickard, who was chairman of the company I was working for and president of the Western Province Rugby Football Union. He is congratulating me following the capping ceremony after my first Springbok Test against England in 1984 in Port Elizabeth.

helped rewrite the Liquor Act of 1957, and had worked for SAB in the eastern Cape. So I had contributed to the statutory control of the industry and had vested roots in it.

Rauch van Reenen, the son of Springbok George van Reenen, was the CEO of Union Wines, and we had an excellent relationship. But then he took ill with cancer and the previous managing director, Danie Terblanche, was brought back to run Union Wines in a caretaker capacity. And I found out that Union Wines had been put on the market.

So I tried to buy the company, but in the process I made a big mistake that taught me a lot about business.

At the time I was negotiating a deal in the United Kingdom that would make us the first South African liquor company to have a shareholding from one of our principals in the UK – Allied Hiram Walker. We wanted to create the first company here where the principal owner of the rights had a shareholding in either the marketing or distribution segments of the company. At the time, it was standard industry practice to hold the local distribution rights. We wanted to break the company into three parts, namely, production, distribution and marketing/sales, and then we also had the retail arm comprised of the Picardi bottle stores and hotels. The strategy was for Jacques Kempen, Darron Swersky and Orion Meyer, who were running the Drop Inn liquor stores, to take over the retail division as part of the deal. I had been doing many other deals with Allan Snelling, the managing director of Allied Hiram Walker, and he had agreed to take up a shareholding in the newly formed company and at the same time to put all his brands into the new company for distribution, as Union Wines had 12 depots and distribution units, as well as four production units.

Our company's presence was strong in the wine category, with brands such as Bellingham and Culemborg and production facilities throughout the country. But we needed a strong spirit brand portfolio, and Allied Hiram Walker had that.

Hiram Walker controlled most of Douglas Green's spirit brands, so we basically agreed a deal in principle with Allan Snelling in which they would give us their spirit brands in exchange for a share in our company.

Unbeknown to me, Graham Beck – whose coal-exporting business was then one of the largest clients of Safmarine – had heard about the deal I was negotiating via a former marketing director I had employed. Graham was also in business with Sol Kerzner's Kersaf, which owned Douglas Green. Buddy Hawton, the CEO of Kersaf, phoned Graham to tell him that Douglas Green was under pressure. So Graham decided to have a look at Union Wines and maybe combine the two. Graham realised that if Hiram Walker joined forces with us, there would be nothing left for Douglas Green.

The next thing I knew, Jan Pickard was selling Union Wines to Graham Beck for six cents a share less than what we'd offered them. This was in 1990. I was flabbergasted, but looking back, I realise that I was naive. I should have done that deal at arm's length. After all, how could a rugby player try to buy a company from the former president of his provincial rugby team? And such a young rugby player at that? I should've found a more mature person to do the deal on my behalf. In the end, Graham offered me an opportunity to be part of finalising the deal and making sure the Allied Hiram Walker brand stayed within the new group. But he also taught me a valuable business lesson. He once said to me, 'Give me your big five.' I thought, is he talking about animals or what? He replied, 'What's in it for me?' I left the company, having completed my agreement with him eight months earlier than we had anticipated.

But farming and the wine industry have remained a constant throughout my life. I enjoy everything about the relationship between the farmer and the land.

In my opinion, a wine estate is the perfect symbiosis between the various blocks of vines and how they mature outdoors in nature, and the process of maturation that takes place in the cellar. Man is the manager of this process and should not try to dominate it or force his will upon it.

As far as I'm concerned, wine is made in the vineyard. Everything and everyone in this process is of equal importance.

You cannot make a good wine with bad grapes. And there is also no better masking agent for poor wine than wood. In South Africa, many of our wines are hopelessly over-wooded.

But there is so much that goes into the process of making the wine, and I believe wholeheartedly that the human hands involved are merely custodians of this process. As I've said, I am just the custodian of this land. The French say it best: 'The dear Lord provides. We on earth can only care for it.' Once a year, the land I farm affords me the opportunity to harvest my grapes and make wine.

You'd be surprised to know that a vine intimidates me. If I plant a vine today, I'll only know in six or seven years' time if it produces well. In the wine industry, mistakes are amplified in that sense. Anything you do is expanded over this extended period of time in the process. So if you're spraying and you make a mistake, you have to wait a whole year to rectify it.

I'm a perfectionist; I like to do things properly. But wine can make you question and doubt yourself. Wine has such a long run in the making of it, and there are so many people involved. You need your workers to prune and spray properly, to look after your vineyards, to put the wine into barrels. It's a complicated process. But I still take immense pleasure in being able to produce something lasting – to know that some of the vines I've planted will long outlive me.

I don't think many South Africans realise that you cannot drink the same quality of wine we have for the same price anywhere else in the world. I'm proud of that. Every year is different – the environment tells us this. We're part of a changing ecology, and we need to learn to treat the environment with dignity and respect. If we don't, there will be nothing left for the generations that follow.

26

OF HEART TRANSPLANTS AND SCREW CAPS

THE THINGS I SAY often get me into trouble.

As I've said before, I believe you should have an opinion, and also be willing to listen to the opinions of others.

One opinion I hold is that we are currently living through the sixth extinction of the Earth. There have already been five mass extinctions, and I believe the sixth is happening now. I also believe in Darwinism. Once, when I discussed my beliefs with a dominee, his response was swift and direct: 'Jy is die Antichris' (You are the Antichrist).

Once I was trying to describe to a wine-tasting group, without losing my audience, the benefits of resveratrol, a compound found in wine, particularly red wine. Resveratrol is part of a group of compounds called polyphenols that act as antioxidants. Some people asked why it was important to have antioxidants. In answering, I said that antioxidants can neutralise free radicals, to which an older man stood up and said, 'So are you telling me that the more red wine I drink, the more I can neutralise the Economic Freedom Fighters?' That's when someone else piped up, 'That is most probably why they wear red uniforms.' Wine tastings, as unconventional and interesting as I like them to be, can throw you many curve balls.

On another occasion, I nearly got into trouble for something I said during a wine tasting I hosted in KwaZulu-Natal. I was there to market my wines, and a woman who owned several of the biggest guest lodges on the North Coast was in the audience. My agent had informed me that she would be attending, and he pleaded with me, 'Schalk, please don't get on her wrong side.' This lady was basically the doyenne of that stretch of coastline and all the locals were a bit wary of her.

Anyway, we had the wine tasting, which included my Chardonnay and Chenin Blanc, both of which have screw caps instead of corks. The woman was quiet the entire evening, until I opened the floor for questions at the end of the tasting. She was the first to stand up. 'It's disgusting,' she said, 'these barrel-fermented white wines of yours.' I looked at my agent, and he nodded. This was indeed the woman he had warned me about. Well, we had just received quite a few awards for both of our white wines, so I was a bit perplexed by her outburst.

So I asked her, 'Madam, is there, in your opinion, anything structurally wrong with my wines?'

She said no, on the contrary, the wine was magnificent. But she was disgusted that I had put such good wine into a bottle with a screw cap.

So I told her one of my stories. I told her the story of Dr Chris Barnard. In 1976, there was a programme on Springbok Radio called *Call Back the Past*, and one of the episodes was about Chris Barnard and the first heart transplant operation in 1967. The Roman Catholic Church had denounced the operation, as the donor of the heart was technically still alive at the time the organ was removed. So there was Chris Barnard in his white coat, addressing a news conference in front of Groote Schuur Hospital, and in that high-pitched voice of his he declared, 'I would just like to say that the church has now denounced my operation. But the heart, the heart you know, the heart is only but a pump.'

The woman asked me, 'What on earth has that got to do with what I said?'

'Madam, similarly, the cork, like the screw cap, is only but a closure. It doesn't change the wine at all.'

Surprisingly, she accepted that answer. However, the stigma attached to the screw top continues to exist. Somehow, people consider wine in a screw-top bottle to be inferior, perhaps because they think a cork helps to age wine. It doesn't. It's just a cap. In the past, cork was simply the easiest way of capping a bottle and it stayed that way.

For me, wine is more about passion than about how you cap a bottle. When I started collecting art, my approach was that somebody had produced something with passion, and if I liked it, I liked it. I never looked at the name of the artist.

I feel people should have the same approach to wine. If you like it, drink it. And the rest be damned. There is perhaps nothing more personal to you than your palate.

PART SIX

SEDIMENT
A few things drifting around in my mind

27

SOUTH AFRICAN RUGBY'S COACHING DILEMMA

I'LL NEVER FORGET the late Western Province rugby player and Springbok wrestler Cliffie Etzebeth once being interviewed by the English media. They wanted to know what lay behind the strength of our Western Province team in the 1980s. Cliffie knew that the Afrikaans word was 'gees' but he couldn't think what it was in English. So he responded: 'It's the ghost in our team that makes us strong.' The English reporter was rather perplexed, as if there was some sinister ghost that allowed us to be better than most of the teams we played against.

Cliffie was right, of course. Team spirit plays a major role in success on the field. But we were also blessed to have some highly intellectual individuals coaching us. To be honest, I don't believe we have that level of intellect in modern rugby coaching. As a result, I don't see coaches in South African rugby who are redesigning the game and creating anything unique at the moment.

Nothing in our game suggests a particular South African style or identity. We are preoccupied with playing rugby like New Zealand, which suits the Kiwis down to the ground. The more we try to play like the All Blacks, the easier it is for the All Blacks to play against us, because they understand that game.

I believe the closest game to rugby is chess. Every piece has a very particular role it must play. And, similarly, every piece has something it cannot do. You can't get a pawn to do a rook's job. That is the big mistake modern rugby makes. Coaches are trying to take a player who is a rook and turn him into a bishop in their game plan. The modern game confuses me, because I don't know what some of the players' roles are any more. You can't make an elephant roar like a lion.

When we had rugby dominance over New Zealand and the rest of the world, what made it difficult to play against us was that we played to our own pattern. We had strong basics. We only took chances in the other team's half. The quick loose ball was the backs' ball, not the forwards' ball. These days, the quick loose ball is being recycled by the forwards. Why? As a defending team, which ball don't I want to go wide? The quick ball, of course.

There is a simplicity to excellence in rugby.

A successful team has to have confidence in what they can do. The greater the level of confidence, the greater the chance of executing exactly what you want to do. So therefore it also means that successful players need to have confidence in what they can do. And when it comes to players, identity is important.

A good coach will allow enough latitude for a player to express himself through his skills. To be able to do this, a player needs confidence in what he can do, and he can only develop that confidence if he's allowed to do it from school level. But at this time in South African rugby, I believe our coaches are selecting too many physically strong players and not enough mentally astute ones. And then they are coaching them into a prescribed pattern that ignores the player's individual skills.

For example, our flyhalves now stand in the same place every time. How easy is it to defend against that? You want variation. You need to keep the opponent guessing and thinking. When your opponent starts trying to follow what you're doing, that's when you can dominate him.

South African rugby looks rushed, because we're predictable. That's precisely why a new young player makes a big impact at first – nobody knows about him. Two years later, though, he's been worked out, mainly because he's been coached into a set game plan that's not evolving.

There are so many matches these days that just don't interest me, and I feel sorry for the players who are being forced into this preprogrammed way of playing the game.

It starts at school level, where a kid is not allowed to make a mistake. How the heck does a player find out the limit or extent of his talent if he's not given the freedom to push the boundaries and make mistakes? When you just drop a player into a preprogrammed style of play, he becomes a robot.

Wernher von Braun, one of the fathers of rocket technology, claimed that if some of his rockets hadn't exploded, he would never have figured out how to improve them. Mistakes need to be made in order to learn. That's why I love sport and believe it's a vital part of a child's education. What better way to find out how a kid reacts to pressure, to taking orders, to winning and losing? There is nothing better than sport to reveal this.

But we seem to be forgetting the bigger picture at school level in the chase to win and produce preprogrammed players we can send to Craven Week, so that we can pat ourselves on the back for the number of Craven Week players our school has produced.

For these reasons, I don't believe there is a single coach in South African rugby today who would be capable of coaching a player like Danie Gerber. He was a genius, but there's no room for his kind of genius in the minds of modern coaches. Imagine a coach of today giving Naas Botha the kind of freedom he enjoyed, and which in my opinion made him one of the best match-winners of any generation.

Modern rugby union has become too much like rugby league. There is very little space between the attackers and defenders, and there are few original moves to create more space. You have scrumhalves now doing most of the kicking, which is bringing the catchers closer to the ball chasers.

The positive things I see in today's players, though, are an increased level of fitness and conditioning, an ability to travel and play away from home better, and the impressive way they deal with the demands on their time, both commercial and familial.

But, from an overall perspective on the game, it seems to me as if there is a lack of intellect in the modern game, and if rugby is not a debate, it won't have a future.

For example, I carried my fascination with mechanics and aerodynamics into my rugby. During my time playing rugby with Western Province, I worked with my teammates to develop the very flat and hard ball thrown to number four in the lineout. For us to pull that move off, we had to get the ball spinning a lot early on. A spinning ball travels further and faster through the air. That's why I don't understand how the coaches of today tell young players not to torpedo-pass a rugby ball, and how so few kickers in the game today can kick a torpedo kick. My old rugby friend Dawie Snyman and I had a lengthy debate with Hawies Fourie, when he was still the coach of Maties, about the value of a spinning ball in the modern game.

Look at the modern hookers and their throwing in the lineouts. They struggle to throw a ball in the wind because they use both hands, so they cannot generate enough spin to get the revolutions on the ball that will make it travel straighter through the wind. I remember spending hours on a Saturday morning, on a lawn in front of the hotel where we were staying, with my Western Province teammate and hooker Shaun Povey as he practised his throws. He had good hands, having been a provincial water polo player. Standing on a hotel lawn, with supporters and cars all around us, I was working on my jumping and he was perfecting the trajectory and spin speed that the ball had to have to get to me.

Another trick that Shaun and I had was that we would walk the east and west touchline boundaries of a field during our captain's practice the day before the match. He would throw and I would jump, and then he would memorise the position of an advertising board or a specific spectators' suite so that, during the game, when the field was full of spectators and players were jumping around, he would have a target to throw at. It was after a particular match against our archrivals, Northern Transvaal, that they said to me I had the highest success ratio of any lock in the country, and especially when I was under pressure. I did have a range of different calls and balls, but Shaun gave me confidence and it was not uncommon in an important match that if I nailed a great take, my hooker could be heard shouting, 'Great fucking take, Burger.' Obviously, you wanted to jump even higher the next time.

When I was interviewed about the state of South African rugby late in 2018, I spoke out about how rugby is being run in this country. I asked how SA Rugby could spend R144 million on the PRO14 when the Free State Cheetahs are right at the bottom of that competition. How, I wanted to know, could that be good for our rugby?

I really believe that South African rugby needs a reboot. We need to go back and decide how *we* want to play the game, and not try to copy how the rest of the world is playing it.

You have coaches today who haven't grasped the fact that rugby is a proactive, not a reactive, game. In 1994 Ian McIntosh and I had a lengthy debate about this. Ian told me that his strategy was to identify his 15 top players and coach them on his game plan. I said that that was the wrong approach. First you decide on your game plan, and *then* you select the 15 players who can play to that game plan. There's a simple reason why you do it that way round. Because, under pressure, a player will always revert to his natural style of play.

And as for the size of the coaching staff on today's teams, my mind boggles. Your average professional team these days has a large coaching staff. The Springboks had *nine* coaches for the 2015 Rugby World Cup. Now, please tell me, as a player, which of those nine coaches do I listen to? I can't help but feel that if I'm confused, the players must be feeling the same.

World rugby has stagnated with regards to allowing unique players to express themselves in other areas of the game beyond just through chance or broken play. Broken play has become more and more formalised, providing even less opportunity for individual brilliance. I believe one of the reasons for this has been that coaches want to have more control of the game from the stands other than the player having control over what he can see and what he can do on the field. Danie Gerber was a great example of a player who saw and did things differently, which made him very difficult to play against.

Another current belief in the game is that the ball carrier must be protected by referees. I disagree. The ball carrier determines play by the mere fact of creating uncertainty as to whether he's going to pass, kick or take the man on. He needs to be left to play, not protected, and let the contact be 50-50. And let the creative players to do what they do best.

I once had a big debate with former UCT player and coach Gus Enderstein, who said you need to pass the ball to move forward in rugby. I told him there is a fundamental flaw in that thinking. You can't go forward by passing, because that's a forward pass. There are only two ways you can move forward in rugby and that's by kicking and carrying the ball. That's how simple the game is.

The role of the scrumhalf has also changed drastically over the years. In June 2019 I had a debate with the English referee Wayne Barnes when he came to one of my wine tastings in London for the Sporting Wine Club. I asked him why a scrumhalf cannot be played if he puts his hand on the ball. He informed me that referees have decided that the ball is only in play once it's picked up. Why then, I asked, is it a knock if the scrumhalf knocks the ball on while trying to pick it up? Technically, according to their interpretation, that ball is not yet in play. He didn't have an answer for me. So the interpretation of the laws is murky.

Looking at the 2019 Rugby World Cup and the Springboks, I think we can all agree that their victory, much like in 1995, was an act of God, in my opinion, in terms of how it all came together and the impact it had on our country. I was really happy for Siya Kolisi, Rassie Erasmus, President Cyril Ramaphosa and the whole team and country. We needed to become proud again as a nation.

On a personal note, I would love to have played in a World Cup. I was so looking forward to possibly being part of the 1987 World Cup, especially after we'd beaten New Zealand in 1986. But that didn't happen for political reasons.

In 1995 it was great for me to be part of the organisation around the World Cup in South Africa. Then in 2007 it was very special for me to be there when Schalk won it with the Springboks.

Going into the 2019 World Cup, I don't think many people gave South Africa a chance. They played their way through the pool stages, and come the final against England I believe the Springboks knew psychologically that they had the better of them. And I think Eddie Jones made a critical mistake in changing his whole game plan against South Africa.

In that magnificent semi-final against New Zealand, England attacked the second and third channel and brought the ball back fast. The All Blacks had no clue what had hit them. I'll never forget the look on Kieran Read's face: he was shell-shocked. He didn't know what was happening to them.

Then came the final. I believe Eddie thought he had the players who could literally bump us off the ball. But you don't bump Springboks, especially in a World Cup final.

One scene that I remember is of the England prop Kyle Sinckler lying on the field out cold, with his tongue nearly touching his left ear, and teammate Maro Itoje looking down at him with his eyes as big as saucers. You could see the panic in his eyes. England just tried to bump us out of the World Cup, and we stood up to it. Our tight five were outstanding, and I believe the real tight games are won by the tight five. There were pieces of individual brilliance by Cheslin Kolbe, though. I don't think our defensive pattern is as good as we say it is, and New Zealand exposed that.

But I think what really counted in the Springboks' favour was that the team was a close unit.

The sad thing is that 17 of those 33 players are now playing overseas, and that's an indictment of the management of the game in South Africa. Your main players must play in your main competitions. We have the money in this country to keep them here, but we do have too many professional rugby players. You're starting to lose it when you contract players at 13 or 14 years of age, as has been the case in this country.

I think we've lost our way in terms of talent identification. Three of the best props I ever played with were Henning van Aswegen, Keith Andrews and Bill Nieuwoudt. But I honestly believe they would never have made it today, because at Under-20 level they were still playing as loose forwards. If they'd been contracted so early, they might never have grown into the great props they became.

I do feel, though, that rugby is headed for a bit of a shake-up globally. I think the next World Cup will look very different, and it should, otherwise rugby won't survive.

I've been fortunate to be involved in rugby at all levels of the game, from player to coach to marketing and advertising and contracts and stadium management. I've seen the game evolve. I believe the intrinsic aspects of the game should be run by amateurs. Look at golf, where The R&A (Royal and Ancient) and the United States Golf Association (USGA), two amateur bodies, control a game that's created more millionaires than any other, and that as a business in the USA is larger than the gross national product of many countries. Golf has the most technical rules, but attracts the least scandal.

When it comes to rugby, let the competitions be run by fully commercial marketing specialists who can commercialise these competitions to their maximum. Let the teams be as commercial as they want to be. But the running of the game – the rules and the intrinsic elements of the game – should be managed by amateurs. And I do not mean they should act as amateurs. I believe that this is key for the survival of rugby in the long term. The reason is simply that a paid official runs the risk of making subjective decisions based on his or her position in the game, rather than the best decisions for the game.

We must never lose sight of what is in the best interests of the game as a whole. In the days before professionalism, most coaches went through the coaching system while also holding down day jobs. Rugby clubs in those days were a mix of all members of society, both on the field and in the administration – the doctor, church minister, traffic cop, prison official, farmer, teacher, attorney, advocate, businessman, banker, and so on. To be a great coach, you had to have more than just a knowledge of the game. You also had to be a great communicator to get such an eclectic group of people to click on the field of play. As such, it was always interesting to me to see how certain coaches just seemed to fit into the environments that they were coaching in. Here I look at Ikeys, Stellenbosch, Uitenhage, Despatch, SA Police in Pretoria and, for that matter, all the police teams. The successful coaches developed a rapport with their players and the supporters, and their brand of rugby reflected this. They were masters at understanding their opposition.

Many of these coaches went on to become provincial coaches, and their way of thinking and deciding on a plan of action for the match stayed the same. I remember many a time at the post-match receptions where coaches would chide each other that they had caught the other man out with their superior game plan.

Those coaches were real students of the game, and nobody played according to a national prescribed style of play. To them, every match presented the question: what game plan do I need against this particular team, and which players can execute that successfully? It wasn't a question of blindly following one style of play from one match to the next.

I feel that this kind of coaching creativity and nuance has been lost in the modern game.

28

GOODBYE, NEWLANDS

ON SATURDAY 23 JANUARY 2021, I witnessed something I thought I would never see happen. Newlands Rugby Stadium, the grand old dame of South African rugby stadiums, with a history dating back to the late 1800s, hosted its last rugby match.

After the Currie Cup match between Western Province and the Sharks, Newlands, that hallowed turf that has witnessed so many iconic moments in South African rugby, and which is a part of the very soul of every Western Province rugby player who has been privileged to play there, shut its gates for the last time.

I don't want to go into the details of why this happened and the alleged mismanagement within the union, or the wisdom of Western Province's taking up a new home at the Cape Town Stadium. Enough ink has flowed on this subject, and those are not the memories I would like to have of Newlands.

Newlands has played a special part throughout the Burger family's rugby history, and we have been playing rugby there since 1943.

My father played at Newlands when he played rugby for Paarl Rugby Club's First XV in 1943. I played my first rugby match at Newlands in 1973 as a member of the Western Province Schools team. My last official match at Newlands was in 1987. After that I played an exhibition match in 1990 as part of the Newlands Centenary between Maties and Villagers, which Villagers won 10–6.

Schalk Jnr played his first rugby match at Newlands in 1995 as a member of the Boland Under-13 team against Western Province. Of course, he had a wonderful career with Western Province and also played many a Springbok Test at Newlands. His final match for Western Province at Newlands was in 2016 before he left to see out his career with Saracens.

Tiaan played provincial rugby at Newlands, representing Boland Under-21 against Western Province.

My brother Johann played many a club rugby match at Newlands as a member of Paarl Rugby Club's first team.

That is 78 years of our family's history tied up in Newlands Rugby Stadium. It breaks my heart to know that Newlands is no more – now to be turned into yet another property development.

But, similarly, it gives me great comfort to know that I was a part of Newlands' history. Newlands was my temple, where I won three Currie Cups. It holds a lifetime of rugby memories for me. Memories of taking off my rugby boots, still thick with the turf, and the smell of Dubbin rubbed onto them before I packed them away for the next match. That smell would seep into my dreams – boyhood dreams of Newlands heroes, the dreams of a man playing to the cheers of the Newlands faithful, and the dreams of a father taking his sons to Newlands and giving them enough money to buy a pie and a Coke, and cheer on their heroes.

Then the drive home as they've fallen asleep on the back seat. And you put them to bed, remembering how you too came home spent as a young boy from an afternoon watching rugby at Newlands with your dad, and fell asleep still clutching that Super Springbok rugby ball.

And with Newlands, its sounds and smells, drifting through your dreams.

29

MY KIND OF PEOPLE

I LIKE PEOPLE WITH STRONG PERSONALITIES because they challenge my thinking.

In my rugby-playing days, I loved the characters of the game, people like Morné du Plessis, Doug Jeffery, Andrew Johnston, Danie Gerber, Boelie Serfontein, Tobie Hanekom, Rob Louw, Bill Nieuwoudt, Divan Serfontein, and the Du Plessis brothers – Willie, Carel and Michael.

Outside rugby, I have a great friendship with Mosiuoa 'Terror' Lekota, who left the ANC in 2008 to co-found the Congress of the People. I was introduced to him by Steve Tshwete, another great friend of mine. I loved Steve for the same reasons I love Terror. Steve was an honest man with a great sense of humour, but he could also be serious. I think he respected me for knowing a bit about Xhosa history. Terror is real man of principle who I believe is too honest for politics, but he should have a place somewhere in the leadership of our country.

Jannie Geldenhuys was another great friend. Not many people know that he wrote books, many of them children's books. Apart from saving me from attending army camps, Jannie was also very good to my brother Johann. When Johann was a Recce in

32 Battalion, he was shot up pretty badly one time. He had been operating out of range of his own forces in southern Angola when he encountered the enemy and was seriously wounded. He sent out a casevac (casualty evacuation) call and it was picked up by Willem Ratte, another highly decorated Special Forces soldier. Ratte in turn relayed Johann's casevac call to the South African Air Force at Ondangwa, near the Angolan border, and they sent two helicopters to pick him up. The choppers flew straight into enemy fire in order to rescue Johann. But Johann said if it wasn't for Ratte and him staying in constant contact with one of the helicopter pilots, Captain Trevor Williamson, he wouldn't be alive today. Johann says that in 1986 he took two boxes of wine I had sourced for him as a thank-you gift to Williamson and his co-pilot. Williamson told him that during the rescue, Ratte was constantly on the radio saying how important it was for them to 'Fetch my friend Joe Burger'.

My mom later received a telegram saying that Johann was in hospital in Pretoria. But we couldn't get any further details or even speak to him, because he'd been involved in a clandestine operation. So the army just stonewalled our attempts to find out if he was all right.

I phoned General Geldenhuys on a Sunday morning and explained to him our predicament.

He told me to stay on the line, and on his other line he phoned 1 Military Hospital in Pretoria and was put through to the ward. He asked to speak to Captain Burger. After a while I heard him say, 'Captain, what are you doing in hospital while your troops are fighting the enemy?' Johann was flabbergasted. He had been reaching for some ammunition when he was shot in the hand. The doctors wanted to amputate Johann's left hand.

Then General Geldenhuys turned the two telephones so that the speaker and the part that you spoke into were across from each other, and so I was able to speak to my brother while he awaited his fate in the hospital. Once Johann was off the line, Jannie promised to ensure that he got the best treatment. It was he who made sure that one of the world's leading hand specialists, Professor Louis Wessels of the University of Pretoria, took over Johann's case.

Dr Kenny Wienand, an orthopaedic surgeon, was due to perform the operation. Johann recalls how Professor Wessels walked with him as he was being wheeled into the operating theatre, and how Wessels told Dr Wienand, 'Save this man's hand at all costs.' Professor Wessels, who was also the dean of the University of Pretoria's Medical School, then added, 'Ek het julle mos baie mooi geleer' (I taught you well).

Johann had to undergo a highly complicated series of operations, and he was told to prepare himself for a possible amputation. But they managed to save his hand; he only lost his ring finger. Johann told me that the operation was later used as a case study that was presented at an international orthopaedic conference in the United States. One of the doctors attending the conference commented that had it been an American GI, he would most surely have suffered an amputation.

Jannie also made sure that my mother's call, after the operation, was put through to Johann's ward so that she could at least hear that her son was fine.

Whenever I would bump into Jannie at a post-match reception at the height of the Border War, I'd ask him, 'General, who is being attacked tonight?' And he'd reply, 'You'll find out next week.'

When I was captain of Eastern Province, my bridge partner was former prime minister John Vorster. He had retired to Oubosstrand in the Eastern Cape, and would come to Port Elizabeth to watch some of the EP matches and stay over in his flat, which was next to that of our team doctor, Win Smith. When Schalk Jnr was born, Win handled everything for us. Myra often jokes that when you're married to a rugby player, the team doctor becomes your family doctor as well.

It was the same with old Justus Moolman, the Test referee who was also a dentist. Justus used to look after all the players' teeth. We played bridge against him as well. On one occasion, Justus and Doug Jeffery were playing against each other, and Doug, who had a problem with his teeth, said he'd play Justus for a new set of teeth. The good Lord responded favourably by allowing Doug to beat

Justus. A few days later, at practice, Doug went up to Justus and said, 'So, I've come to fetch my toofs.'

It was Justus who first invited me to play bridge with him and John Vorster. Mr Vorster and I were always partners. On one occasion we were playing against Gert van Vollenhoven, a founding member of the University of Port Elizabeth. As the evening went on and Mr Vorster was enjoying his Klipdrift brandy and Rothmans cigarettes, I thought it was a good time to tell him a story.

On 6 September 1966, Prime Minister Hendrik Verwoerd was assassinated by Dimitri Tsafendas in Parliament. 'It happened on my youngest brother's birthday,' I told Mr Vorster. 'Then it was announced that you were going to take over as prime minister of South Africa. And my mother burst into tears, because with her leftist leanings she was convinced you were going to drive all the English people into the sea.'

The bridge game came to halt and there was an awkward silence. Mr Vorster looked at me and said, 'Are you talking about your bridge partner?'

'Yes, Mr Vorster,' I replied. I always called him Mr Vorster.

'You can call me Oom John,' he said. And that was that.

He was a highly intellectual person and I admired him for that. He and Louis Luyt actually shared a lot of the same mannerisms. Some people might ask why on earth I would've played bridge with John Vorster. But I also had dinner with Eugene Terre'Blanche. I remember him drinking three bottles of Bellingham Johannisberger wine and relating long pieces of Latin. To this day I do not know if he was making any sense, but to the people who supported him he sounded like the pope.

I have an extensive library of autobiographies because I am interested in people, and it doesn't really matter to me what side of the political spectrum you are on. If I'm interested in you, I'll spend time with you.

My friendship with Johann Rupert is one of my most treasured. I always knew about Johann when I was at school, as his cousin Jannie Rupert was in the same class as me. He married Cecile Wahl,

In 2002 at the Under-21 World Rugby Championship in Oxford, with a lot of South African supporters. Schalk Jnr was captain of the South African side and received a red card following two yellow cards. To my left are the Rupert family – Anton, Caroline, Gaynor and Johann – and my dear friend Alan Lamb. In front is Eben Calitz.

daughter of the great Springbok scrumhalf Ballie Wahl, who also was in our class. I spent some days at Jannie's house in Stellenbosch, which was also next to the river, close to Johann's family home.

Following school, I saw Johann again at university. But we really became good friends when I had an office in London at the top of Hill Street, in Mayfair, where his offices also were. He always says that his mother knew me better than her own son. We did a lot of business together through Megapro, and Johann would invite me to join him on his annual golf tour, which would often end at the prestigious Dunhill Cup, where countries would send teams of golfers to compete on the Old Course at St Andrews. South Africa won it in 1997 with the fabulous team of Ernie Els, David Frost and Retief Goosen.

Over the course of our friendship we've been through a lot together. Johann is one of the most principled South Africans I know, and I don't think the country has had a bigger philanthropist in its history. Most people don't even know about most of his philanthropy, because he keeps it all under cover. Just look at what he's done for South African golf, founding the South African Golf Development Board, which has made a huge difference in the lives of so many disadvantaged young golfers.

Johann is passionate about sport, and gets very excited when he sees our young golfers do well on the world stage. He is also incredibly loyal, and the people who work with him have done so for ages. I'd go so far as to say Johann is the best modern-day ambassador for South Africa.

Johann has created a great many jobs through his various companies, which is only one of the many things he has done for South Africa. In fact, the entire Rupert family has done a great deal for this country. I've been very privileged to be so close to them. Through Johann I have met wonderful people, such as the actors Michael Douglas and Catherine Zeta-Jones, and musicians Don Felder, Mike Rutherford, Huey Lewis and Tico Torres.

I've also had a good relationship for many years with Gary Player, who achieved the pinnacle of sporting success under very trying circumstances. He has also been a fantastic sports ambassador for South Africa.

Dr Chris Barnard was also good company. He was an entertaining and very interesting man, always laughing. It was through Chris that I met Emiliano Sandri. Emiliano came to South Africa from Italy to work on the Blue Train, where he met many of our leading politicians, one of whom suggested he open his own restaurant. Emiliano started the famous La Perla restaurant in Sea Point, and later went into partnership with Chris and opened La Vita restaurant and Die Wijnhuis, in Newlands and Stellenbosch, respectively, and which his sons now run.

Sir De Villiers Graaff also made a big impact on me. When I was captain of Western Province, he invited me to his wine farm, De Grendel, on a number of occasions. I once told him how we'd actually met for the first time when I was a kid. Every year, the agricultural show would come to Paarl, and to earn a bit of pocket money, I used to parade the prize bulls for the exhibition and to be judged. One day, I ended up walking De Villiers' bulls. He always told me that I had a way with animals and would give me an extra tip. The announcer would call for the animal to be walked to the left and right, and then to be brought to the middle and face the pavilion. It was important here that the front and the hind legs had to splay so that the bull had a great stance, which was not always easy to achieve. A few of my friends would end up kicking the animal's hind legs, with the inevitable consequence of their being hoofed back by one of these big animals.

As I've mentioned, Nelson Mandela was very good to us when we went through our toughest times as a family. He phoned when he heard about René's ordeal, and when Schalk was in hospital fighting for his life. He was someone with a natural empathy for people.

Frik du Preez and I are also good friends. We have hunted together and I love his company. One of the first sports autobiographies I read was his book *Rugby Reus*. My father gave it to me on my birthday. My dad wrote *Excelsior et excelsior* (Higher, always higher) in the book for me. For many years I thought he had written those words to get me to jump higher in the lineout. As a kid, I remember sitting in the front row of the Paarl cinema watching Frik du Preez score *that* try against the 1968 British Lions. To a young boy, it felt like he'd run from one side of the screen to the other. It felt so real to me that I could almost smell the grass, wintergreen and sweat.

The Springbok Tommy Bedford and I also became friends. We were on the same wavelength politically. It's because of him that I love to write in green ink to this day, as he always used to write in green ink on yellow paper. His uncle was Sir Laurens van der Post, so Tommy and I always had great debates and conversations. One of my all-time favourite books is Sir Laurens's *The Lost World of the Kalahari*.

I met Ian Smith, the former prime minister of Rhodesia, in Salisbury in 1979 when I played for the Goshawks against the Kwaggas at the Police Grounds on a sweltering day. The Goshawks were a team much like the South African Barbarians. A team of selectors chose the players who would play certain representative and exhibition matches in Rhodesia. The Kwagga team comprised mostly fellow South African players. I was one of only two South Africans in the Goshawks team that day.

This match was always played in July, on Founder's Day, and I remember Smith arriving without too much show in his Peugeot 404, which he drove himself. He was introduced to the players of both teams. Following the match I spent more time in conversation with him, and we stayed friends after that. I saw him many times at the after-match functions of big games or Tests, and we always made an effort to get together for a beer and talk about the situations in both our countries. Once I was walking on the platform of Victoria Station in London and I heard this voice, 'Who is this big shadow gliding here in front of me?' He had just returned from the Conservative Party conference in Brighton, probably in the hope of doing a deal for his country. We had coffee together. No security, just him, his briefcase and a mind full of dearness and good stories.

I also used to go and visit him at his home in Harare whenever I was in what had become Zimbabwe. I'd knock on his front door, hear the footsteps coming down his hallway, and then from behind the frosted glass would come the words, 'Who's this big hulk standing at my front door?' He'd open the door and greet me with a hug. I would always say to him, 'Mr Smith, where is your security? Don't you think we should bulk it up a bit?' To which he would reply, 'All the security is over there.' He would point to State House, where Robert Mugabe resided. 'He needs it more than me. Just the other day, when I challenged him that when both of us walk up and down Independence Avenue, he on the one side and me on the other, I walk without security, he said it's because they are doing a great job keeping me safe. I said to him that at the top we could have a cup of tea and then cross over and come down the other side of the street. He still has not answered me.'

He later stayed in an old-age home in Kalk Bay, and in 2007, three months before he passed away, he spent Mother's Day with us on our farm.

Former Springbok coach Jake White is another interesting person. In 2019 I spent a few days on the back of a bakkie hunting with Jake. We had a good time talking about life and rugby and doing the occasional bit of hunting. Also, it was the first time I ever spoke to him about Schalk Jnr and about his time coaching my son, which was enlightening to say the least, as I stayed away from the team dynamics wherever my children were involved in sport. It was a day I will always remember.

I like Jake in that he's honest. He tried his best as Springbok coach and he was under immense pressure. He's also proved himself around the world, and he's not one to court popularity. He's very much an old-school type of thinker. I think he performed exceptionally well as Springbok coach, within his ability and in a very difficult time politically. I mean, being called back while on tour with the Springboks in 2006 must have been very degrading for him. It shows how single-minded and driven he was to still go on and win the Rugby World Cup. But then to be booted out as the coach after you've won the World Cup sends, in my opinion, the wrong message to many people.

Jake is a loyal servant of the game and for that I have a lot of respect for him.

30

CLIMBING KILIMANJARO

I WAS MOTIVATED TO CLIMB Kilimanjaro by what motivates me more than anything else in life – somebody told me that I couldn't.

Some of my friends took bets against my reaching the summit. So not only did I reach the summit, I completed a golden summit at just after 7 am. And I'm extremely proud of that. Remember, at the summit of Kilimanjaro you are higher than Everest Base Camp (5 364 metres). And I climbed it with some serious climbers who had all the necessary fancy clothing and equipment. Actually, they were the ones who lost their minds at the summit. They were falling around like drunks. It was hysterical. We had two Comrades athletes in our group. They kept asking me, 'Schalk, what's your VO2 max?' Bloody hell, I thought they were speaking Mandarin to me. I had no idea what the heck that was.

The night before we started the climb, I was enjoying some Kilimanjaro lagers. We called them 'Kili beers'. The rest of the group gave me a lecture about alcohol, which they said reduces the oxygen in your blood. I said to them, 'Stuff that. I'm thirsty.' So then we had to lay out all our gear. We were limited to 20 kilograms each. I forked out extra so that I could take an extra five kilograms on the basis that I was bigger than anybody else on the climb.

So we started to lay out our gear, beginning with our shoes. I noticed that some of the guys had shoes made from some fancy materials; you could probably have climbed Everest in those if you wanted to. I laid out my Timberland boots, which got a few skew looks. Then they asked me, 'Schalk, where are your inner synthetics?' Once again, I'm hearing bloody Mandarin out of their mouths. I was duly informed that these were socks you wear under your socks. So I hauled out my socks, a pair I'd bought in New Zealand in 1994. They were a mixture of mohair and wool. The rest of the team warned me that natural fibres would let moisture in and result in my toes freezing.

I said, 'Ag, dammit, can we just get on with the packing, please?' Then they asked for our leggings. So I hauled out my pair of long johns from the army. They were so old they were yellow. But I figured that they'd kept me warm in Upington, so they should be good enough for Kilimanjaro. Now I'm watching as the rest of this crowd pulls out leggings that are all fancy and stretched tight over your legs, basically holding your calves and hamstrings together in case you can't do that for yourself.

Then we moved on to the gear for the top half of our bodies. There were inner layers and outer layers, and then outer layers for the inner outer layers. It was crazy. I had an old T-shirt, two white vests, two lumberjack-style shirts, and a jacket. They asked where my rain suit was. So I pulled out the rain suit I wore for golf. By now the group leader was exasperated, and said in no uncertain terms, 'Burger, you are going to die up there.'

Then we moved on to scarves. Can you believe it?

I honestly didn't know you had to be so well dressed to climb a bloody mountain. I didn't have a scarf, so I took the pair of old rugby socks I was wearing, tied them together and used that as a scarf. I had my old army balaclava to cover my head. To be honest, it was the only thing that would fit my head. I'm a big man, so I can't just go to any old shop and buy a hat or something for my head. And my gloves were a pair of old motorbike gloves. When I took them out, one of the guys said, 'What the hell are those?'

I said, 'They're my gloves, and look, they still fit me like a charm.'

The others had fancy water bottles that prevented their water from freezing. I had a Thermos flask. My reasoning was simple. If a Thermos flask keeps the warmth in, then that means it must be able to keep the cold out. I thought in reverse.

And then I remembered my mother telling me about Tiger Balm. Whenever I played rugby in Johannesburg at high altitude, I'd dab a bit of Tiger Balm in my nostrils; it helps you breathe easier. Also, if you put it behind your ears or on your neck, it can help ease headaches. And finally, I had a poncho, which I'd bought on a trip to the Andes.

So now we begin climbing. I didn't trust the food, because I knew that if I got an upset stomach, I was a goner. So I took two beers up the mountain with me, which I mixed with water. I basically survived on the beers and bits of chicken that I asked them to fry until it was as hard as a rock to ensure it wouldn't upset my stomach. We

The unlikely achievement of a 135-kilogram man who, after vehemently resisting the idea of going up Kilimanjaro, was then rewarded with a golden summit on Africa's highest peak at 7.30 am. I was amazed that I made it. But the worst was to follow – going downhill is not for heavy people.

were already halfway up the mountain when some members of the group got poepskyte (the runs).

We bumped into some Japanese climbers, and when we stopped to rest, they started doing these odd, funny breathing exercises. They kept saying to me, 'Big man, you too.' Jeez, so there I was, doing bizarre arm movements and breathing exercises with this lot. Then we carried on climbing, and I was chatting to everybody about life and all the questions on my mind. We stopped for the night and made camp.

The next morning they wanted to summit, but I had a look at the weather and it didn't feel right to me. It looked like there was a blizzard at the summit. So I told them I was going nowhere, and I started making some alterations to my shoes. They were slipping a bit, so I took out my knife and cut some grooves into the soles. The next thing, the party returns with the news that three people had died of hypothermia on the mountain. There was a bit of a panic then, and the tour guides wanted us all to sleep in their quarters.

I said, 'Not a donner. With all due respect, it's riddled with lice in there.' So I did what we used to do in the army. I dug myself a hole in the shale on the side of the mountain, and I slept outside that night. They woke me at 11 pm and we started summiting at midnight. Just before we summited, I approached our camp commander and asked him for three beers. He looked at me and said, 'Big man, how much do you weigh?' I told him around 135 kilograms. His response was, 'You're not going to make it. This mountain isn't kind to people over 100 kilograms.'

So there it was again: you can't.

I summoned my finest English and said to him, 'Stuff you. Give me my beers.' And we started to summit.

Now, let me tell you, I saw some funny things up there. People crapping in their pants. People walking sideways. One guy walking right in front of me fell over a stone and shat in his pants all at the same time. It was one of my friends, Johan Pauw, a raconteur of many a hunting, crayfishing and fishing trip, who after many bottles of wine had convinced me to go on this trip. I had always said I do not jump out of planes, go down deep mines, or climb steep mountains. Yet here I was. Johan wanted to go to the toilet and just started walking towards the edge of the mountain. I grabbed him before he walked right off it. I tied a rope around him, so that he was basically hanging off the edge with his arse in the air having a crap. But I tell you, my poor friend was so far gone with altitude sickness or whatever he had. I had already given him my handwarmers that I had brought back from Scotland: they contain these little crystals in a pouch that you rub together and it gives off heat. He put them in his boots to help with the cold in his feet. Furthermore, he suffers from high blood pressure and is very competitive, so I was scared that he would overexert himself trying to stay with me. So I left him in the capable hands of another two climbers in our group.

By now, the only thing making me question what the bloody hell I was doing on this mountain was the funny smells all over the place.

As I left Johan there, I was really worried about what effect climbing higher would have on his blood pressure, and hoping that he would at least make Gilman's Point, one of the three summit points.

At 5:45 am I reached Gilman's Point, which is on the rim of the volcano crater. From here, you still need to reach Uhuru Peak. We were now doing what is known as the 'Kili shuffle', where you are literally just putting one foot in front of the other on the path up to the summit. Our two Comrades runners? Gone. They'd left us on day three and headed back. Evidently, their famous VO2 max had failed them.

Everything in me was also pretty much gone by this point. You are struggling to breathe and you can hardly put one foot in front of the other. Strange things were also happening around me as other stragglers were falling over, and some nearly falling off the cliffs. It reminded me of the final runners arriving at the finish line in the last hour of the Comrades Marathon. Everyone is battling. So I would try and help somebody until they said they wanted to rest, and I then put my head down and kept going and reached the summit at 7:25 am, with a beautiful sunrise.

I took a few photos and then helped quite a few others who were on the verge of altitude sickness and could not operate their cameras, before the guide beckoned to me to follow them down as I had already stayed there too long.

Let me tell you, coming down is where that mountain got me. Being as big as I am, it was hell going downhill. Two of my toes are still not quite normal after that experience.

But I made it.

Johan and I spent a relaxing six days in Dar es Salaam and Zanzibar to recover.

31

OPERATION SAVE ROB

I WILL NEVER FORGET the day I heard that one of my closest friends, fellow Springbok Rob Louw, with whom I'd played most of my rugby, from Craven Week days, was dying of cancer. The doctors had given him three months to live.

Rob and I first became friends at the start of high school. We met at the Craven Week trials, which also was where I met the cricketer Garth le Roux. Garth and I ended up going to the army together and were in the same company. In fact, I remember our regimental sergeant major (RSM), Jorrie Jordaan, informing us that he was going to arrange a cricket match between the PFs and the CFs (Permanent Force and Citizen Force). With great pride, he told us that this match would be played on his beloved parade ground. He ordered a brand-new mat and we proceeded to lay it down and mark out the boundary with chalk.

Garth was to have the honour of bowling the first over. But Garth was frightened of a few things in the army. One was the tough-as-nails nurse who used to draw our blood. She smoked Texan cigarettes while she performed this task. Garth was so frightened of her that on one occasion, as he stood up, he fainted and knocked over the two vials she had filled with his blood. So she had to do it all over again, and Garth nearly fainted again at the prospect.

So Garth opened the bowling. Jorrie Jordaan was fielding at first slip. Garth's first ball was wide, and the ball hit the side of the mat and ricocheted towards the RSM, who was fielding with only his beret on his head. The ball hit him square between the eyes and knocked him out cold. Garth took off like a bullet, because he was convinced that as soon as the RSM woke up, he'd be dead.

Anyway, back to Rob Louw. We went through Craven Week together, as well as Maties Under-20, Western Province Under-20, the Oribis team and then the Springboks. Rob is very close to all of us, so it was a tremendous shock when we first heard he had cancer.

In November 2009, I was on my way to visit Duimpie Baily, a dear friend of mine from the wine industry. It was his 70th birthday, and a party was being held in Stellenbosch. Then Schalk Jnr phoned and said he'd been at the Rocking the Daisies music festival in Darling over the weekend, where he had seen Rob. But he said that Rob didn't look well. After speaking to Schalk, I phoned Rob. He was with his doctor at the time. And that's when he told me straight: 'Schalk, they say I'm going to die, and you know I don't die easily.' Rob has survived a rubber-duck accident and a plane crash.

He went on to tell me that he'd been diagnosed with cancer – a melanoma on his gallbladder – and given three months to live. I'd lost a dear family friend, Nico Gey van Pittius, whose cancer had started the same way, so I said, 'Rob, you need to be careful and take this seriously.'

At Duimpie's birthday party I bumped into Johann Rupert and I told him I needed a favour. We went for dinner at the Big Easy restaurant in Stellenbosch, where I told Johann about Rob. Johann simply said, 'Leave it to me.' This was on Monday. By Tuesday, Johann had managed to get Rob admitted to the MD Anderson Cancer Center in Houston, Texas, and had bought him a plane ticket to leave that Friday. Rob needed an emergency visa to travel. While standing in the lengthy visa queue at the US embassy, Rob found out that one of the officials was passionate about rugby. Within 45 minutes, Rob had his visa.

Of course we thought we were on track; Rob was packed and ready to fly. But on the day of his flight – in fact, only a few hours before departure – Johann phoned me and said that we had a problem. Rob's visa was only for the United States, but he had to fly via London and needed a British visa as well. It was a strange regulation at the time, because he was simply going to be in transit, but British Airways insisted that without the visa they wouldn't let him board his flight, which was supposed to depart at 8 pm.

Once again, Johann was brilliant. He immediately phoned Keith Williams, then the chairman and chief executive of British Airways, and asked him how long they could delay the flight departure. Keith said a maximum of two hours, after which they would lose their landing slot at Heathrow. Johann's wife, Gaynor, had met the then British High Commissioner in South Africa, Nicola Brewer, through her horse-racing ties.

Gaynor got on the phone and contacted the High Commissioner to explain the emergency. It turned out that Nicola Brewer's father had played rugby for Wales, so she was a massive rugby fan as well. She authorised all the official documents, and was even kind enough to send them with her driver straight to Cape Town International Airport. The documents arrived in time, and Rob was able to board the plane and travel to Houston for the surgery. This all happened in less than a week after we decided to launch Operation Save Rob. It was an amazing display of goodwill by so many people, and it quite literally saved Rob's life.

Johann let Rob convalesce at his home in the Bahamas, and he asked people like Sean Connery and Kelly Slater to visit Rob and raise his spirits.

At the same time that Rob was in hospital in Houston, I went to India with Johann. India is such a spiritual place. We were visiting the Taj Mahal, in the city of Agra, and were struck by the realisation that you have a very special bond with the people around you. Johann had lost his father two years before and his mom just before that, and the whole Rob experience had touched both of us deeply. Johann then put a challenge to Rob. He told him to get

Rob Louw and I have been good friends since 1969, and every year we make a pilgrimage to St Andrews – the Home of Golf – for the Alfred Dunhill Links Championship. Since Rob's remarkable recovery from cancer, we cannot wait for our annual week together playing golf and enjoying one another's company. Life is so short, but can be so beautiful.

himself healthy, and then he would invite him to play in the Alfred Dunhill Links Championship in Scotland. Rob held up his end of the bargain, and so did Johann. So every year Rob and I take our week-long sabbatical as old teammates. We stay in the same hotel room overlooking the 18th hole of the Old Course, and in 2019 we celebrated Rob's tenth year since his comeback. We have the greatest times in the Rusacks Hotel with fellow competitors Shane Warne, Michael Vaughan, Kevin Pietersen, Mark Boucher, Mark Nicholas, Jacques Kallis, Ian Botham and the irrepressible Allan Lamb, who keeps us all awake. I am so privileged to be able to spend time every year in the company of these friends and playing these beautiful courses with incredibly talented professional golfers.

It's beautiful to think that, years later, Rob found himself playing in a fourball with Kelly Slater at this tournament. It was a wonderful moment for them both.

Fortunately, Rob made a full recovery. But it is thanks to so many amazing people, and the family of world rugby, that Rob is still with us today.

There is another great story involving Rob that happened when we took a trip to Mauritius.

In the 1980s, when I was involved in negotiating a better financial deal for us rugby players, we met with Jan Pickard, who was the manager at Western Province, and also my boss at Union Wines. Jan said his hands were tied; he'd just been voted onto the IRB executive as head of finance. If he paid us, we'd be declared professionals.

The players, especially Michael du Plessis, were pretty insistent that if they weren't going to be paid better, then they weren't going to play. At the time, we were earning R165 per match, and the players were lobbying for R700. Jan said he could maybe push the

On the Swilcan Bridge, following a social round on the Old Course with Boris Bekker, Morné du Plessis and Ian Banner. It doesn't get more iconic than this – walking over the bridge and up to the 18th green with The R&A clubhouse to welcome you.

fee to R300, but that was it. The players were having none of it, though.

So, after a long lunch, Jan told me that he had a compromise: he offered us a holiday in Mauritius with our wives and girlfriends. The only hotel I knew in Mauritius was Sol Kerzner's Le Saint Géran, so I suggested we stay there for the ten-day trip. Jan agreed, but added, 'Okay, but then you need to win the Lion Cup and the Currie Cup this year.' I said I'd convey the deal to the players and hear what they had to say.

We would normally start practice at 6 pm, so that day we agreed to meet at 5 pm to discuss the deal. The players arrived in good spirits because they were expecting news of a pay increase. We sat down. I had just told them that I had good and bad news when in walked Dawie Snyman, our coach in those glory days. I don't know if he had been tipped off or not, but now we couldn't very well talk about the deal. 'Okay,' said Dawie, 'if we're all here, let's start practice.' I think it must have been the earliest we'd ever started practice in those days. Usually the players would arrive just a few minutes before practice started.

As we ran out, Rob, being as inquisitive as always, asked me what the bad news was. I told him there would be no pay increase. 'And the good news?' he asked. I told him the deal about Mauritius and our winning the Lion Cup and the Currie Cup. The next thing Rob was running around the field telling all the guys, 'Boys, we're going to Mauritius.' And we did, because we won both cups, as agreed.

While in Mauritius, Princess Caroline and Princess Stéphanie of Monaco were also staying at the Saint Géran. Calla Scholtz had a great time playing tennis with Princess Caroline, and Princess Stéphanie took quite a liking to Rob, even though his wife was there. One night, I danced the Mauritian Sega with Princess Caroline. It was a fabulous trip.

I also met the renowned (and enigmatic) photographer Monty Shadow on that trip. We were lying by the pool one day, having had way too much rum the night before, and talking about the princesses, who had arrived the previous day by private jet. And

Many a time I've had to apologise to world-renowned photographer Monty Shadow for thinking he was the bodyguard of Princess Stéphanie and Princess Caroline of Monaco when I tackled him into the pool at the Saint Géran hotel in Mauritius. Here he is with me and Gaynor Rupert in 2013.

among their group was this big guy who we said was a security guard masquerading as a photographer. As we lay there, the guy came walking past. The boys dared me to tackle him. And of course I did, hitting him with a thunderous tackle straight into the pool. Then I swam away before he could attack me, as I assumed a bodyguard would do.

As I surfaced near the pool bar, he was still standing there in the pool trying to get his big mop of curly hair out of his eyes. He was a great sport about it, and we shared three beers after that. He became our introduction to his group.

Monty was also on his way to Sun City to take photographs for Sol Kerzner, who arrived the following evening to take the whole group with him two days later. We also ended up gambling with Sol, and received some free chips after Nick Mallett asked him for some dosh to gamble. Monty and I remained very good friends afterwards, and we met up in many weird and exotic places around the world. He even visited Welbedacht for a braai.

The world of rugby has certainly opened up a world of friendships, all of which I treasure.

32

RAISING A SPRINGBOK

I REGULARLY HAVE PARENTS come up to me and ask, 'How do I make my son a Springbok, like yours?' I always feel uneasy about answering this question, for two reasons. First, because I honestly do not know. And, second, because I never set out to make any of my children a Springbok.

Throughout my children's sports careers, it was never important to me if they won or lost. It was about their experience of the game. Did they enjoy it or not? What did they learn from it? Those factors were more important.

Sure, I was always very competitive on the sports field. I hated losing. But when it came to my own children, I always tried to take the approach that sport is like a subject at school and part of their education. But I believe it's a very important subject, because it teaches you so many important things. However, it's still just a subject, and one that has its place in the overall make-up of a child.

I also exposed my children to my love of culture. If I took them to Wimbledon or a Grand Prix or to watch a Rugby World Cup or Cricket World Cup match, I also took them to see Luciano Pavarotti. I wanted them to be exposed to everything life had to offer.

My mother always supported her children in everything we did. I could do no wrong in her eyes, and I took the same approach with my own children. I always told Schalk and Tiaan that if they wanted to, I wouldn't mind if they became ballet dancers, as long as they wanted to be the best ballet dancers in the world, and they understood what it took to become the best and were prepared to work at it.

I would put little motivational sayings above their beds, encouraging them to follow their dreams and set big goals for themselves. I believe wholeheartedly that kids must be allowed to dream. They must inspire themselves with dreams. If you dream about owning a house or a car or having a job, then you need to understand what you should do to obtain these things. If you have a dream, you connect the dots to see what pattern forms. Then you can see where you're at now, and what steps you need to take to achieve your dream.

I have always tried to see the world through my children's eyes. You can't live their lives through your own eyes, because they see and feel things differently. Only when they ask you questions can you understand what their minds are trying to conceive.

I have been blessed in that my children were always great listeners. I never had to chase them out of a room when I was having a meeting or seeing some of my friends; in fact, I encouraged them to sit in on meetings so that they could learn something. In the natural world, the lioness takes her cubs on the hunt with her, but human beings leave their children out when they're occupied with the so-called important things in life. We should include our children as much as possible, so that they can learn.

Although I thought it essential that my children learn how to hunt, fish and play golf, beyond that they were free to pursue whatever sport they wanted. I felt that those three sports were the best for character formation – especially golf. Golf is one of the few sports where you first learn to compete against yourself before you compete against the rest of the field. In golf, you have to really understand yourself, and learn to control your emotions, before you can beat either the course or your opponents.

Golf is the game that most closely resembles life, because it's not fair. And of course life is also not fair, and I taught my children not to expect it to be. I think I may have leaned too hard on that message; maybe my children grew up always expecting the worst. But when it came to sport, I never forced them into anything. They always made up their own minds about what they wanted to pursue.

I've seen the downside of parents who expect too much from their children on the sports field. I never felt that pressure as a child, and I didn't want my children to experience it either. I never wanted to be in a situation where one of my children turned around and said to me, 'You forced me into this.' They had to want it for themselves, not for me.

Once they knew what they wanted to do, I helped them where I could. So my approach was to find out what their dream was, and then see how I could help them achieve it. What do my children expect of me as their father/mother? It's a question I think we need to ask ourselves as parents. We need to know what our children want, rather than forcing our will on them.

I always played a lot of games with my kids, mostly sport-related, I suppose. If we went to the beach, I would take along the whole house. I'd have to make two or three trips to the car to haul out the balls and bats and things. And it didn't really matter what sport we played as a family. It could be beach cricket or surfing, for all I cared. I just loved playing games with my kids.

As I mentioned, I encouraged them to learn about all aspects of life. By the age of 12, when they were at the dining table with me and Myra, I'd give them a glass of wine to enjoy and to teach them to appreciate the finer things in life. Or, if we were on the yacht together in a particularly icy wind, I'd give them a sip of sherry, just as my uncle used to give me – to warm the soul a bit. Some people might criticise my approach, but I would talk to them about the wine's origin and make-up; I wanted them to experience the delights of wine with me, their father, rather than discovering these things with their friends.

I'll never forget when Schalk turned 13. Myra and I asked him what he'd like for his birthday, and he said he wanted to play golf on a 'serious' golf course and watch a Test match at Ellis Park. So with my air miles, I booked the three of us (myself, Schalk Jnr and Tiaan) business-class tickets to Johannesburg. I arranged for us to play the Wanderers golf course, and then they would join me for the Springbok Test against Samoa at Ellis Park, where I was commentating with Hugh Bladen.

On the flight to Johannesburg, the flight attendant came past and offered me a glass of wine. That's when Schalk put up his hand and asked politely if he could also have a glass of wine. The flight attendant looked shocked, but I said it was perfectly fine with me. So then she turned to Tiaan and said, 'En jy? Jy wil seker ook wyn hê?' (And you? You probably also want wine?) To which Tiaan replied, 'Nee dankie. Ek wil vonkelwyn hê' (No thank you, I want sparkling wine). I laughed so hard at that.

I never allowed any photos of my own rugby days to hang in our homes. I didn't want my children to grow up with a photo on the wall of their dad in his Springbok jersey, arms folded, glaring down at them, with the subtle message, 'You will one day also play rugby.' It might sound strange, but that's how I saw it, and I never wanted that for them. So to this day you will not find a team photo, or even a team jersey, of mine framed and displayed in any of our homes. Most of the photos in our tasting room at Welbedacht are of Schalk's rugby career.

So when parents come to visit me to find out how I went about creating the perfect Springbok, I tell them their notion is misplaced.

I never set out to turn any of my children into professional sportspeople – or, in fact, to become anything beyond what they themselves wanted to be. I don't believe it's a healthy thing for any parent to do. Besides, research proves that it's out of a parent's control.

There's a fascinating book by Daniel Coyle called *The Talent Code*, which discusses the importance of myelin, a kind of sheath around the nerves in the brain, which acts like the insulating rubber around electric wiring. Myelin protects the nerves, including those in the brain and spinal cord. Coyle's theory is that the thicker the myelin, the more efficient and faster the electrical impulses that can be transmitted along the nerve cells. But researchers have also discovered that really talented people rewire their brains, so to speak, through the age-old method of making mistakes and learning from them. This teaches the brain to route the right paths for the transmission of these electrical impulses.

So the conclusion is that talent is not only something you are born with; it can also be developed. Or, to put it another way, talent can be learnt through experience. For example, a sportsperson will make mistakes. Learning from those mistakes is what makes them better at their craft. Similarly, you can't protect your child from making mistakes. Mistakes foster learning. A sportsperson who hasn't failed under pressure and learnt from it cannot move forward. Gary Player put it very well in *Don't Choke: A Champion's Guide to Winning Under Pressure*: 'Everybody has nerves ... some have more control of their nerves than others. A player has no greater asset on the golf course than the power of his mind ... The mind is what makes you a superstar ... I proved that you are able to train your mind to strengthen your nerve.'

All this raises the question: is it the hardware (so-called natural talent) or the software (nurtured talent) that makes a great athlete? Well, one of the best attempts at answering that is David Epstein's *The Sports Gene: Inside the Science of Extraordinary Athletic Performance*, a remarkable book that analyses everything from the influence of malaria on the world's fastest runners to how outstanding athletes develop their skills through a combination of 'software' and 'hardware'.

My personal experience in sport is that it is the mental ability of a sportsperson that is the most critical component of their success, and mental ability is developed in a whole variety of ways – often just during the normal experiences of being a child – rather than any single structured approach. A child discovers more about themselves just by playing, as children do, than through any particular type of activity.

For example, future success can come down to something simple, such as how we teach our children to catch a ball. Once, I was on a flight from Berlin to London, and sitting next to me was an official of the Russian Tennis Federation. We began chatting about how Russia had been able to produce so many excellent young tennis players. He asked me how I'd taught my kids to catch a ball.

As he pointed out, grown-ups tend to throw the ball in the air for a child to catch. According to him, that's wrong. You should rather bounce the ball towards the child, so that the child can learn where the ball's zero point of gravity is. If you want to be a good tennis player, he went on, understanding where the ball's zero point of gravity is will affect your decision on whether to hit the ball early or late. That knowledge is acquired by the child's catching a bouncing ball rather than an airborne one. It was a simple shift in focus, with a major result for Russian tennis.

A lot of what I encounter in school sport these days is of major concern to me. Many parents seem to be vicariously living their children's lives. It has become vitally important to the parent that their child should make the A team, or a provincial team, when the child should be setting the bar for themselves. The parent should stand aside and only help the child if they really need help.

Because I was a Springbok, there were some expectations that my children would follow in my footsteps. I was never a pushy dad on the sports field, however. I hardly even attended their practice sessions. And when I went to watch their matches, I kept my distance. I preferred to help outside the ropes.

With sport having turned professional, it's been a shock to me that parents of 12-year-olds are trying to turn them into professional sportspeople. At that age, sport should just be another subject at school. Parents should be more focused on what sport reveals about their child's character. No subject at school will reveal more about a child's make-up than sport. How do they handle losing? More importantly, how do they handle winning? Therein lies a character appraisal of your child that is vital to the kind of adult you want them to become.

I believe it is wrong that South African schools are taking a professional approach to Under-13 and Under-15 sport. American sports researchers have proven that it's only at the age of about 21 that you really know biomechanically what a young sportsman will become. For example, Garth le Roux only really hit his straps with his fast bowling when we were in the army in 1974. He grew six inches taller, and in 1977–1978 was the Player of the Series in the World Series Cricket competition organised by Kerry Packer. All the evidence suggests that we're trying to identify future champions at too early an age.

Morné du Plessis played fullback at school. If he'd already been typecast in that role, would he ever have been allowed to develop into the great forward he became, or would he have been overlooked in the modern era?

I am also against a Craven Week for primary schools, as I think the children are too young for that kind of tournament to have any meaningful impact. Less than one per cent of junior Craven Week players go on to play senior rugby. What does that tell you?

So when parents ask me how their child can become a Springbok, I say, 'By leaving them alone. If they can't do it on their own, how are you going to help them? Let them dream and create their own goals.'

Let your children find their own way in life. Give them the freedom to be themselves. I am not saying they should not have the right coaching and training, but they will let you know what they are going to be good at.

33

DREAMS

HOW DO YOU LOOK back on a life?

I thought about this as my boat drifted on the ocean off Kleinmond. Below the deep blue water, my crayfish nets were lying on the seabed. Life's a lot like that, actually. There's this vast openness as the world and a lifetime of choices lie before you. You can't see where those crayfish are. So you prepare as best you can, drop your nets in what you think is the right spot, and then you hope.

You hope you're in the right place at the right time.

If I had to live my life again, what would I change and what would I do all over again? I was just a poor boy from Paarl who had some dreams. Some of those I fulfilled, and some not. Carly Simon has a song called 'Letters Never Sent'. I suppose in a sense my life has been a case of a lot of letters written, some of which I never sent. Some of them I've opened here, in this book, for the first time for others to read.

I've tried not to live with regrets, although I've made many mistakes. There are things I should never have said, and times when I said nothing when I should have spoken up.

And, like most people, there are things I would've done differently, and things I still hope to achieve.

I would have loved to have attempted the Cape to Rio yacht race with Schalk and Tiaan. You get to know one another really well on that kind of trip.

I would've loved to go running with the bulls in Pamplona with my two sons. Perhaps we can still do it one day.

I also wish I had discovered golf earlier in my life, maybe at school, and not at the ripe old age of 24, and that I could have had proper golf lessons right from the start. Despite this, I've been privileged to play at some of the most amazing golf courses in the world.

My life has been a lucky one.

I was lucky enough to play rugby for South Africa, even though I wish it had not been during our sporting isolation.

I'm proud that I stood up against apartheid, the National Party and the Broederbond, even if it cost me a place on the 1981 Springbok tour to New Zealand.

I wish I'd played more cricket. I really do, Dad.

I've been lucky to have shared the stage with a lot of superb musicians, and even luckier to call many of them my friends.

It has become a party trick of mine to join the band at a function I attend, and it's even become an auction item for Danie Gerber, who has made some good money for charities by auctioning me to play a few songs with the house band. But the older I get, the more the broken fingers in both my hands hamper the actions required from them. I've resorted to pressing chords or plucking the strings, but it hasn't stopped me from holding my own on stage.

I wish I'd spent more time with my children while they were growing up. But I was building a business, like so many men do.

In my desire to have another Y2K type of adventure, we embarked on an amazing family trip to Namibia in June–July 2019 as part of Myra's 60th birthday celebration. It was a great occasion for us because Schalk and his family could join us, having just arrived back from their three-year stay in England. While Schalk was still overseas we did some work on his beloved, but thirsty, Hummer V8. I equipped my Ford F250 with some extra electrics for refrigeration, and Tiaan got his newly acquired Ford Ranger 3.2 ready for this trip.

What a great family adventure this turned out to be. The three vehicles drove in convoy, and we even had walkie-talkies to communicate between vehicles. I had Myra, René and Bella with me in the F250, which was loaded to the max with camping equipment, food and drinks. Unfortunately René's husband, Marco, couldn't join us because of work commitments. Tiaan had his wife, Thalia, and his son, Francois, a boisterous two-year-old, in his vehicle. Schalk had Michele, Schalkie Jnr and Nicol in his car, plus all their bikes and more on his roof.

During our journey we would pull off the road onto a gravel strip and the kids would ride around on their bikes while we made food. We slept over in guesthouses and rented apartments. We travelled all along the Orange River to Sendelingsdrif and then through Rosh Pinah and Aus to Lüderitz. From there we did the desert mining town of Kolmanskop and slept the night at Helmeringhausen. We followed that with a few nights in Sesriem, where the kids climbed the mighty dunes of Sossusvlei. Then it was on to Walvis Bay and Swakopmund, where we stayed in my dear friend Jean Engelbrecht's beautiful house on the beach. Myra booked a trip, which the two of us had done previously, called Tommy's Living Desert Tour, in which guide Tommy Collard takes you into the Namib Desert and teaches you about all the animals there. You cannot believe the life in the desert.

With my love for Africa, I was delighted to see my grandchildren staring absolutely mesmerised as Tommy plucked a sidewinder adder out of the sand right in front of their eyes. And this after they had told him they were convinced nothing lived in the desert. We marvelled at the nocturnal palmato gecko, with its beautiful colours. It was extraordinary to see my grandchildren delight in this new world that was being shown to them, especially the two who had just returned to magnificent Africa from England.

A highlight for me was when my eldest grandchild took control of a fishing rod on the beach, just as I was pouring a gin and tonic, and exclaimed, 'Oupa, this rod is pulling!' I told him it was just a wave while adding more ice to my drink. 'Oupa, it is really pulling!' he shouted again. As I looked up the rod was bent all the way over. 'Start reeling!' I told him. After a good battle he landed the fish all on his own, catching his first kob. It was a beautiful moment for me. I was over the moon, and far too few photographs were taken. Not long after that we cooked the fish, with some galjoen, over an open fire on the beach.

We also spent time at Gert Joubert's exquisite game farm, Erindi, where we had two lodges next to each other overlooking a water hole. It was magical to fall asleep to the cry of a nearby hyena and then later to the grunting of a pack of lions. We had a fabulous game drive where we witnessed not only wild dogs but also a wild dog kill of a brindled gnu (blue wildebeest), as well as three leopards hunting for a late-afternoon meal. And we were chased by a grumpy white rhino.

The day ended with all of us sitting around a campfire telling stories about what we'd seen. It was a perfect 60th birthday present for Myra to spend it with her grandchildren like this.

The stories our grandchildren were already telling, the lessons they'd learnt about the bush and how to track animals, made me go to sleep that evening happy that no matter where in the world they may one day find themselves, Africa had become part of their DNA.

I would love it if this country of ours is able to offer my grandchildren the best life. Like the one I have had. Yes, we had to make sacrifices. We lived through some pretty scary times. Times that cost us as sportsmen and put a cap on all our dreams. Times in which people lost their lives on the border. But we got through it.

Now, as a tenth-generation South African, I am passing the baton to my children. I hope that they will remain children of South African soil and add value to this country, and that our country will give them the space in which to do so. So that they can also catch an abundance of crayfish in our oceans, and fish in our rivers, and hunt throughout Africa.

I'm grateful to have had wonderful relationships. Myra has allowed me the space to go out into the world and be myself.

I've had good friendships, too, the closest of which is with Johann Rupert. We enjoy the same types of conversation and debates, and we've had great times together going hunting and fishing. What I appreciate most about Johann is his honesty, his patriotism and what he's done for the less privileged in South Africa. I don't believe South Africa has ever seen a philanthropist of his calibre.

Look at what he's done with the Laureus Sport for Good Foundation, and more recently launching the Michelangelo Foundation to protect the real remaining craftspeople of the world. He doesn't just give his money away. He really positions his wealth with a specific reason to help.

Unfortunately, I think there have been political parties in South Africa that have used him as a pawn for their own gain.

What people perhaps don't know about Johann is how well-connected he is. I don't know of any other South African with a contact list like his. He has the numbers of the most powerful people in the world, and all of them – from presidents to kings – will take his call.

I wish I had had more adventures with my father. Like the camp at Melkbos we used to go to on 2 January every year. We'd take a big canvas tent and camp out with other farmers and their sons. Every year, we'd compete in traditional Boeresport games, one of which was a strongman competition where you had to load bags of wheat onto a truck. Those bags weighed around 100 pounds each. I loved watching that competition and trying to predict the winner. I'd always look for the man with the biggest muscles and think that surely he would win. But my dad would whisper in my ear that it's not always the man who looks the strongest who wins. And he was right. A wiry old man from Malmesbury with sloping shoulders and thin legs won one year. Forever after, if I saw a man with sloping shoulders, I knew he was strong. It's a bit like spotting a good rugby prop: if his legs are shorter than his body, he's a tighthead. Especially if he has shoulders that slope downwards.

I would still like to visit the island of St Helena, to see my grandfather's grave. For years, I desperately wanted to take my mom there

On 24 September 2020, at the christening of Tiaan's son Reinhardt, the youngest of my grandchildren, at Welbedacht. Trust Tiaan not only to get married on National Braai Day (Heritage Day), but also to christen both of his sons on the same day. The whole family is here: standing (from left) are Schalk Jnr, Michele, Marco, René, baby Reinhardt, Thalia and Tiaan; seated (from left) are Myra, Schalk Jnr (Jnr), Nicol, Bella, Francois and a proud grandpa.

to see where her father was buried after he died on the voyage to England.

But, for now, I work hard on the farm and I love what I do. My friends say I've become a recluse, but that's not true. I'm just busy with what I enjoy. I'm not there in the madding crowd. That's just who I am. I see some people socially, and that's that. Sometimes people misunderstand that about me.

You might call me a rugby player. A Springbok. A winemaker. A Boer. A farmer. A businessman. A liberal. A contrarian.

I'll tell you that I'm an African. I'm an Afrikaner.

DREAMS

Maybe I'm just a kid who grew up on the poor side of Paarl. A kid who used to ride his bicycle and deliver 58 newspapers a day. A kid with a few dreams of his own.

And I'm proud of that.

ACKNOWLEDGEMENTS

THIS BOOK HAS BEEN a journey in which I have regaled the reader with the route I have taken so far. No journey is without turnoffs, destinies that get changed, and friends and fellow travellers who get on the bus and then get off again. It is these fellow travellers who provide the energy and fuel for the journey, allowing me to climb the steep slopes and enjoy the downhill on the other side, while also being able to enjoy the view from the top down or from the bottom up.

To all my fellow travellers, I thank you for the time we have spent together and the energy and fuel you have contributed to the journey. Here I must single out the family I grew up with: my father, Tiny, mother Mavis and siblings Johann, Laura and Paul, and half-sister Gaeleen and (still to be met) half-brother Otello, if he is still alive. Then there is Myra, my long-supporting wife, my beloved children, Schalk, Tiaan and René, their respective partners, Michele, Thalia and Marco, and the most recent navigators of the South African landscape, Schalk, Nicol, Bella, Francois and Reinhardt – 12th-generation Africans and my beloved grandchildren.

The most prized journeys are those that are etched into the memory and create that unique library that provides the firewood and energy for the journey ahead. May I, with this recollection of moments, thank my fellow travellers for your contribution to a life less travelled on tarred roads but driven by love and passion, with the major thought being that you cannot walk forward by looking back, as you may bump into something. If any of my recollections have offended anyone or any organisation, my defence is that this is how they are etched into my mind. I have done my best to research the details as they are set down by statisticians or historians. Most of these stories are of a very personal nature and have never been heard or declared before, as I have always kept them to myself.

Why undertake something like this? Well, when the publisher asked me to put together an honest book about my early years, I had to declare that I had no intention of revealing much about my past, my journey, my family or the circumstances that made me. Here I must thank Michael Vlismas for dragging these moments out of my memory bank and putting them together.

My journey has been a varied and unique one. It is my hope that maybe, in the process of healing my beloved country and celebrating the diversity that exists within it, my stories of a simple poor boy's dreams can help others to understand a lost period in South Africa, the forces that controlled it, and how one individual navigated the minefields, made mistakes and had some interesting times, in particular the highs and lows of parenthood and business and family life, on a continent that is unique in every way.

The word 'just', as an adjective, means to be based on, or to behave according to, what is morally right and fair. It completes the title of this book, which could also read as 'A Moment of Just(ice)'. As we all know, every now and then we find ourselves in contradictory and onerous discussion due to another's lack of background knowledge of a particular issue, and usually the following is used to interrupt such a conversation:

'Just a moment ...'

Schalk Burger Snr

TO MY WIFE, URSULA, thank you for always being my first reader. Your first read of this manuscript contained the most important piece of advice I needed to hear. Thank you for the support you give me, and the endless cups of tea you make for me.

What began as a drive out to Welbedacht farm for a golf magazine feature with Schalk Burger developed into this book of memoirs. There were just too many good stories to limit them all to one magazine article. Thank you, Schalk, for opening up and sharing all the colourful details of your life, and for trusting me with some of your most personal and cherished memories.

Many of these stories were told over lunch in the Welbedacht manor house. Thank you, Myra, for the magnificent lunches you treated me to. The wildspastei was a particular favourite.

Thank you also to Schalk Jnr, Tiaan and René for being willing to share, through your father's memories, the triumphs and tragedies of your lives in this memoir.

To Jeremy Boraine at Jonathan Ball Publishers, thank you for your enthusiasm for this book and for the opportunity to publish it. It is always such a pleasure to work with you. To Alfred LeMaitre, thank you for your expert editing and the always constructive feedback, and your commitment to making this the best book it can be.

And to my sons, Jack and Ethan, you always hear the 'first draft' of everything in the stories I tell around the dinner table, and are always so enthusiastic. Thanks for always listening.

Michael Vlismas

Lightning Source UK Ltd.
Milton Keynes UK
UKHW022304210621
385916UK00012B/2981

9 781776 190843